Graphic Inquiry

Annette Lamb • Daniel Callison

LIBRARIES UNLIMITED

AN IMPRINT OF ABC-CLIO, LLC
Santa Barbara, California • Denver, Colorado • Oxford, England

Library of Congress Cataloging-in-Publication Data

Lamb, Annette C.
  Graphic inquiry / Annette Lamb and Daniel Callison.
    p. cm.
  Includes bibliographical references and index.
  ISBN 978-1-59158-745-3 (pbk. : acid-free paper)
  1. Visual education. 2. Teaching—Aids and devices. 3. Graphic arts. I. Callison, Daniel, 1948– II. Title.
  LB1043.5.L275 2012
  371.33'5—dc23   2011040644

ISBN: 978-1-59158-745-3

15 14 13 12 11   1 2 3 4 5

Libraries Unlimited
An Imprint of ABC-CLIO, LLC

ABC-CLIO, LLC
130 Cremona Drive, P.O. Box 1911
Santa Barbara, California 93116-1911

This book is printed on acid-free paper ∞
Printed in Korea

Contents

Acknowledgements

This book would not have been possible without the generous contribution of visuals from many of our friends and colleagues, students, public sources, organizations, along with subscription services. Also, thanks to Anne Roecklein for her efforts in securing permissions.

Thanks to all of our graduate students. Their wonderful class projects and discussions inspired many of the examples found in the book.

Thanks to Nancy Bosch for all her work with teachers and children. She provided lots of great student projects as well as ideas for using primary sources in the classroom.

Thanks to the teachers and students at the IPS Center for Inquiry for their great work and inspiration.

Thanks to the many organizations including the American Association of School Librarians, International Society for Technology in Education, and Mid-continent Research for Education and Learning who are providing leadership in the development of standards that emphasize the importance of inquiry. Their work inspired the standards sections of the text.

Thanks to Sharon Coatney for her patience and encouragement.

Annette expresses her personal thanks to her husband, Larry, for encouraging her to think over the edges and outside the box.

Danny expresses his personal thanks to his brother, Norman, for being an inspirational teacher to him personally as well as to thousands of students in Norman's high school and college classes.

Finally, thanks to our families for their love and support.

Introduction

As a high school social studies teacher, I'm exploring strategies to promote deep thinking.

As the technology coordinator, I'm seeking techniques to connect tech tools with visual literacy.

I'm a parent volunteer looking for ideas to help at-risk kids.

I'm an elementary teacher looking for approaches to meet the diverse needs of my students.

As a school librarian, I'm looking for ways to incorporate graphic inquiry into the curriculum.

Intended to provide a practical approach to incorporating graphic inquiry across the curriculum, this visually-rich book provides numerous standards-based inquiry activities and projects that incorporate traditional tools and resources, as well as emerging social and collaborative technologies.

Designed to bridge theory and practice, this book provides applications for new and practicing educators and librarians. Although research will be cited and references provided, lengthy text passages will be avoided in favor of practical, visual examples rooted in best practice. It's hoped that you will view this book as a quick reference to timely, realistic activities and approaches as opposed to a traditional textbook.

Let's explore some possibilities.

While a camera creates a recorded version of what is seen by the photographer, other tools such as pencils, markers, and electronic paint tools can be used to create unique images like or unlike the real world.

I read as a means to visualize an environment and relationships... visuals can provide a more complete view of the world than words sometimes can. As a school librarian I strive to share this perspective with others.

In **Mind's Eye: Our Emerging Visual Culture**, photographer Lloyd Eby notes that photography brought about profound changes in human culture "taking us from a literary culture, based primarily on words and printing, to an increasingly image-based, or visual, culture." (p. 22). He states that the Internet has brought a convergence of these written and visual cultures requiring people to be educated in this hybrid of communication applications.

In **Visual Thinking**, Rudolf Arnheim states "visual education must be based on the premise that every picture is a statement. The picture does not present the object itself but a set of propositions about the object; or, if you prefer, it presents the object as a set of propositions." (p. 308)

Why graphics? Tony Buzan states that "Images are more evocative than words, more precise and potent in triggering a wide range of associations and thereby enhancing creative thinking & memory."

The quality and perspective of any graphic is impacted by the information selected as well as how the user interprets and presents the information.

It's important that young people have access to well-designed visual content. Without an effective graphic, a student may have difficulty judging the difference in scale between the planet Earth and Jupiter.

Students consume thousands of words, orally and visually, and they need a variety of communication methods to summarize their own sharing of information and knowledge. Illustrations serve to aid the student researcher who wants to grow and mature in communication skills through the use of graphics that enhance, condense, quicken, direct, heighten, or inspire the message.

This book is divided into seven sections focusing on different aspects of graphic inquiry.

As you explore each section, think about how you will design engaging learning environments for young people.

Also, consider how graphic inquiry might enhance your own personal inquiries.

1 Graphic Literacy, Fluency, Inquiry, and Life-long Learning

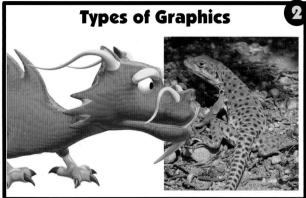

Types of Graphics 2

3 SCORE IT! Standards and Deep Thinking

Skills and Strategies 4

5 Interdisciplinary Approaches and Individual Differences

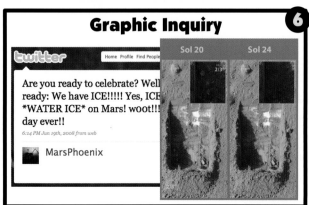

Graphic Inquiry 6

7 Learning through Graphic Inquiry

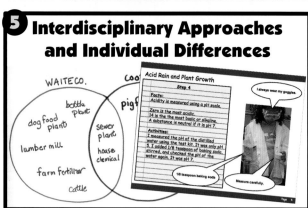

Graphic Literacy, Fluency, Inquiry, and Life-long Learning

Whether unlocking clues found in historical photographs from the Library of Congress or National Archives for a child labor unit ...

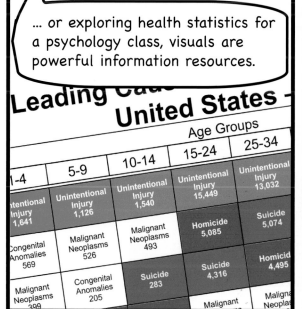

... or exploring health statistics for a psychology class, visuals are powerful information resources.

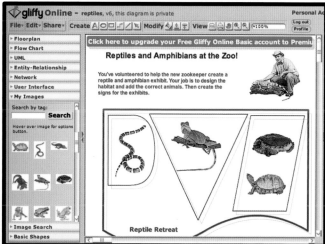

Technology tools such as the collaborative, online concept-mapping tool gliffy.com help students share their understandings of topics such as reptiles and amphibians.

Graphic inquiry involves extracting information from and presenting information in visual formats such as cartoons, diagrams, maps, photos, charts, tables, and multimedia.

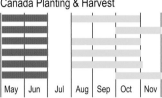

Through a recursive process of questioning, exploring, assimilating, inferring, and reflecting...

.... student information scientists and their instructional specialists use graphic inquiry as a means to answer questions, draw conclusions, solve problems, and make decisions.

Literacy involves gathering, selecting, analyzing, synthesizing, evaluating and communicating.

Inquiry extends these basic activities to include the ability and desire to...

question
share — | — explore
knowledge
create — | — discover
apply

... to solve problems
(personal, workplace, and academic)
in authentic situations (Callison 2002).

Let's explore graphic literacy, fluency, inquiry, and life-long learning.

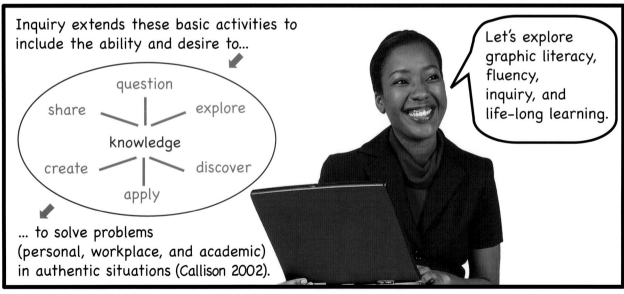

Graphic Literacy

Visual literacy is the ability to understand and use images. This includes to think, learn, and express oneself graphically.

Young people need to be able to evaluate and place value on graphics in personal, academic, and workplace situations.

Graphic Literacy

(Callison & Lamb, 2007)

read & comprehend graphics

design & create graphics

Graphic literacy involves the ability to...

analyze & interpret graphics

use & apply graphics

After reading the graphic story **Persepolis**, I wrote my own graphic memoir using Comic Life.

As a volunteer at the hospital, I use the first aid charts to help me remember basic bandaging techniques.

I have been studying the anatomy of snails. It's interesting to compare photos with diagrams.

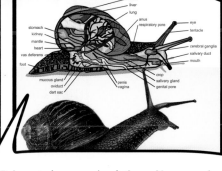

Personal Situations   Academic Situations   Workplace Situations

In 1657 John Amos Comenius published the first picture book for children using labeled diagrams to help young readers. Titled **Orbis Pictus,** the name is now used for a children's book award.

Children learn to read pictures before they read words. Unfortunately, we often stop visual teaching once children can read words. From billboards to television ads, young people are bombarded with visuals, making graphic literacy a critical life skill.

In the 1960s, IVLA (International Visual Literacy Association) was formed to help people learn more about visual learning, visual thinking, and visual language.

In **Teaching Visual Literacy**, Nancy Frey and Douglas Fisher, both professors at San Diego State University, state that "visual literate learners are able to make connections, determine importance, synthesize information, evaluate and critique. Further, these visual literacies are interwoven with textual ones, so that their interaction forms the basis for a more complete understanding." (p. 1)

Historical photos, scientific sketches, and mathematical drawings are all important resources in teaching and learning, yet these visual message are rarely assessed or valued in a formal way. I encourage my students to use visuals as a way to find meaning and express understandings.

While reading **A Single Shard** by Linda Sue Park, I used Google Earth satellite images, photos, and historical maps to trace Tree-Ear's journey through 12th-century Korea. I wondered how the journey and art would be different today so I made a chart to show the comparisons.

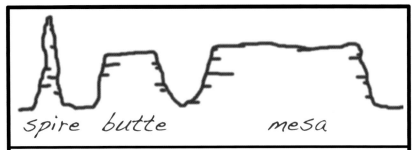

spire   butte   mesa

Textbooks often provide basic definitions and a single image to illustrate a concept. While students might be able to replicate the image above for an exam...

Sedimentary rock - sandstone
Balanced rock formation

harder rock

softer rock

harder rock

softer rock

Wind and water erosion and weathering caused the softer rock to crumble.

wind blows sand causing erosion

water seeps into the cracks in the rock

freezing and thawing causes rock to crack and crumble

By providing a variety of examples using different types of graphics, young people can more easily assimilate the information and be ready to apply these concepts in new situations.

It's not always possible or practical to provide a live experience, photos, or other concrete visuals, so young people need skills in using more abstract graphics to understand people, places, or events.

Sketches have been used throughout history to record battles.

...they might have difficulty when asked to apply what they know in a real world setting.

Many researchers have described the need for a continuum of concrete to abstract experiences.

Concrete

Live Experience
Virtual Reality
Photographs
3-D Images
Line Drawings
Diagrams
Icons
Words

COW

Abstract

Decades of brain research supports the theory that using multiple communication channels increases comprehension, understanding, and learning.

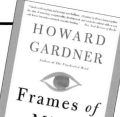

In a 1969 study, Schnorr and Atkinson found that encoding words visually helps students remember twice was much as verbal-only encoding.

In **Frames of Mind**, Harvard Professor Howard Gardner noted that the human brain houses a unique combination of intelligences including spatial/visual intelligence.

Noted researcher Allan Pavio found that visual and verbal information are encoded through separate channels in the brain. When information is presented using both visual and verbal channels, it's more likely to be remembered by students.

In a 1999 study using EEG brain activity measures, Ivan Gerlic and Norbert Jausovec found more active cognitive processes when learning from multimedia versus text formats.

In **Classroom Instruction that Works**, Robert Marzono, Debra Pickering, and Jane Pollock identified nonlinguistic representation as one of nine categories of effective instructional strategies. Because most instruction is presented in linguistic forms such as lectures and written work, young people need experiences using and creating nonlinguistic images to understand and retain new information.

How do you define poverty through graphics?

Graphic literacy involves much more than simply illustrating a term paper. Our students build skills by learning how to read, interpret, apply and create graphics. Activities may involve seeking patterns in graphs, categorizing items using graphic organizers, using photos as evidence in an argument, or building diagrams to represent scientific processes.

Graphic Fluency

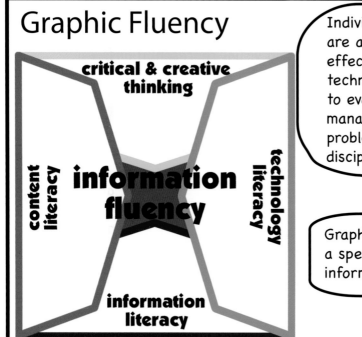

critical & creative
thinking

content literacy

information fluency

technology literacy

information literacy

Individuals who are graphic fluent are able to move efficiently and effectively across graphic types, technologies, and formats. They're able to evaluate, select, assimilate, apply, manage, and create visuals to solve problems and communicate ideas across disciplines (Callison & Lamb 2007).

Graphic fluency is a specific type of information fluency.

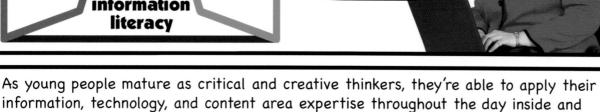

As young people mature as critical and creative thinkers, they're able to apply their information, technology, and content area expertise throughout the day inside and outside school to address authentic problems. As students move from basic literacy skills to information fluency, their use of graphics becomes more seamless.

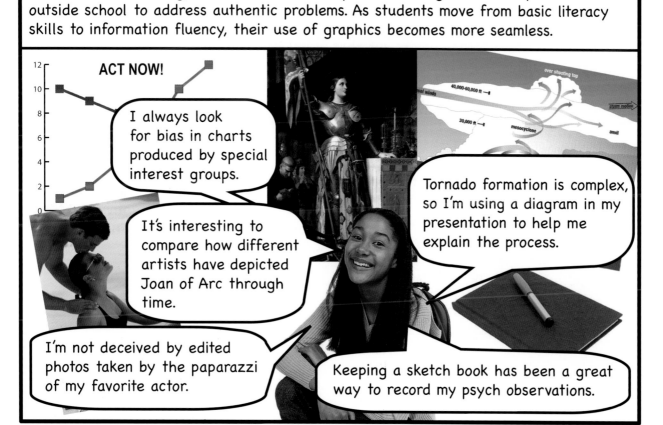

ACT NOW!

I always look for bias in charts produced by special interest groups.

It's interesting to compare how different artists have depicted Joan of Arc through time.

Tornado formation is complex, so I'm using a diagram in my presentation to help me explain the process.

I'm not deceived by edited photos taken by the paparazzi of my favorite actor.

Keeping a sketch book has been a great way to record my psych observations.

People who are graphic fluent are able to:

> Read, comprehend, analyze, interpret, use, apply, design, and create graphics;
> Identify bias, misinformation, and errors in visual representations;
> Use and produce graphics to visualize problems and solutions;
> Apply techniques of critical and creative thinking to graphic projects;
> Apply visual design principles to the creation of effective communications;
> Appreciate and enjoy effective visual messages.

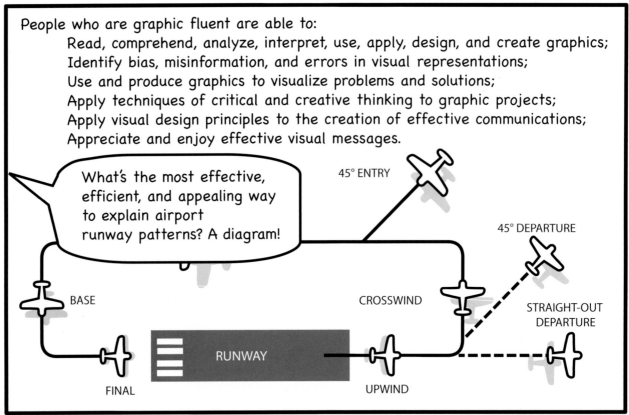

In **I See What You Mean: Children at Work with Visual Information**, Steve Moline points out that visual communications can be highly complex and should not be viewed as an academically "soft option" since graphics can be equally demanding to produce as texts. Moline stresses that students need practice in selecting the most effective tool for a particular communication.

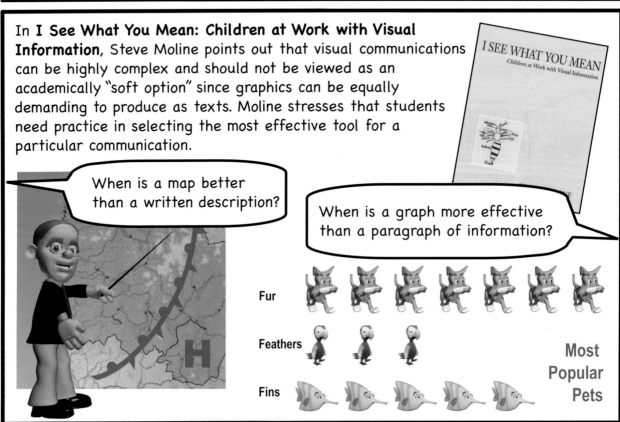

Young people are adept at reading for specific information, but they may struggle when trying to draw inferences from content. Students who are graphic fluent use images to stimulate deep thinking and create visual communications that reflect deep understandings.

Gettysburg

Pickett's Charge

Land monitors

A cross between a tank and a submarine, the "Land Monitor" was one of many inventions during the Civil War that was rejected. How might history be different if it had been built?

When designing instructional materials and creating learning environments, apply graphic skills to materials selection and production, as well as assignment design and evaluation. Also, be thinking about how to create a bridge between academic activities and real-world uses for this knowledge.

Standards-based Lessons

Authentic Applications

I'm learning to use graphic tools and technologies to explore and address global issues. Today in class we used GIS and Google Earth to analyze the changes in major cities around the world.

I feel comfortable using online mapping and GIS tools. I have the address for the Astronomy Club Star Party. I could use Google Maps on my iPhone or the GPS in my car to find it.

I wonder how global warming will impact major coastal cities like Rio de Janeiro Brazil? I'm going to do some projections.

Before I leave for the party, I'm going to use Google Sky to preview the star field that's available in our area.

Helping young people become graphic fluent involves much more than simply using pictures in my classroom for motivation. It has required a change in the way I think about my content and the skills young people need in today's world.

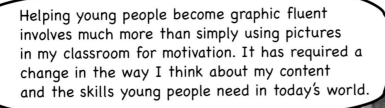

Like reading and writing across the curriculum, I infuse graphic skills development throughout the learning environment. As students become graphic fluent, they're able to transfer these skills to situations inside and outside school.

Whether organizing a personal scrapbook or putting a magazine photo in context, young people need to be able to identify elements of a historical photo that reflect the time when the photo was taken. Rather than simply showing photos that match the time period being taught, young people are learning to categorize photos based on content. When were automobiles introduced? When did children play leap frog and wear these fashions?

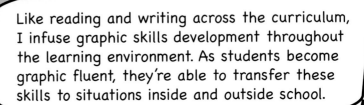

When studying acid rain, I tried to figure out how the graphs from two different companies using the same government data can be so different. We looked at the units, dates, and scales. Now I understand why it's important to always analyze graphs.

20
10
Reduced Emission Levels
0
1916   1946   1976

20
Acid Rain Emissions of SO2
15

10

5

0
1990   1995   2000   2006

Rather than just reading about gears in our textbook, we're examining gears and creating diagrams to show how they work.

Graphic Inquiry

Graphic inquiry is a cyclical, recursive process of investigation using visual information resources and tools to question, explore, assimilate, infer, and reflect.

(Callison 2002)

questioning & exploration

task or need

reflection

assimilation & inference

Questioning & Exploration

We were looking at the map and noticed that there's volcanic activity all over the Pacific Northwest. When will one of our volcanoes erupt? Are we ready for the "big one"? What plans do we need to make?

Assimilation & Inference

As we're finding information, we've been creating diagrams of our volcanoes showing likely eruption patterns. We're also collecting data for our graphs to help us predict the next eruption.

Reflection

We created a graphic organizer showing the process we went through to plan for a volcano disaster. This made us think about other threats such as earthquakes and tsumanis, so now we're going to begin planning for other disasters.

In **Guided Inquiry: Learning in the 21st Century**, Carol Kuhlthau, Leslie Maniotes, and Ann Caspari state that "inquiry is an approach to learning that involves students in finding and using a variety of sources of information and ideas to increase their understanding of a specific area of the curriculum. It is not simply answering questions and getting the right answers. Inquiry learning engages, interests, and challenges students to connect their world with the curriculum. Inquiry does not stand alone but is grounded in the content of the curriculum, which motivates students to question, explore, and formulate new ideas... Inquiry is a way of learning that prepares students to think for themselves, make thoughtful decisions, develop areas of expertise, and learn throughout their lives." (p. 133)

As the school librarian, I collaborate with teachers to build mini-lessons and units to scaffold student inquiry.

Inquiry flourishes in well-designed, nurturing learning environments. Using ancient Socratic questioning methods along with modern techniques and technologies, today's educators create exciting real and virtual experiences where our next generation of decision makers and innovators can think critically and creativity.

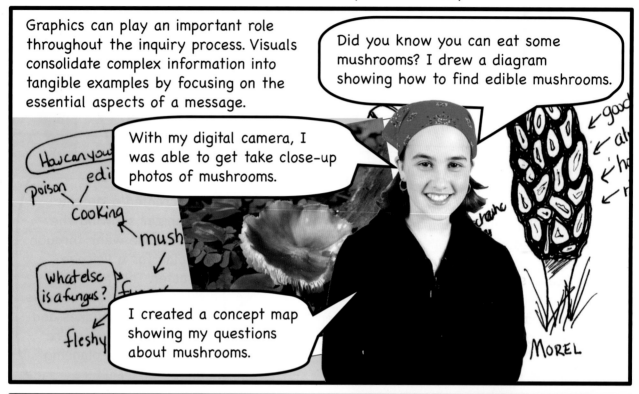

Graphic inquiries can occur inside a formal setting like school or in everyday life.

Fire Danger is High!

The ongoing drought and windy conditions have increased fire danger th the state. Those residen near National Forests re-examine their fire p plan and be certain th defensible space is p around their property. This includes removal of dead tree reduction of plants and replacement of flammab increase the moisture content other poss

Become an observer. Get in tune with the world around you. Turn your problems and concerns into questions.

> Could the house in the photo have been saved through better fire protection? Is my house at risk?

Brainstorm ideas, search for information, and make connections. One piece of information may lead to more questions and areas of exploration. It's a cycle of questioning and exploration.

> The map shows that my house is in a high risk area. How do I defend my home against fire?

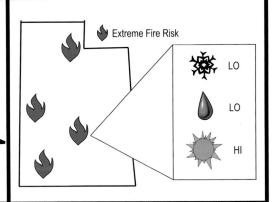

Extreme Fire Risk

LO
LO
HI

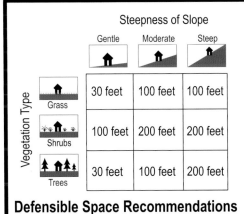

Defensible Space Recommendations

Steepness of Slope

Vegetation Type	Gentle	Moderate	Steep
Grass	30 feet	100 feet	100 feet
Shrubs	100 feet	200 feet	200 feet
Trees	30 feet	100 feet	200 feet

Discoveries are added to prior knowledge and organized in meaningful ways. By analyzing and synthesizing information, patterns, clues, and perspectives are identified. Through a cycle of assimiliation and inference, evidence is used to make decisions and create plans.

> We have shrubs and steep slopes, so we need 200 feet of defensible space around our house. It's time to get out the chainsaw and clear some brush.

Sharing plans with others, gaining feedback through discussions, and reflecting on the process leads to a new round of opportunties for inquiry.

> I wonder if my neighbors are aware of the need for defensible space. I think I'll share my photos and start a local firewise program.

As you design inquiry experiences, consider whether a controlled, guided, modeled, or free inquiry environment will be most effective in meeting student needs, addressing specific standards, and promoting deep thinking (Callison 1999b).

Controlled Inquiry

The classroom teacher and/or media specialist chooses the topic and identifies materials that students will use to address their questions. Students are often involved with specific exercises and activities to meet particular learning outcomes such as retelling stories, evaluating sources, or comparing approaches. Students may create a specific product such as a Venn diagram, paragraph, or poster.

Write a letter to the king to let him know what's happening in Jamestown.

Guided Inquiry

Students have more flexibility in their resources and activities; however, they are expected to create a prescribed final product such as a report or presentation.

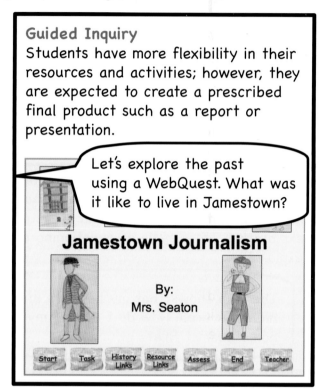

Let's explore the past using a WebQuest. What was it like to live in Jamestown?

Modeled Inquiry

Students act as apprentices to a coach such as a school librarian or classroom teacher. The student has flexibility in terms of topic selection, process, and product. The educators and students work side-by-side engaging in meaningful work.

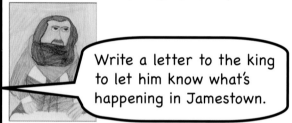

What was it like to live in a house in Jamestown? How were the houses made? Where did they get the building materials?

Free Inquiry

Students work independently. They explore meaningful questions, examine multiple perspectives, draw conclusions, and choose their own approach for information dissemination.

Why did men wear wigs? Did they have hair salons and barber shops?

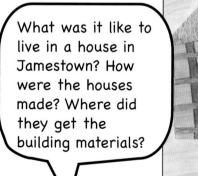

Graphic Inquiry & Life-long Learning

I've got lots of questions about getting a tattoo.

Our society values writing. From a young age, children are encouraged to move away from drawing and use writing as their main method of communication. However for some people, writing is a frustrating process filled with spelling errors and inadequacy. Sketching, drawing, diagramming, taking a photograph, or creating a simple chart or graphic is an efficient, effective, and appealing way to record and share ideas.

In **How to Interpret Visual Resources**, Harry Stein (p. 13) notes that "graphs and charts have indeed become a part of everyday life for most Americans. In the working world, for instance, employers may ask applicants to read graphs on pre-employment tests. And employees often find that supervisors use graphs and charts to explain production steps or company procedures, whether in fast-food restaurants, factories or corporate offices. Complex procedures or statistical information is given to new employees in this way with the expectation that knowledge will quickly and efficiently be put to use on the job."

I created a pros and cons chart based on information I found at the FDA website. I also watched videos of the process on **YouTube**. Once I made the decision to get a tattoo, I explored designs and began sketching ideas.

Guidelines for Plating

I use the NCAA Basketball Tournament Bracket every Spring.

I love to hike. I use Google maps.

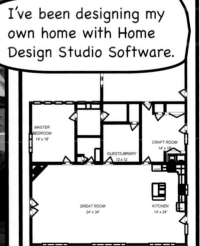

I've been designing my own home with Home Design Studio Software.

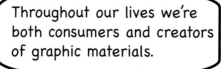

Throughout our lives we're both consumers and creators of graphic materials.

Life-long learners are constantly asking questions, exploring resources to address these questions, assimilating information, drawing inferences, and reflecting on what they've learned.

The map shows a chair lift that will take us to the top.

I attended a city council meeting and watched presentations from both sides of a land development project. I sought accurate information, so I had to screen out phony promises, evasive answers, and misdirection. I carefully analyzed the architectural drawings, graphic organizers, and 3D maps used to illustrate their points.

When developing a presentation for my local garden club on native plants, I tried to differentiate facts from opinions. I showed photos, maps, and charts. I wanted to be sure the participants understood their options so they could make good decisions about their garden planning.

In the book **Beautiful Evidence**, Edward Tufte (p. 141) states that "making a presentation is a moral act as well as an intellectual activity. The use of corrupt manipulations and blatant rhetorical ploys in a report or presentation... suggests that the presenter lacks both credibility and evidence. To maintain standards of quality, relevance, and integrity for evidence, consumers of presentations should insist that presenters be held intellectually and ethically responsible for what they show and tell. Thus consuming a presentation is also an intellectual and a moral activity."

As we think about graphic inquiry and life-long learning, consider how we can provide experiences in school that can be applied to life outside the classroom. Rather than depending on others to make decisions or jumping to conclusions based on limited information, mature information scientists are independent thinkers who use visual resources to collect evidence and graphic tools to build effective communications.

Encouraging questioning in school promotes active thinking in everyday life.

How does gravity work in the real world?

My sister is afraid of roller coasters. How can I convince her that she won't fall out?

I learned desktop publishing techniques in high school. As an adult, I apply these skills to everything from creating professional documents at work to designing my annual family Christmas letter.

Providing experiences using a variety of graphic tools in school lays the foundation for use of these tools in leisure and work situations.

Children as well as adults often make choices based on visual preferences. Donis Dondis stated that "a bias toward visual information is not difficult to find in human behavior. We seek visual reinforcement of our knowledge for many reasons, primary among them is the directness of the information, the closeness to the real experience."

I read the weather map on the TV news.

Are you more likely to pick up a book with an interesting photograph? We use visuals all the time. In a single day, I may go through the graphic inquiry process a number of times.

I read the clothing labels for washing instructions.

I read the symbols on the medicine bottle.

I compared grills, bought one, and followed instructions to put it together.

Think about your own inquiry experiences. How were visuals used in questioning, exploration, assimilation, inference, and reflection?

After years of waiting, our parents have finally given us permission to get a dog. I want a dog that likes to run and play outdoors, while Isabel wants a small dog. We need a graphic inquiry.

We took an online survey to help us figure out what dog would fit our family best. We wanted a breed that would meet all of our needs. The survey helped us narrow our search to three breeds: beagle, kelpie, and collie. As a family, we made a chart showing the pros and cons of each option.

Once we chose the beagle, we began another cycle of investigation. Should we purchase a dog online, at the local pet store, or through the humane society? We located a beagle breeder in our state. She sent us photographs to examine before making a visit to choose our new dog.

At school, work, and play, graphics can play a role throughout the inquiry process. As you think about graphic literacy, fluency, inquiry, and life-long learning, consider the many ways that educators can support visual learning.

Select a topic you'd like to investigate, a problem you need to solve, or a question that's been on your "to do" list. Conduct your own graphic inquiry by placing emphasis on the visual aspects of your investigation. During your investigation you may read, comprehend, analyze, interpret, use, apply, design, and create graphics.

Types of Graphics

Although graphics may simply provide a visual illustration of a concept, they often include numbers, words, and other symbols.

Graphics are visual representations created on paper, the computer screen, or other surfaces to communicate information.

Graphics may represent fiction or nonfiction content.

An artist may create a 3-D picture of a fantasy world using imaging software,

... while a geologist may draw and label a cross section of a mountain.

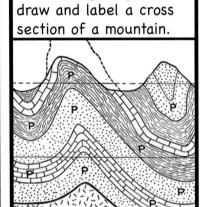

Stories can be told through words, but they can also be expressed visually. Just as paragraphs can define a concept, so can diagrams. Think about the many ways that skull images can be used to explain, entertain, and engage.

Selecting, designing, or creating a graphic to meet a particular need can be difficult.

Although technology can enhance charts, some techniques can distract from the data. Professional Graphic Designer Nigel Holmes suggests that developers avoid 3-D effects, colored backgrounds, and ornate fonts.

As an opening to his classic, **The Visual Display of Quantitative Information**, Edward Tufte writes: Excellence in statistical graphics consists of complex ideas communicated with clarity, precision, and efficiency. Graphical displays should:

➤ show the data;

➤ induce the reviewer to think about the substance rather than about methodology, graphic design, the technology of graphic production, or something else;

➤ avoid distorting what the data have to say; make large data sets coherent;

➤ encourage the eye to compare different pieces of data;

➤ reveal the data at several levels of detail, from a broad overview to the fine structure;

➤ serve a reasonably clear purpose: description, exploration, tabulation, or decoration;

➤ be closely integrated with the statistical and verbal descriptions of a data set.

The Visual Display
of Quantitative Information

EDWARD R. TUFTE

In **Teaching Visual Literacy** Nancy Frey and Douglas Fisher stress that student's success is often dependent on their ability to master visual messages. Unfortunately many lessons don't address or assess visual communications. Look for opportunities.

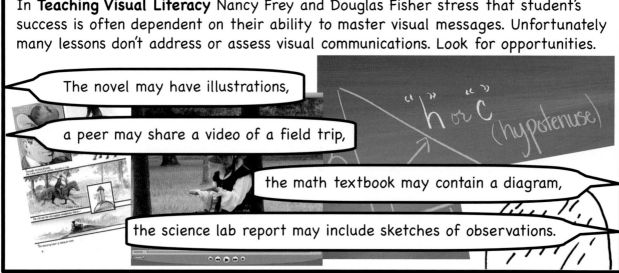

The novel may have illustrations,

a peer may share a video of a field trip,

the math textbook may contain a diagram,

the science lab report may include sketches of observations.

Graphics help young people grasp the gestalt. Thinking spatially, students are able to see relationships and patterns in data. They can use this information as evidence solving a problem or expressing an idea.

> The Standards for 21st Century Learners from the American Association of School Librarians (AASL 2007) stress the need for young people to be able to locate and create graphic communications.

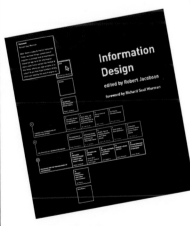

Information Outcome: Apply information presented in varied formats to collect evidence, make inferences, create arguments, and draw conclusions.

Mathematics Outcome: Applies concepts of probability, statistics, and data analysis to solve real-world problems.

Through the use of charts and graphs, the **Chances Project** from NCES at http://nces.ed.gov/nceskids/chances/ helps young people understand that what appears to be "good luck" can actually be explained with probability and statistics.

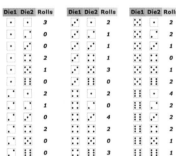

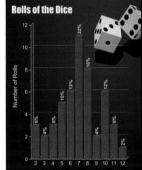

Die1	Die2	Rolls	Die1	Die2	Rolls	Die1	Die2	Rolls
		3			2			2
		0			1			2
		0			1			1
		2			1			0
		1			3			1
		0			0			2
		2			2			4
		1			0			2
		0			4			2
		2			2			2
		0			0			1
		0			3			1

Edited by Robert Jacobson, **Information Design** explores the newest of design disciplines. Robert Horn states "Information design is defined as the art and science of preparing information so that it can be used by human beings with efficiency and effectiveness. Its primary objectives are:

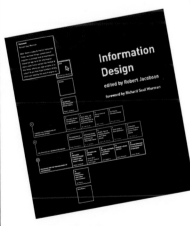

1. To develop documents that are comprehensible, rapidly and accurately retrievable, and easy to translate into effective action.
2. To design interactions with equipment that are easy, natural, and as pleasant as possible. This involves solving many problems in the design of the human-computer interface.
3. To enable people to find their way in three-dimensional space with comfort and ease – especially urban space, but also, given recent developments, virtual space...

...What we need is not more information, but the ability to present the right information to the right people at the right time, in the most effective and efficient form." (p. 15-16)

From professionals graphing data during field work to young children finger painting in the classroom, a widge range of graphics are created every day.

In **Effective Instruction: A Handbook of Evidence-Based Strategies,** Myles I. Friedman, Diane H. Harwell, and Katherine C. Schnepel stress that research evidence indicates that integrating graphics organizers into the teaching of subject matter enhances the academic achievement of students across grade levels and subject areas. The use of these unifying schemes may elevate student achievement by as much as five times (p. 152-3).

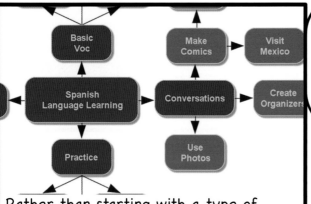

Rather than starting with a type of visual you want to create, begin with the ideas and information you want to convey.

If you want to share information that answers questions such as "how much" or "how many" then a chart might make sense. However if you're interested in showing relationships among physical locations, a map might be more useful.

Since graphics are used in many different contexts and involve overlaying techniques, it's difficult to create a definitive list with distinct divisions.

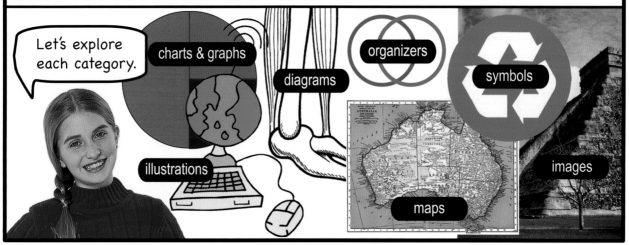

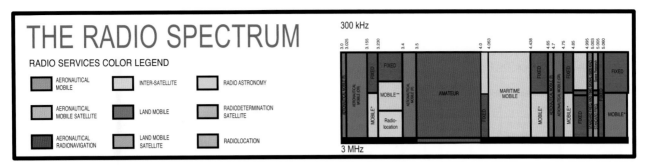

Charts and Graphs

Numeric data are often represented using charts and graphs.

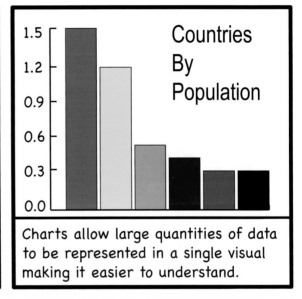

Countries By Population

Charts allow large quantities of data to be represented in a single visual making it easier to understand.

Although there are many different types, charts share some of the same elements.

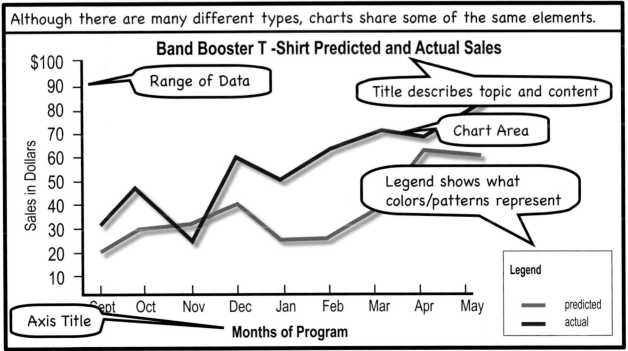

Band Booster T-Shirt Predicted and Actual Sales

Range of Data

Title describes topic and content

Chart Area

Legend shows what colors/patterns represent

Axis Title

Months of Program

Legend
— predicted
— actual

Let's explore a few examples of different types of charts and graphs.

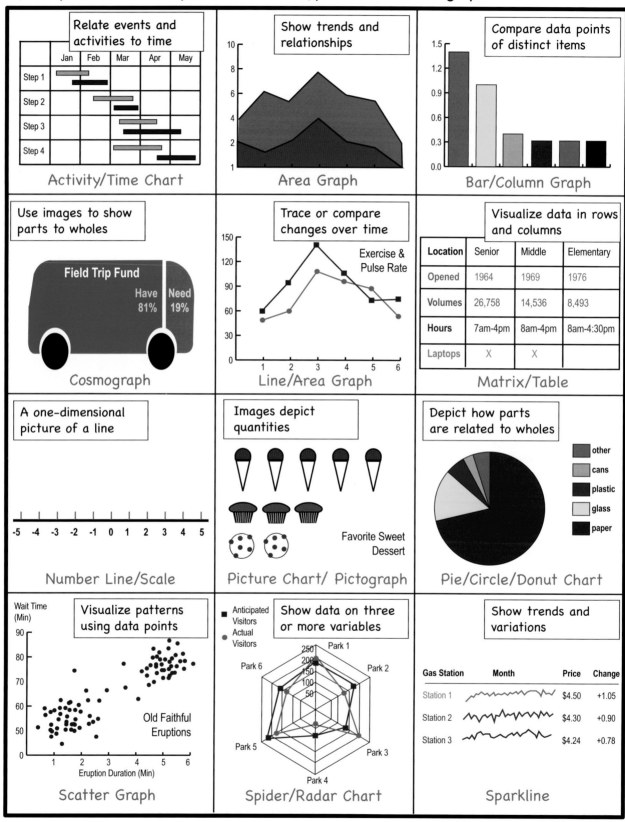

Relate events and activities to time — Activity/Time Chart

Show trends and relationships — Area Graph

Compare data points of distinct items — Bar/Column Graph

Use images to show parts to wholes — Cosmograph

Trace or compare changes over time — Line/Area Graph

Visualize data in rows and columns — Matrix/Table

A one-dimensional picture of a line — Number Line/Scale

Images depict quantities — Picture Chart/ Pictograph

Depict how parts are related to wholes — Pie/Circle/Donut Chart

Visualize patterns using data points — Scatter Graph

Show data on three or more variables — Spider/Radar Chart

Show trends and variations — Sparkline

Charts usually give information in tabular format using rows and columns. Some charts are well-known and have become the standard way of data access such as the periodic table or lunar calendar. Graphs show how one variable quantity changes in relation to another variable and may show trends.

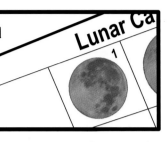

The advantage of using technology to produce charts is the ability to enter the data once, then try many different graph views. The use of software such as Microsoft Excel makes this process easy.

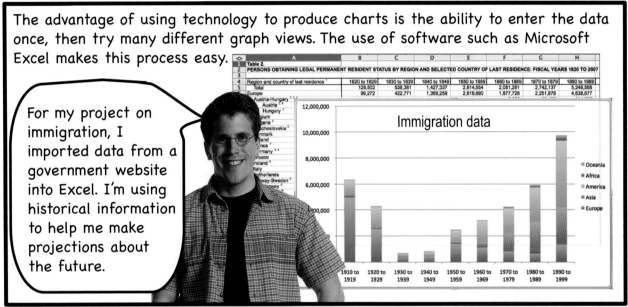

For my project on immigration, I imported data from a government website into Excel. I'm using historical information to help me make projections about the future.

Involve young people in examining professionally produced charts from newspapers such as USA Today, articles from scientific journals, and government websites. Ask them to consider different ways that the data could have been presented.

Where did this data originate?

How does the layout and use of color impact understanding?

Why is the data being shared?

What is this data really saying?

Can bias be found?

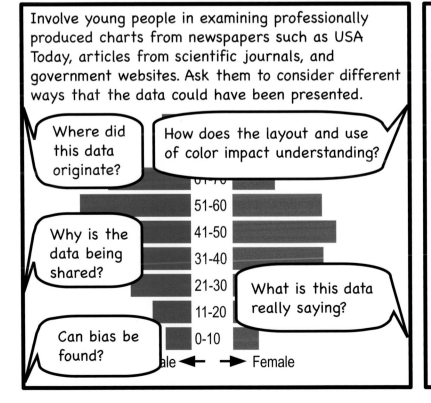

Introduce an inquiry-based assignment focusing on the collection of data to involve young people in gathering data, identifying ways to display this information, and creating their own graphs and charts.

Think of unique ways to present data using charts and graphs.

Charts and graphs are useful tools throughout the inquiry process. Consider the many ways that data can be visualized.

Questioning & Exploring

Think about how a chart might help get you started with an inquiry. Use graphs to identify problems, arrange background information, and organize ideas.

People with Disabilities by Age

(Bar chart: Percentage vs. Age Category — 15-24, 25-44, 45-64, 65-74, 75+)

My Question:

Over 50% of people over the age 75 have a disability. I've noticed that not all places have the same number of parking spaces for disabled people. What guidelines are used to decide how many parking spaces are provided?

> I found the Americans with Disabilities Act. It was established in 1990 to address the needs of disabled people.

PARKING BY DISABLED PERMIT ONLY

250.00 FINE

Assimilating & Inferring

Charts are powerful tools to display data, but it's important to select the best type of visual for the job. Tables work well for data presented in rows and columns, while pie charts work for showing parts of wholes.

More Questions:

I found a table with the Americans with Disabilities Act guidelines for parking spaces. Does our school have the required number of parking spaces?

5% accessible spaces

95% regular spaces

> My pie chart shows we have more than the minimum spaces.

ADA Minimum Number of Accessible Parking Spaces

Total Spaces	Total	96"	60"
1 - 25	1	1	0
26 -50	2	1	1
51 - 75	3	1	2
76 - 100	4	1	3
101 - 150	5	1	4
151 - 200	6	1	5
201 - 300	7	1	6
301 - 400	8	1	7
401 - 500	9	2	7
501 - 1000	2%	1/8	7/8
1001 +	*	1/8	7/8

Reflecting and Sharing

Charts can be used in presenting conclusions to others. Online tools such as **Create a Graph** are useful in creating simple charts and graphs.

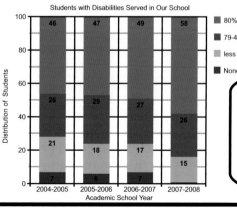

Students with Disabilities Served in Our School

Legend: 80% + | 79-40 | less 40 | None

Distribution of Students vs. Academic School Year

2004-2005	2005-2006	2006-2007	2007-2008
46	47	49	58
26	29	27	26
21	18	17	15
7	6	7	

My New Questions:

Besides parking spaces, how does our school meet the needs of the people with disabilities?

> This project has made me think more about the students at our school with disabilities. I don't think most people realize that this year almost all of the students are in the regular classroom.

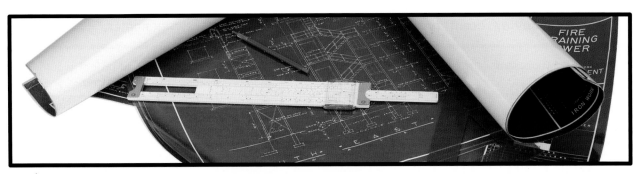

Diagrams

A simplified visual representation of an object, concept, or idea is often called a diagram.

Usually a line drawing, diagrams provide a quick reference to information that would otherwise be complex and difficult to understand.

Diagrams often show the relationships among parts and wholes such as the anatomy of the human body or the operation of a machine.

Technology has made the creation of diagrams much easier.

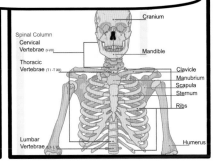

From the technical drawings of Leonardo DaVinci to the schematic etched in the Pioneer spacecraft, diagrams are classic tools to visualize concepts.

The ability to show complex concepts using simple lines and shapes is the key to effective diagrams.

There are many different types of diagrams. Let's explore a few examples.

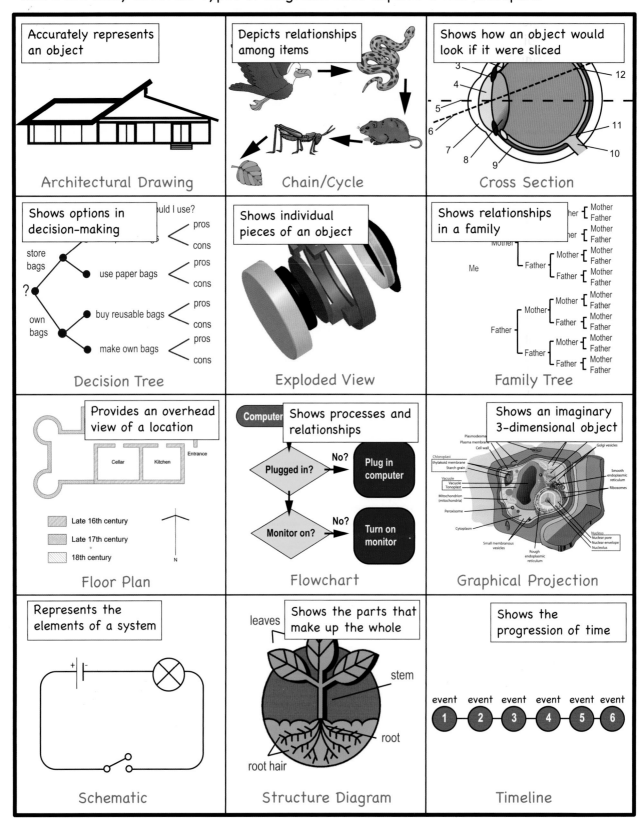

Accurately represents an object
Architectural Drawing

Depicts relationships among items
Chain/Cycle

Shows how an object would look if it were sliced
Cross Section

Shows options in decision-making
Decision Tree

Shows individual pieces of an object
Exploded View

Shows relationships in a family
Family Tree

Provides an overhead view of a location
Floor Plan

Shows processes and relationships
Flowchart

Shows an imaginary 3-dimensional object
Graphical Projection

Represents the elements of a system
Schematic

Shows the parts that make up the whole
Structure Diagram

Shows the progression of time
Timeline

In **The Rapid Vis Toolkit**, Kurt Hanks notes that a schematic can provide structure, meaning, and accesssibility to information. It provides a place to "hang information on." (p. 114)

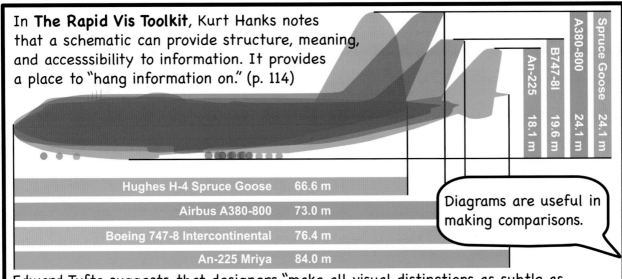

Diagrams are useful in making comparisons.

Hughes H-4 Spruce Goose	66.6 m
Airbus A380-800	73.0 m
Boeing 747-8 Intercontinental	76.4 m
An-225 Mriya	84.0 m

Spruce Goose	24.1 m
A380-800	24.1 m
B747-8I	19.6 m
An-225	18.1 m

Edward Tufte suggests that designers "make all visual distinctions as subtle as possible, but still clear and effective... the idea is to use just notable differences, visual elements that make a clear difference but no more – contrasts that are definite, effective, and minimal." (p. 73) Also in **Visual Explanations**, Tufte suggests using very light grids and outlines so they don't distract from a graph or diagram. Rather than coded lists of parts, use direct labels on objects.

Technical drawings provide accurate representations of objects to be used by an architect, engineer, or machinist.

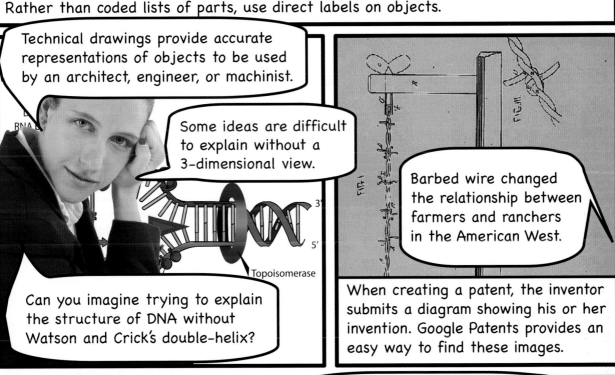

Some ideas are difficult to explain without a 3-dimensional view.

Topoisomerase

Can you imagine trying to explain the structure of DNA without Watson and Crick's double-helix?

Barbed wire changed the relationship between farmers and ranchers in the American West.

When creating a patent, the inventor submits a diagram showing his or her invention. Google Patents provides an easy way to find these images.

Rather than show details, a diagram generalizes by simplifying. Cross sections show the layers of rock.

Diagrams are useful tools throughout the inquiry process. Consider ways that inquirers can use existing diagrams as well as create their own.

Questioning & Exploring

Diagrams can jumpstart an inquiry by stimulating questions, providing background information, and visualizing problems or procedures.

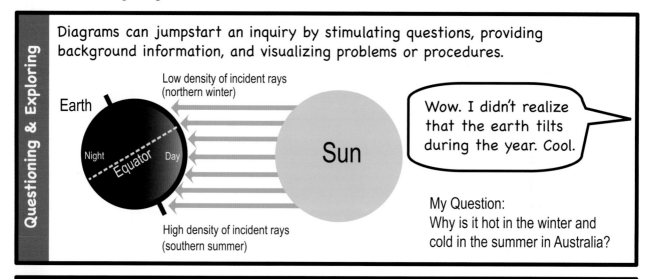

Low density of incident rays (northern winter)

Earth

Night   Equator   Day

Sun

High density of incident rays (southern summer)

Wow. I didn't realize that the earth tilts during the year. Cool.

My Question:
Why is it hot in the winter and cold in the summer in Australia?

Assimilating & Inferring

Diagrams are helpful in providing visual explanations and information. Use diagrams as you look for insights, make comparisons, and build connections between existing knowledge and new information. Ask yourself: how does this diagram help me better understand this object, system, or procedure?

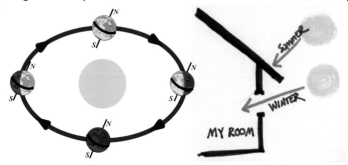

I notice that in the winter the sun shines in my bedroom window. However in the summer it doesn't. I think it's because of the angle of the sun.

SUMMER
WINTER
MY ROOM

Reflecting and Sharing

Building a diagram is an excellent way to demonstrate understanding and share this knowledge with others. In addition, use diagrams as a way to reflect on learning and generate new questions.

Stonehenge is an example of how much early civilizations knew about the sun and the seasons.

My New Questions:
What did ancient cultures know about the sun and seasons? How did they share this understanding?

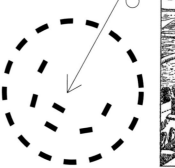

Illustrations

Drawings, paintings, sketches, and etchings are examples of illustrations. These visual representations are intended to communicate an informational or artistic message.

With editorial cartoons, the message is often social or political. A century ago when most citizens couldn't read the newspaper, cartoons could reflect the depth of corruption of the Boss Tweed politcal machine in New York City or concerns about a war in Europe.   4.7828

Artists during the Middle Ages crafted murals and stained glass scenes to tell the Christian story. Illustrations helped to communicate across a wider audience as well as give emphasis and drama to the narrative details available to those who had mastered reading and writing.

In graphic novels, picture books, and tales by children today, illustrations are still used to tell the story.

There are many different types of illustrations. Let's explore a few examples.

Cartoon	Collage	Drafting/Technical Drawing
You make me SICK! When germ relationships go bad	*Assemblage of varied forms into one visual*	*Communicate technical information*
Drawing	Graffiti	Information Graphic
Visuals created by marking a surface	*Images marked on property*	*Represents info, data, or knowledge*
Poster	Painting	Printmaking
Process that applies color to surface	*Impression created from a matrix*	
Sequential Art/Comic	Sketch	Visualization
Series of images to convey a story	*Quick drawing to record impressions*	*Communicates a visual message*

Essential ideas sometimes become lost in text-heavy communications. Use illustrations along with a few key words to produce memorable messages.

I'm interested in fashion design. Most fashion drawings include varied angles and close-up views, along with brief descriptions.

Drawing pictures of idioms is a natural connection between graphics and standards.

a feather in my cap!

Painting can provide realistic or abstract representations.

Before the invention of photos, illustrations such as paintings and etchings were used as a way to record events and capture the likeness of individuals.

In **A Practical Guide to Graphics Reporting**, Jennifer George-Palilonis stresses the importance of "putting all of the pieces together in a rhythmic, orderly, interesting design...the design of the graphic can have a direct impact on the audience's ability to follow the information that is presented in an efficient and logical manner." (p. 83)

Information visualization uses computer tools to represent large amounts of abstract data. Infographics are used where information must be explained simply and quickly.

This mosaic provides a macro view of all English Wikipedia and those areas that are identified as "hot."

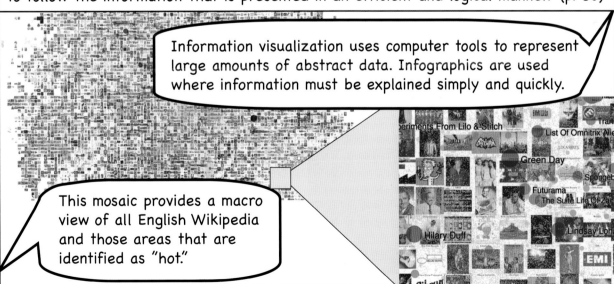

Whether using existing resources or creating your own, illustrations play an important role in the inquiry process.

Use the illustrations you find in books, newspapers, and websites to stimulate thinking and questions about a topic. When were these visuals created? How do they reflect a particular time, place, or situation? What questions do the images trigger?

Native Americans used ledger books to record their experiences through drawing.

My Questions:
What was it like to go on a buffato hunt?
How far did they travel from home to hunt?
What did their homes look like?

As you examine illustrations, create visual notes such as sketches to remind you of what you've seen and read. Continue to enhance your graphic notes as you find new information.

Pueblo
Adobe or sandstone
inside   outside

As you think about what you've learned, go back and revisit illustrations you examined earlier in your investigation. What new questions have emerged?

My New Questions:
How do the images created by Indians about their own experiences differ from those created by European observers?
How was buffalo hunting different for Indians and Europeans?
How did the Indians hunt buffalo before the Spaniards brought horses?

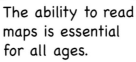

The ability to read maps is essential for all ages.

Maps

A map provides a visual representation of an area showing relationships in space. When you hear the word "map" you probably think of geography. Cartography is the practice of creating maps of the Earth including road maps and treasure maps...

We made treasure maps and wrote stories about finding a buried treasure!

...however there are many different types of maps. A knowledge domain map is used to visualize information making it easier to understand and access.

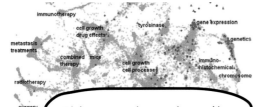

This map shows how the medical research in the area of melanoma can be visualized.

Consider how maps can be used by young people to draw inferences.

I'm not very good at reading, but I love pictures. I learned a lot about the province I'm studying by reading the map. My province is next to the ocean, so people probably use boats and ships.

There are many different types of maps. Let's explore a few examples.

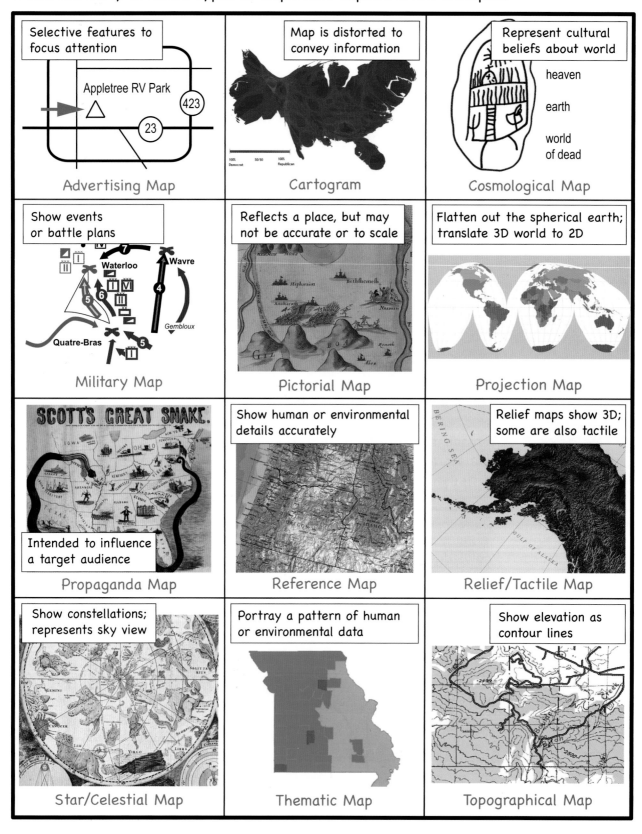

Selective features to focus attention — Advertising Map	Map is distorted to convey information — Cartogram	Represent cultural beliefs about world (heaven, earth, world of dead) — Cosmological Map
Show events or battle plans — Military Map	Reflects a place, but may not be accurate or to scale — Pictorial Map	Flatten out the spherical earth; translate 3D world to 2D — Projection Map
Intended to influence a target audience — Propaganda Map	Show human or environmental details accurately — Reference Map	Relief maps show 3D; some are also tactile — Relief/Tactile Map
Show constellations; represents sky view — Star/Celestial Map	Portray a pattern of human or environmental data — Thematic Map	Show elevation as contour lines — Topographical Map

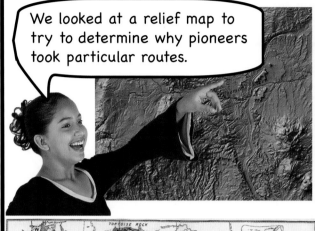

We looked at a relief map to try to determine why pioneers took particular routes.

In a special issue of **Knowledge Quest** on the topic of maps, Debbie Abilock noted that "as a tool for thinking, a map may help us grasp the gestalt, understand findings, analyze relationships and patterns, or define and solve problems." (p. 8)

However, according to Mark Monmonier in **How to Lie with Maps**, "there's no escape from the cartographic paradox: to present a useful and truthful picture, an accurate map must tell white lies.... a single map is but one of an indefinitely large number of maps that might be produced for the same situation or from the same data." (p. 1-2).

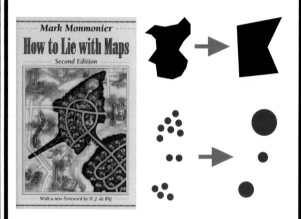

Since symbols take up more space than the features they represent, Monmonier notes that clarity requires geometric generalization. Lines might be simplified, displaced, smoothed or enhanced (p. 25).

Before using a map, try to determine who created the map and why. Was it designed by a well-known cartographer or respected historian? Was it created for advertising or propaganda purposes? Does it exaggerate data? Do the symbols, lines, and colors contribute or distract from the map?

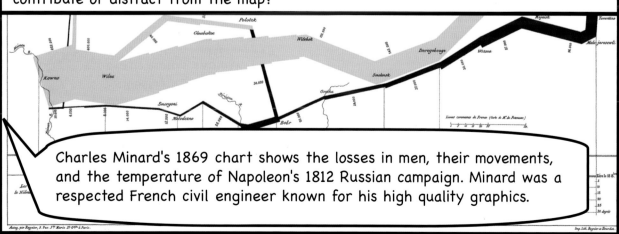

Charles Minard's 1869 chart shows the losses in men, their movements, and the temperature of Napoleon's 1812 Russian campaign. Minard was a respected French civil engineer known for his high quality graphics.

Maps are effective for conveying a wide range of information. During inquiry, look for ways that maps can be used to access, analyze, and share data and information.

Questioning & Exploring

Use maps to jumpstart inquiry. Maps ignite curiosity, generate questions, visualize patterns of movement, and stimulate brainstorming activities.

We've been watching an interactive map showing the migration of hummingbirds through the Journey North Project. We even added our own sighting.

My Questions:
What other creatures migrate? Why do some animals migrate and others stay in one place?
Where do tarantulas live? Do they migrate?

Assimilating & Inferring

As you examine maps, think about ways to adapt and build your own maps as a way to organize what you're learning. Add notes, symbols, and color to help you record information.

I've been reading about tarantulas. They're found all over the world, even here in Branson. They live south of the Missouri River. Missouri Tarantulas move about a mile during mating season, but don't migrate.

Reflecting and Sharing

As you think about what you've learned, consider new questions. Think about the many types of maps that could be used to convey data and information. Ask yourself: how could maps show movement or changes over time?

I wonder when fire ants will come to Missouri.

My New Questions:
What's the difference between migration and invasion?
How and why do plants and animals invade?
Why do some creatures thrive and others die?
How do we make decisions about what to keep and remove?

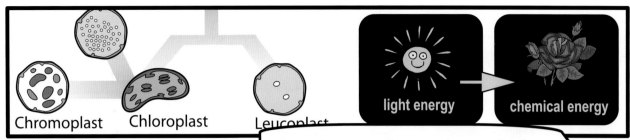

Chromoplast   Chloroplast   Leucoplast

light energy   →   chemical energy

Organizers can be complex or simple.

Organizers

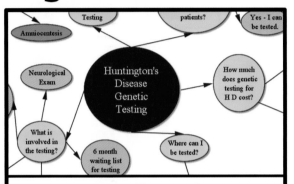

Organizers are effective for showing relationships among data, connections like cause and effect, chronologies of events, and comparisons such as the pros and cons of alternative solutions.

Joseph Novak developed the process for using concept maps as a way for students to gain a better understanding of associations in subject matter and retention of concepts. In **Learning How to Learn**, Novak and Gowin stress that students identify and develop new concept relationships in the process of drawing concept maps. This experience fosters creativity. As young people begin labeling connections and reviewing their maps, they're able to demonstrate their deep understandings.

needs

The use of graphic organizers in teaching and learning emerged from David Ausubel's research in the 1950s and 1960s on the benefits of advanced organizers. He found that student learning improved if young people had a structured method for organizing information.

Concept maps help people show interconnection of information and ideas. Circles and boxes cluster ideas together. Lines and arrows are used to show relationships. Colors can add emphasis and draw interest.

I'm just learning to write, but I can show what I know through pictures, shapes, lines, and arrows.

Let's explore examples of different kinds of organizers.

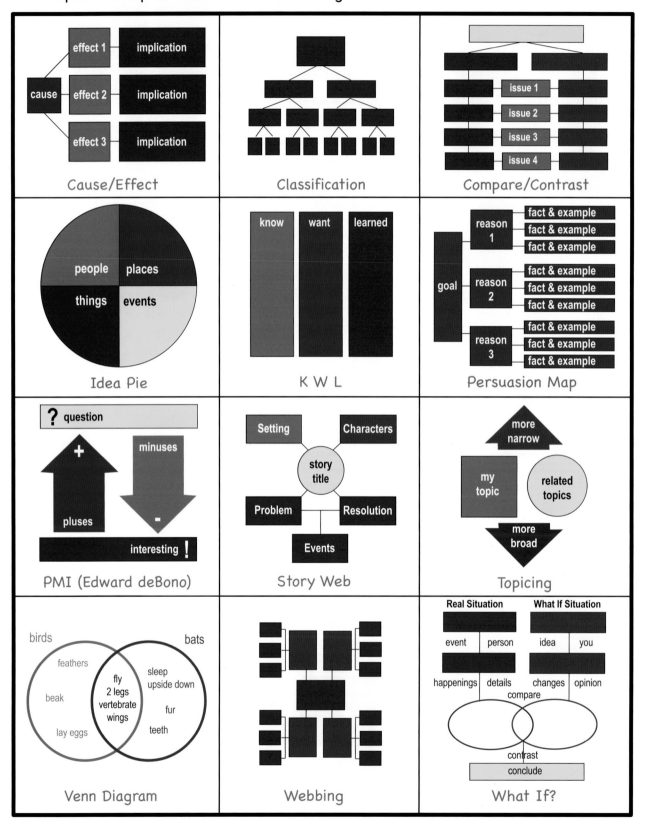

In **Graphic Organizers**, Karen Bromley, Linda Irwin-De Vitis, and Marcia Modlo identify four basic patterns of knowledge organization:

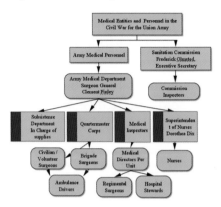

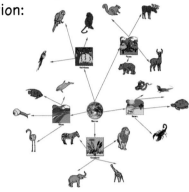

Hierarchical - main concepts and levels of subcategories. (generalizations, classifications)

Conceptual – central idea with supporting facts or examples (mind maps, Venn diagram)

Sequential – arranges events in chronological order (timeline, problem solving)

Cyclical – a continuous sequence of events forming a circular process (chains, cycle)

> I'm organizing information about polar ice caps and climate change.

> Organizers can take many forms. However the key is selecting the most effective method of structuring the data. Ask yourself: What information needs to be organized? How can visuals convey this structure?

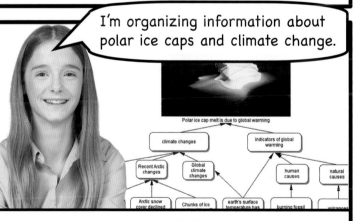

Marian Martinello and Gillian Cook believe students can benefit from being taught how to visually organize the information they gather to show connections between and among ideas. In **Interdisciplinary Inquiry in Teaching and Learning** they note that the conceptual web helps young people show connections among ideas, while the Venn diagram helps them find the features when making comparisons.

Organizers are useful tools throughout the inquiry process. Think about how they can be used in brainstorming, synthesizing information, and presenting alternative ideas.

Questioning & Exploring

Consider how graphic organizers can be used to help you visualize concepts and explore "big ideas." Use organizers to visualize topics and subtopics.

KINGDOM – – – – – Cars

TYPE – – – Imports   Domestic

LOC – Japan   Germany   USA

MAKE–Honda Toyota   Mer BMW   Chrysler Ford GM

SUBS – – – – – – – – – Jeep Dodge Chrysler

MODELS

> I'm studying taxonomies in biology. My teacher said practically everything can be organized into kingdoms.

My Questions:
How can cars be classified?
How will a car tree help me better understand the idea of taxonomies?

Assimilating & Inferring

Organizers can provide scaffolding for learning new concepts and assist you in visualizing the relationships among data and information. Ask yourself: what's the best way to organize these ideas? How can a visual help me understand?

> The electronic database "What Tree Is It" is arranged as a taxonomy. We're using it to help identify and map the trees in our community.

Needles	Scales	Broad	Flattened

Reflecting and Sharing

Think about how to apply the things you've learned to new situations inside and outside the school setting. Use organizers in real-world settings.

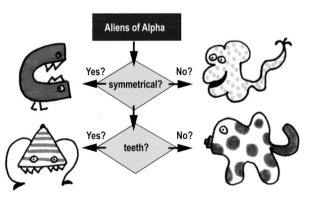

Aliens of Alpha

Yes? — symmetrical? — No?

Yes? — teeth? — No?

> I want to be a computer game designer. I'm working on a game called Aliens Attack.

My Questions:
Will a classification system help me create a world for the Aliens Attack game I want to create?

Images

Many devices can be used to capture an image. You're probably most familiar with using a camera for photography.

Tomography involves creating images like x-rays and ultrasound visuals using technical equipment like a CT or MRI.

Digital imaging is the process of creating digital images from a physical object.

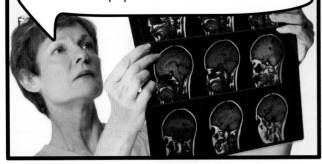

**Processing
Compressing
Editing
Printing
Storing
Displaying**

In **Ways of Seeing,** John Berger states "an image is a sight which has been recreated or reproduced. It is an appearance, or a set of appearances, which has been detached from the place and time in which it first made its appearance and preserved – for a few moments or a few centuries. Every image embodies a way of seeing." (p. 10)

A photographer composes an image through techniques such as angle, field of view, and depth of field.

Photographs are useful in reflecting real people, places, and things. They can capture a moment in time, show a sequence of activities, and provide different perspectives on an event.

Many examples can be found of photography and other types of imaging. Explore a few.

Images taken from the air of the ground	Images taken of astronomical objects	Obtaining photos through a spotting scope or telescope
Aerial Photography	Astrophotography	Digiscoping
Light captured beyond the visibile light range	A close-up that shows actual size	Using a camera on a microscope
Multi-spectral Imaging	Macro Photography	Microscopy Imaging
Images with a wide field of vision	Images produced by radar detection	Visualized data from aircraft or satellite
Panoramic Photography	Radar Imaging	Remote Sensing
Visualize muscles and internal organs	A radiographic image is created to show structure	A series of photos taken over time
Ultrasonography	X-Ray Imaging	Time-lapse Photography

In **Ways of Seeing**, John Berger states "images were first made to conjure up the appearance of something that was absent. Gradually it became evident that an image could outlast what it represented... no other kind of relic or text from the past can offer such direct testimony about the world which surrounded other people at other times." (p. 10)

By providing images of changes over time, people can start a dialog about issues such as water use, natural disaster preparation, urban development, and climate change.

Compare Grinnell Glacier in 1938 with 2005. Notice how much the glacier has retreated.

How is disaster preparation different now than 100 years ago during the San Francisco earthquake? How would this scene be different today?

 Different views can facilitate learning. A glass terrarium reveals the growth of a plant, while the cross section of a tree provides insights into its growth over time.

From locating existing images to photographing the research process, images are useful tools throughout the inquiry process.

Questioning & Exploring

Images jumpstart inquiry by prompting questions and stimulating comparisons. Photographs serve as useful evidence.

Our class is reading historical fiction books set during the Klondike Gold Rush. I read **Call of the Wild** and **Jason's Gold**. Historical photographs are a great way to explore the setting of the books.

My Questions:
What was life like in the Klondike during the 1890s?
What did the people, places, and things look like?

Assimilating & Inferring

Images serve as useful evidence in problem-solving and decision-making, however it's important that images are carefully analyzed and evaluated. Ask yourself: what's the perspective of the photograph? Why was the photo taken? Are different views available that can be compared?

To get a sense for the geography and climate, I've been looking at aerial and satellite images of Skagway, Alaska. I used Google Earth to retrace the steps of Gold Rush explorers. I can understand why the trip was such a challenge.

More Questions: Which images best represent these settings?
What pictures help me understand the terrain?

Reflecting and Sharing

Images are helpful in sharing ideas and communicating conclusions. Photos taken during the inquiry process can be used to review progress and justify decisions. Scrapbooks of images are helpful in sharing understandings.

Act 2: Scene 1

I've been reading that lots of directors take photos as they scout out film locations. I want to turn the science fiction story I wrote for my English class into a movie. I've created a photo scrapbook to record the locations I'll be using for each scene.

Another Question: What location will I use for my movie?

Symbols

Semiotics is the science of signs and symbols. Symbols are visuals used to represent ideas, concepts, or other abstractions. They can serve as a common language for giving directions or warnings and are often used to represent groups or causes such as a pink ribbon for breast cancer research.

When I looked at the laundry instructions on my new sweater, I realized they were written in Chinese. Luckily, I can read the symbols so I know what to do.

From culture to culture, symbols and colors may be interpreted differently. A leaf may represent nature to some, but to Canadians it's a national symbol.

I'm studying the old west. It's fun to learn about the brands they put on cattle. This is the rocking R.

While the thumbs-up sign has a positive meaning to some cultures, it may be meaningless to others. Symbols are useful as a quick reference and common global language. For instance, most people would recognize that a red diagonal line through an object means DON'T or FORBIDDEN.

There are many different types of symbols. Let's explore a few examples.

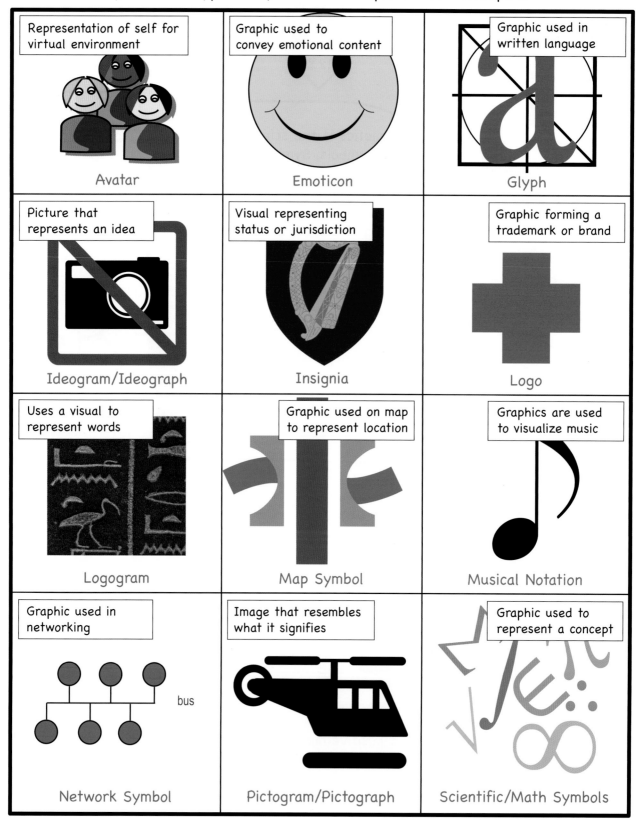

Representation of self for virtual environment	Graphic used to convey emotional content	Graphic used in written language
Avatar	**Emoticon**	**Glyph**
Picture that represents an idea	Visual representing status or jurisdiction	Graphic forming a trademark or brand
Ideogram/Ideograph	**Insignia**	**Logo**
Uses a visual to represent words	Graphic used on map to represent location	Graphics are used to visualize music
Logogram	**Map Symbol**	**Musical Notation**
Graphic used in networking	Image that resembles what it signifies	Graphic used to represent a concept
Network Symbol	**Pictogram/Pictograph**	**Scientific/Math Symbols**

bus

Many of the most common symbols are part of the ISOTYPE – International System of Typographic Picture Education developed by Otto Neurath. A standard set of pictograms are also defined by the international standard ISO 7001. These Public Information Symbols provide a standard so that food handling and chemical hazards are always labeled in the same manner.

Young people are taught the meaning of symbols or have direct experiences with these images. For instance, they need to be able to read the safe handling instructions on meat products.

Symbols can inform, communicate, or express. Let's explore three approaches:

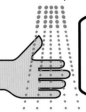 **Concrete** – accurate picture of person, place, thing, or object

 Abstract – simplified graphic remotely resembles the original

 Invented – graphic invented for a specific purpose; doesn't represent a real object

Symbols are often used on maps to show relationships. To understand the map, readers must be able to interpret the symbols. On my map the larger the dot, the higher the percentage of Spanish speakers.

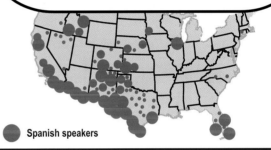

● Spanish speakers

In **Information Graphics**, Robert Harris identifies four types of symbols (p. 380).

Literal
HOUSTON = Largest city
Austin = Medium city
LIVINGSTON = Smallest city

Point
• = small
● = medium
● = large

Line
- - - - - - - bike trail
— — — ATV trail
———— unimproved road

Area/Volume

He also states that symbols serve seven functions in charts and graphs (p. 379).

 Convey quantitative info

 Convey descriptive info

 Austin Designate location

 Differentiate, identify, etc.

 Serve as an enclosure

 Highlight specific info

 Form meaningful displays

Symbols may be used throughout the inquiry process. They may be the object of an inquiry or a means of organizing or communicating information.

Questioning & Exploring

Symbols are useful springboards for inquiry. They can stimulate questions and provide a focus for exploration. They may also be used to organize information and express ideas.

A new school policy prohibits students from wearing political symbols.

My Questions:
What's a political symbol?
Do I own any T-shirts with these symbols?
Why are people worried about political symbols?

I want to learn more about these symbols and why people wear them.

Assimilating & Inferring

Symbols are powerful tools for communication, however it's important to have a clear understanding of their meaning. Ask yourself: what's the origin of this symbol? What's the meaning and how has it been used? How is the symbol like and unlike other symbols?

The peace sign is actually based on the semaphore flag signal system representing D and N standing for **N**uclear **D**isarmament. Developed in 1958 by Gerald Holtom, it became the emblem for the 1960s anti-war movement. My mom gave me her peace sign necklace. I think I should be able to wear it to school!

Reflecting and Sharing

From scientific notation to map production, symbols are often used to produce communications and share conclusions. Think about the many types of symbols that can be used to share understandings.

Learning about the peace sign made me wonder about other peace symbols throughout history. I composed a song to go along with these symbols of peace.

I'm going to make my own peace symbol!

SCORE IT! Standards and Deep Thinking

> In my multi-age classroom, I design learning experiences that help young people think about content in different ways. When I look at a standard, I ask myself:...

> My picture shows my math problem and my solution!

> ...how many different ways can students show me they understand?

Since so much of student communication is text-based, it's easy to see each learning outcome as requiring a written response. However if you examine your standards with an open mind, you'll see many opportunities to incorporate graphic elements.

> **Grade 3**
> I need your help!
> Animals are arriving for the new children's zoo. How do you think they should be organized?

> **Grade 6**
> No one ever visits the anthropods exhibit. Let's help people see how important these creatures are by showing how they are related to other living things.

> **Grade 11**
> Fungi are related in interesting ways.
> We need a graphic for visitors showing these relationships and their connection to other living things at the zoo.

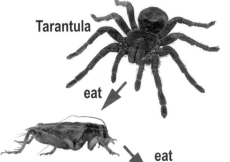

Tarantula

eat

eat

Science Learning Outcomes. Diversity and classification of life
Grade 3. Describes ways living things can be grouped.
Grade 6. Classifies living things using established systems.
Grade 11. Classifies organisms into a hierarchy of groups and subgroups based on evolutionary relationships.

Regardless of the grade level, young people need to be able to do more than answer basic multiple choice questions. To show their understanding, they need to apply their knowledge and skills to authentic situations.

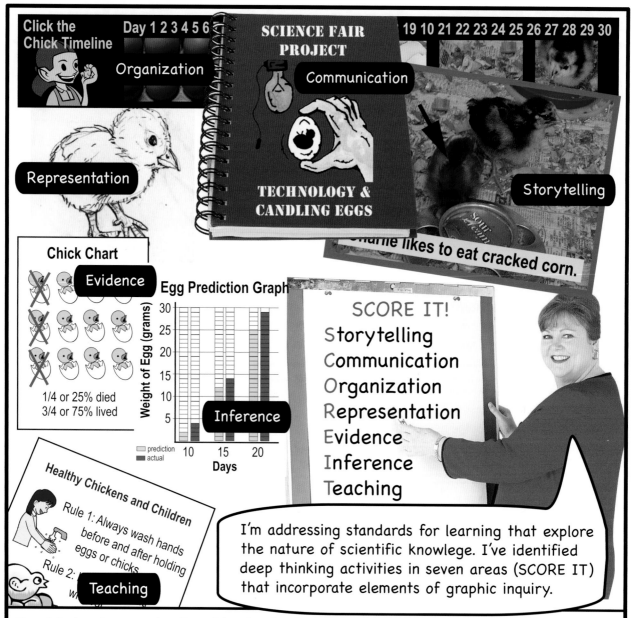

I'm addressing standards for learning that explore the nature of scientific knowlege. I've identified deep thinking activities in seven areas (SCORE IT) that incorporate elements of graphic inquiry.

Graphic inquiry can be found in standards across grade levels and subject areas. As you examine a specific standard, think about the following questions:

√ What ideas does the statement provide regarding how students learn from graphic information and how they might communicate their knowledge through visuals?

√ Which of the seven deep thinking areas (SCORE IT) apply to this standard?

√ Which of the seven types of graphics would be useful in teaching and/or learning the knowledge, skills, and dispositions associated with this standard?

√ What visuals could students read, analyze, use, or create to address the standard?

√ What learning activities in graphic inquiry can be devised to meet this standard?

√ What basic artifacts of student learning can be illustrated through graphic inquiry that represent this standard (Lamb & Callison 2007)?

Once you've thought about the kind of graphic inquiry you'd like learners to experience, match standards with specific assignments and assessments that require deep thinking.

Design Assignments

Assignments describe the task or mission of the inquiry for the student. They also define the parameters and identify what will be valued in their work. Tools, resources, materials, learning activities, and processes are also given with the assignment. Additional scaffolding and assistance is provided as learners face obstacles or have questions.

After exploring resources about owls, think about how the authors and scientists learn about owls.

How do scientists figure out what owls eat?
How and why do we dissect owl pellets?
What role do owls play in the ecosystem?

Owl Pellet Dissection

Science (Grades 6-8): Describes the scientific inquiry including evaluating the results of experiments, observations, and theoretical models. Identifies relationships among living things and their physical environment.

Design Assessments

Assessment is the process of gathering, measuring, analyzing, and reporting data on a students' learning. It helps teachers determine how much children learned and how well they learned it. Assessment can also be used to determine the effectiveness of the instruction and how well students were able to meet a given standard. Interacting with students about their performance is an integral part of the learning process. There are dozens of different assessment tools that can be adapted to fit the needs of your students. These include anecdotal reports, checklists, conferencing, conversations, journals, peer assessments, portfolios, progress reports, quizzes, rubrics, self-assessments, scored discussions, and tests.

Science Inquiry Rubric
Categories:
Dissection log
Checklist of identified parts
Photographs of owl pellet dissection
Sketch of rodent reconstruction
Sketch of owl in food chain

As you work your way through the SCORE IT section of the book, think about how you might design inquiry experiences to address standards in each SCORE IT area. How can existing visuals and student-generated graphics help learners:
- generate meaningful questions?
- explore information and ideas?
- assimilate concepts and build new connections?
- make inferences and share their findings?
- reflect on the experience and transfer learning to new situations?

History (Grades 3-5): Identifies well-known historical figures who contributed to the cultural history of the U.S. such as folk heroes, mountain men, leaders in the Westward movement, and Native Americans.

Question and Explore: Existing Graphics

Buffalo Bill

Visuals are used to show students popular folk heroes. Students select a person to explore and use a concept map to record ideas and information.

Question and Explore: Student Made

Assimilate and Infer: Existing Graphics

Historical images are used to discuss the fact and fiction of folk heroes. Students then draw pictures to synthesize and share what they've learned.

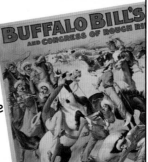

Assimilate and Infer: Student Made

IL   IN   OH

Reflect: Existing Graphics

Local photos along with images from the news are used to talk about modern day heroes. Children choose folk heroes they think are significant from around the world.

Reflect: Student Made

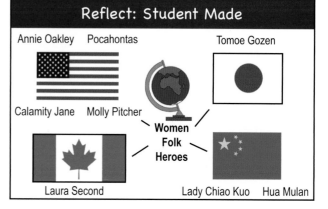

Annie Oakley   Pocahontas   Tomoe Gozen

Calamity Jane   Molly Pitcher

Women Folk Heroes

Laura Second   Lady Chiao Kuo   Hua Mulan

SCORE IT: Storytelling

From ancient petroglyphs to today's comic books and graphic novels, visuals contain the oldest recorded stories. Storytelling is the art of conveying a sequence of events that may use visuals to express character, plot, and setting.

Along with storytelling, seek engaging activities that encourage students to imagine, invent, entertain, re-enact, and illustrate.

Whether describing a math story problem or re-enacting an event from history, students need to be able to retell stories as well as invent their own visual narratives.

Kalyee ⊙⊙⊙ $2×4 = $8
Alex ⊙⊙⊙⊙ $2×5 == $10
Arrion ⊙⊙ $2×3 .= 6
COOKIE SALE $24
$2 per ⊙
— I sold the most Cookies. I win!

During the inquiry process, stories may stimulate questions, trigger personal connections, or illustrate concepts. As a product of inquiry, visually-rich stories may be used to communicate, entertain, or preserve culture.

In **Graphic Storytelling and Visual Narrative**, Will Eisner notes that visual stories are a way to convey information in an easily absorbed manner.

In the Aesop's fable, **The Fox and the Leopard**, children learn that "A fine coat is not always an indication of an attractive mind."

Students retell fables through drawings and comics.

You talk about you.

History (Grades K-2): Describes the main idea found in fables, folktales, and tall tales, along with myths and legends from around the world. Connects the stories to the belief systems of current and past cultures.

I have a new haircut, an expensive sweater, and cool glasses. Do you want to be my friend?

Aesop's Fables Today
The Fox and the Leopard

Friendship isn't about fancy things. I want friends who think for themselves.

Science (Grades 6-8): Describes the Earth's structure and composition.

I want students to do more than simply blurt out an answer. I want them to be able to create their own original example to show that they can transfer information into a new and different situation.

Sharing an anecdote, story, or invention is an easy way to demonstrate understanding and address a standard.

The Story of Antelope Canyon
500 million ago
250 million ago
million years ago
illion years ago

Digital storytelling is an emerging form of personal, heartful expression that enables individuals and communities to reclaim their personal cultures while exploring their artistic creativity.
– Bernajean Porter

DigiTales
The Art of Telling Digital Stories

Think about how standards support use of graphics to imagine, invent, tell a story, entertain or display information.

Think about visual inspiration or story starters across the curriculum.
Start with:

- maps of locations.
- drawings of objects.
- comics or graphic novels.
- works of art.
- a series of photographs.

THE STORM IN THE BARN

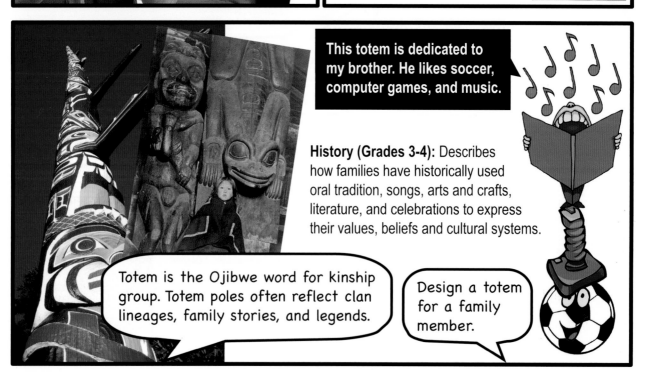

This totem is dedicated to my brother. He likes soccer, computer games, and music.

History (Grades 3-4): Describes how families have historically used oral tradition, songs, arts and crafts, literature, and celebrations to express their values, beliefs and cultural systems.

Totem is the Ojibwe word for kinship group. Totem poles often reflect clan lineages, family stories, and legends.

Design a totem for a family member.

Scenarios can jumpstart an inquiry, re-enactments may visualize concepts, and anecdotes can summarize an experience. Tell the story of people, places, or things using a variety of images. In the book **Story Proof** Kendall Haven notes that humans are predisposed to share their experiences through stories. As we build narratives, we shape our understanding of new experiences.

Tell the story of people through illustrations, photographs, and symbols.

History (Grades 3-5): Describes individuals who made significant contributions in the field of communications.

The Story of Toilet Paper

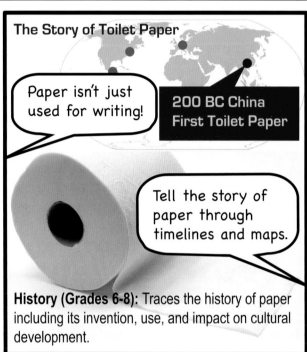

Paper isn't just used for writing!

200 BC China First Toilet Paper

Tell the story of paper through timelines and maps.

History (Grades 6-8): Traces the history of paper including its invention, use, and impact on cultural development.

Language Arts (Grades 9-12): Creates narratives including fiction, biography, and autobiography.

After reading Ann Marie Fleming's illustrated memoir focusing on her search for information about her great-grandfather, I decided to write the story of my great Aunt Laura using primary source documents including photos, her birth certificate, and diaries.

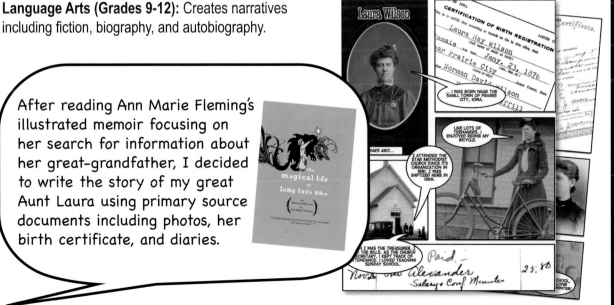

Language Arts (Grades 6-8): Identifies stereotyping and bias in visual media, advertising, and television.

Maria likes the idea of reading a graphic novel rather than a traditional book. As one of the only Hispanic students at her school, she relates to the characters in the book **American Born Chinese** by Gene Yang.

What's a stereotype?
Where do they originate?
Why are recent immigrant groups stereotyped more than others?

I want to tell the story of Chinese stereotyping and the anti-immigration movements of the late 1800s and early 1900s. I see the same thing happening today with stereotyping of recent immigrants.

By comparing the historical story to my personal story, I hope people will see the importance of treating each person as an individual.

Let's examine 100 year old magazines, cartoons, art, and advertisements.

How were Chinese people depicted in the U.S. media in the past? Why? What characteristics were commonly attributed to this group? What stereotypes do you see in media today?

SCORE IT: Communication

Brainstorming questions as a team, reporting results of an experiment to others, and conducting peer evaluations are examples of how communication takes place throughout the inquiry process. Inquiry often involves interacting with others to question, explain, define, report, and share. Through a process of asking and answering questions, young people communicate their understandings.

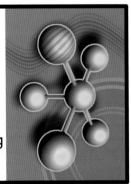

Communication is the process of transferring messages from a sender to a receiver using a common language.

Reports and worksheets are common ways students communicate their understandings, but there are many other options. Young people might collect and publish personal histories or create editorial cartoons.

Communicating visually requires students to transform their ideas into a visual format such as conducting and sharing the results of a poll, survey, experiment, or interview.

Health (Grades 6-8): Applies stress management strategies to deal with personal feelings and peer pressure.

In the **KABAM!** project at http://bam.gov/ sponsored by the Center for Disease Control, students read comics to learn about dealing with stressful situations. Then, they make choices as they create comic communications. Finally, children are ready to build their own comics using the digital camera to visualize situations and share strategies for dealing with their feelings.

Think about how standards support the use of graphics to explain, define, instruct, report and communicate. In **I See What You Mean,** Steve Moline advocates activities that involve "recomposing" or asking students to read in one format and express understandings in a different way such as a diagram, graph, or poster.

The Arizona Department of Health Services and Arizona Diamondbacks **Be SunWise and Play Sun Smart Poster Drawing Contest** asks students to share sun safety advice in a persuasive poster.

Health (Grades 3-5): Describes and applies best practices related to injury prevention and safety.

Award-winning student poster

Consider products such as:

- blogs
- banners
- bulletin boards
- exhibits
- posters
- murals
- reports

We made ceiling tiles for the library showing our favorite book character.

Language Arts (All Grades): Applies skills and strategies of the writing process to create real-world communications that incorporate effective illustrations and technologies.

Let's Recycle!

Metal   Paper   Glass

Look under the metal, paper, and glass flap to find out why recycling is so important to our community! Then, RECYCLE!

I'm investigating the options for local recycling. I want to share what I've learned with members of our community. I've created an interactive poster with information flaps I hope to post at the grocery store.

A peacemaker helps to resolve disputes and conflicts. I am going to nominate Gandhi for the **My Hero** award. I'm using historical photos to document his work.

The online **My Hero Project** challenges young people to explore, identify, and share their heroes through photos, film, artwork, and written communications in a wide range of categories such as artists, earthkeepers, and peacemakers.

Language Arts (Grades K-2): Identifies and describes the main idea in visual media such as photographs, maps, cartoons, and visual narratives.

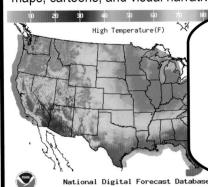

High Temperature(F)

National Digital Forecast Database

> I can read weather maps. We've made our own weather map that shows the weather at my school in Indianapolis and at my grandparents' house in South Bend.

74

69

United States Declaration  **French Declaration**

We hold these truths to be self-evident, that all men are created equal.

Men are born and remain free and equal in rights.

> We're comparing documents. Then we're going to create a visual comparison in the style of Sam Fink's books.

The Declaration of Independence
The words that made America

THE CONSTITUTION
THE UNITED STATES OF AMERICA
Inscribed and Illustrated by Sam Fink

Illustrated and Inscribed by Sam Fink

Government (Grades 9-12): Identifies how various government documents from around the world are alike and different such as the United States Declaration of Independence and the French Declaration of the Rights of Man and Citizen.

PETERSON FIELD GUIDES
Animal Tracks
THIRD EDITION
Olaus J. Murie and Mark Elbroch

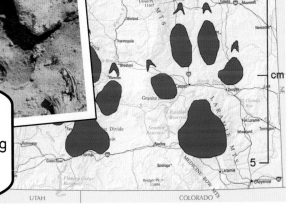

> We're creating animal tracks field guides for our state. It's interesting to learn about the animals in our state.

In **Beautiful Evidence**, Edward Tufte states that "the purpose of a field guide is to combine visual recognition of physical objects with new verbal, geographic, and graphical information...location maps are particularly helpful in avoiding ridiculous identifications." (p. 115)

Science (Grades 3-5): Describes how scientific inquiries involve questioning, exploring, assimilating, inferring, reflecting, and comparing results with what scientists already know about the world.
Uses observations and other evidence along with scientific knowledge to create scientific explanations.
Creates clear, concise communications that reflect the results of inquires.
Selects and applies different types of investigations to address specific types of questions.

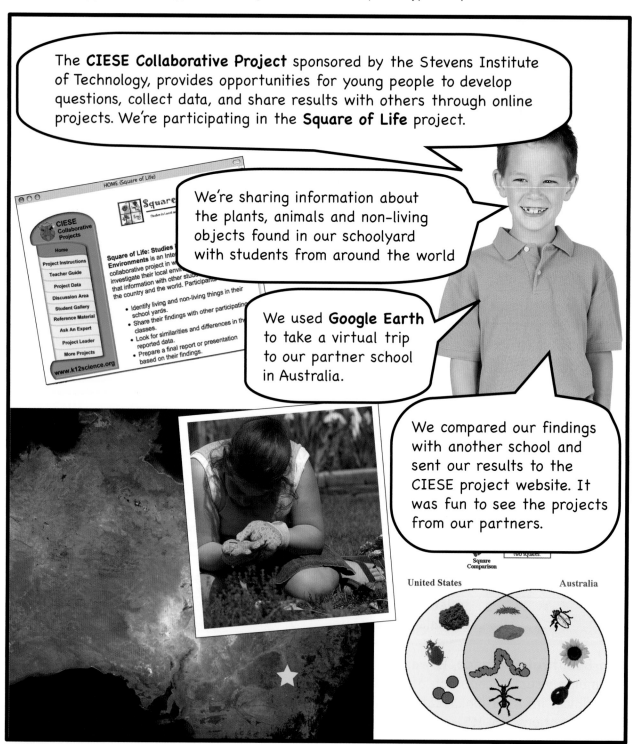

SCORE IT: Organization

Whether creating a concept map to organize ideas, categorizing information to seek patterns, or building a diagram to reflect understandings, organization is critical to graphic inquiry. Individual pieces of data aren't useful until they are put into a context. Young people need to be able to organize data in meaningful ways to express their understanding.

MyPyramid.gov
STEPS TO A HEALTHIER YOU

Science (Grades 9-12): Describes the arrangement of elements in the periodic table and how this organization reflects patterns among elements with similar properties.

Many standards require students to use and apply existing organizers. Rather than simply memorizing boxes, ask students to personalize the visual to fit their needs.

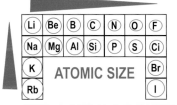

ATOMIC SIZE

I understand the Periodic Table much better after creating charts that focus on patterns like atomic size, electronegativity, temperature, and energy.

I love the outdoors, but I didn't do well in science until I started organizing ideas and information visually.

I match science vocabulary with pictures. Then, I create timelines, visualize cycles, build charts, and solve problems.

Science (All Grades): Describes the structure and function of cells and organisms.

Conifer

Coniferae
/
cone-bearing
\
seed plant

vascular
\
circulates
resources

Conifer Life Cycle

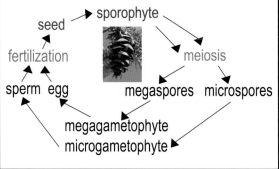

Think about how standards support the use of graphics to illustrate, navigate, map, chart, diagram, measure, organize, categorize and classify.

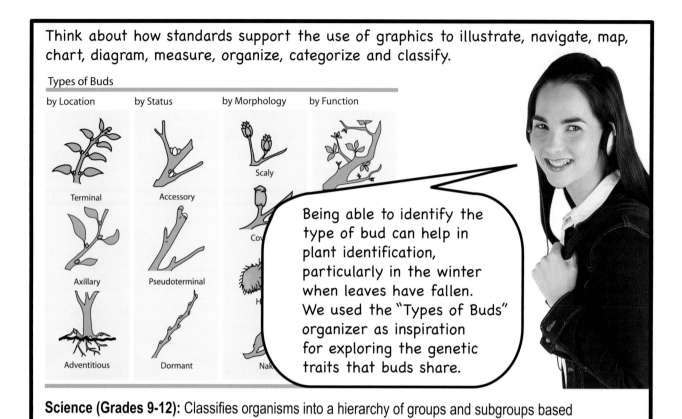

Science (Grades 9-12): Classifies organisms into a hierarchy of groups and subgroups based on evolutionary relationships.

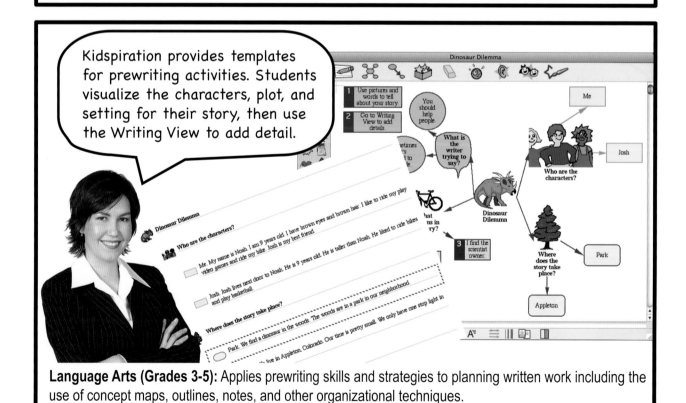

Language Arts (Grades 3-5): Applies prewriting skills and strategies to planning written work including the use of concept maps, outlines, notes, and other organizational techniques.

In **Beautiful Evidence**, Edward Tufte stresses the need to use links and arrows wisely when producing concept maps and other types of organizers. For instance...

Be credible. Provide a coherent story.

Annotate nouns. Label, explain, describe and provide examples.

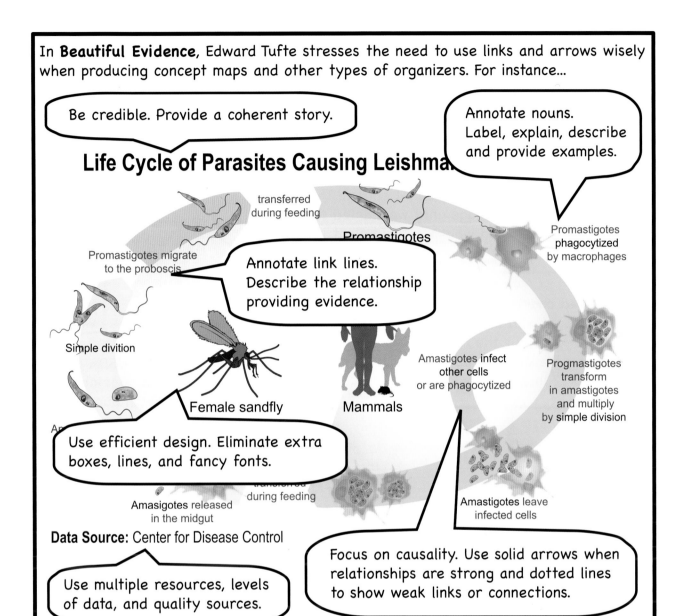

Life Cycle of Parasites Causing Leishma...

transferred during feeding

Promastigotes

Promastigotes migrate to the proboscis

Annotate link lines. Describe the relationship providing evidence.

Promastigotes phagocytized by macrophages

Simple division

Amastigotes infect other cells or are phagocytized

Progmastigotes transform in amastigotes and multiply by simple division

Female sandfly

Mammals

Use efficient design. Eliminate extra boxes, lines, and fancy fonts.

Amasigotes released in the midgut

transferred during feeding

Amastigotes leave infected cells

Data Source: Center for Disease Control

Use multiple resources, levels of data, and quality sources.

Focus on causality. Use solid arrows when relationships are strong and dotted lines to show weak links or connections.

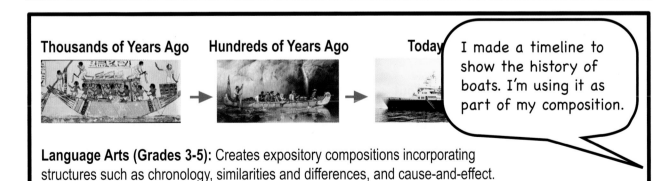

Thousands of Years Ago   **Hundreds of Years Ago**   **Today**

I made a timeline to show the history of boats. I'm using it as part of my composition.

Language Arts (Grades 3-5): Creates expository compositions incorporating structures such as chronology, similarities and differences, and cause-and-effect.
History (Grades 3-4): Traces the development of human constructed marine vessels such as canoes, boats, and ships throughout history.

Mathematics (Grades 6-8): Applies measurements including units, square units, and cubic units. Describes the relationships among linear dimensions, area, and volume.

Science (Grades 6-8): Describes how variations in the scientific method can be used to meet the needs of a particular investigation.

Science (Grades 6-8): Demonstrates how human actions modify the physical environment.

Our math/science class is turning the empty space outside the media center into a garden. The empty courtyard seemed huge until we started to figure out the actual size and what we could plant in the area.

I created charts showing how many plants we'd need. I also had to figure out the cost of covering the entire area with 1, 1.5, or 2 inches of mulch.

We used the USDA map to see what vegetables would grow in our area. I designed a plan for the courtyard and for a pizza garden.

My overall design didn't win, but my pizza garden was selected for Plot #1.

Pizza Vegetable Garden

1 square = 1 foot

I propose to create a pizza vegetable garden. Everyone likes pizza! We'd just need to buy crust and cheese to make our meal. We have a 12' by 12', so we have 144 square feet of land. The first column contains signs and the last row and column is a walkway, so we only have 108 square feet for gardening. Tomatoes need 24" of space, so I planted 8 plants. Green peppers need 12-18" of space, so I planted 10 plants. Onions need 6" of space, so I planted 10 plants. The herbs need 6" of space, so I planted 3 basil, 3 oregno.

I really enjoyed learning about composting. We're using 9-cubic foot tumblers. I've been recording how much plant material goes into my tumbler and how much comes out. We're comparing three tumblers over the entire school year to see which works best. We've divided waste into biodegradable, compostable, and compost-compatible matter.

Tumbler 2: Contents March 6

umbler Contents		
	2	3
8.6	48.6	58.5
2.0	49.8	60.2
	51.0	62.3
	53.1	64.8

SCORE IT: Representation

Many children have a difficult time transferring what they've learned to new situations. Rather than simply restating what's found in the textbook, encourage young people to depict their ideas and illustrate their understandings by creating visual representations that show relationships, demonstrate causality, or express time in ways that are meaningful inside and outside the classroom setting.

History (All Grades): Analyzes chronological patterns and relationships.

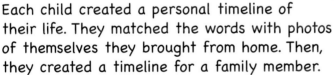

baby   toddler   pre-schooler

> Each child created a personal timeline of their life. They matched the words with photos of themselves they brought from home. Then, they created a timeline for a family member.

Hazel Bolger
1910s

Eleanor Roosevelt
1910s

> Older students created a timeline for a family member or friend and matched it to a famous person.

Young people need to be able to create models to reflect understandings, generate pictures to depict ideas, and design illustrations to represent concepts. Think about how standards support the use of graphics to represent, model, depict and illustrate.

Mathematics (Grades K-2): Applies various strategies in the problem-solving process. Draws pictures to visualize problems. Applies concepts of geometry to represent and describe real-world problems.

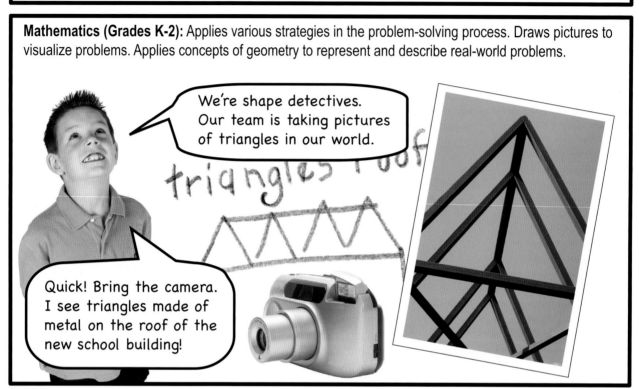

We're shape detectives. Our team is taking pictures of triangles in our world.

Quick! Bring the camera. I see triangles made of metal on the roof of the new school building!

In **Visual Explanations**, Edward Tufte notes that "spatial parallelism takes advantage of our notable capacity to compare and reason about multiple images that appear simultaneously within our eye span. We are able to canvas, sort, identify, reconnoiter, select, contrast, review – ways of seeing all quickened and sharpened by the direct spatial adjacency of parallel elements." (p. 80)

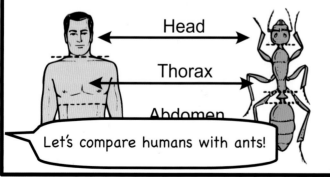

Let's compare humans with ants!

Language Arts (Grades 3-5): Creates narrative accounts through poetry.

Visual poetry, idioms, and word play involve young people in using graphics to depict ideas and concepts.

In **50 Graphic Organizers for Reading, Writing & More,** Karen Bromley, Linda Irwin DeVitis & Marcia Modlo stress that graphic organizers provide a "visual representation of knowledge that structures information by arranging important aspects of a concept or topic into a pattern using labels." (p. 6)

> Learning is enhanced when children create graphic organizers because they are actively engaged with the class content. They demonstrate their ability to identify key concepts and make connections.

Mathematics (Grades K-2): Applies skills and strategies in addition and subtraction of whole numbers to solve real-world problems.

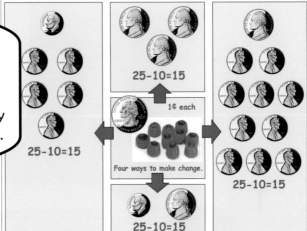

Language Arts (Grades 9-12): Creates expository compositions that organize and synthesize information from primary and secondary sources including books, journals, and electronic databases and cites sources. Develops the main idea through the use of comparisons, chronologies, examples, interesting facts, and illustrations.

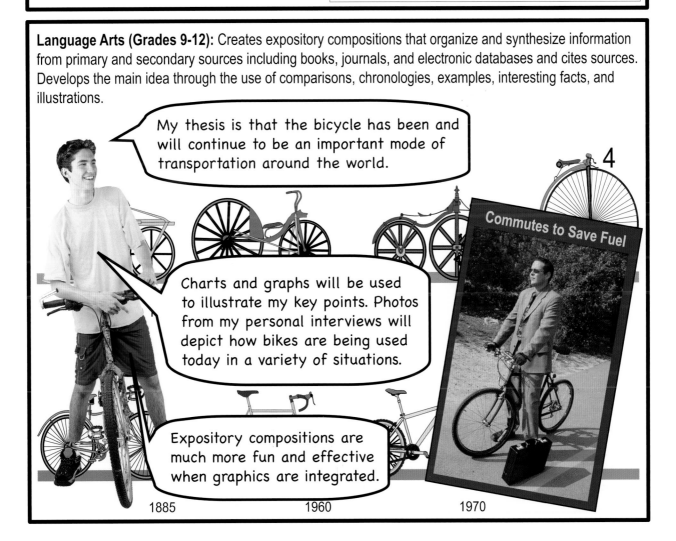

> My thesis is that the bicycle has been and will continue to be an important mode of transportation around the world.

> Charts and graphs will be used to illustrate my key points. Photos from my personal interviews will depict how bikes are being used today in a variety of situations.

> Expository compositions are much more fun and effective when graphics are integrated.

World History (Grades 9-12): Describes the spread of agrarian societies and how new states emerged in the third and second millennia BCE.

SCORE IT: Evidence

Young people need to be able to use and display information in visual ways to support their thinking. They develop deep questions, explore resources looking for visual clues, locate visuals to support their arguments, and design persuasive visuals messages.

Seek out images that provide evidence to support arguments. Involve young people in identifying, evaluating, selecting, creating, and applying images to persuade others.

This photo provides evidence of the important role of bees in pollination.

Language Arts (Grades 3-5): Describes and applies techniques used in advertising in visual media.

We used the Admongo.gov government website to learn the elements of advertising. We evaluated magazine ads and commercials, then wrote e-mails to companies.

To show what we've learned, we helped the local farmer's market create new signs. We turned a boring apple sign into a great sales poster!

Young people need to be able to document, argue and persuade; to make information more likely to be convincing.

In **Beautiful Evidence**, Edward Tufte states that "evidence is evidence, whether words, numbers, images, diagrams, still or moving. The intellectual tasks remain constant regardless of the mode of evidence: to understand and to reason about the materials at hand, and to appraise their quality, relevance, and integrity." (p. 9)

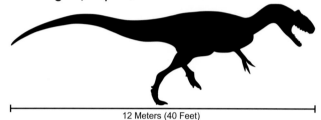

1.8 Metres (6 Feet)

12 Meters (40 Feet)

"Well-designed and thoughtfully mapped pictures combine the direct visual evidence of images with the power of diagrams:
Images' representational, local, specific, realistic, unique, detailed qualities;
Diagrams' contextualizing, abstracting, focusing, explanatory qualities." (p. 45)

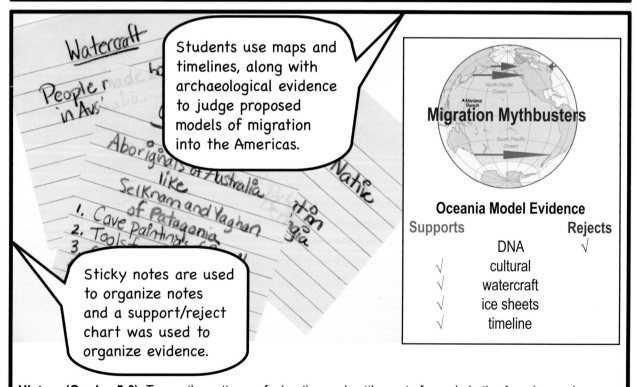

Students use maps and timelines, along with archaeological evidence to judge proposed models of migration into the Americas.

Sticky notes are used to organize notes and a support/reject chart was used to organize evidence.

History (Grades 5-6): Traces the patterns of migration and settlement of people in the Americas using archaeological and geological evidence to support conclusions.

Provide experience collecting, organizing, and applying visual evidence. In **I-claim: Visualizing Argument**, Patrick Clauss identified six ways of visualizing arguments:

Claims. Supported by data to explain, judge, reason, or suggest action.

Context. Provides a format, location, and audience for argument.

Goals. Provides the purpose and motivation.

Support. Justifies the claim and makes it convincing with facts and data.

Multiple viewpoints. Recognizes and acknowledges varied positions and addresses objections.

Logic. Uses reasoning to make generalizations, demonstrations, and a system of inference leading to a conclusion.

How did Theodore Roosevelt go from a game hunter to a protector of the environment? It all starts with his meeting with John Muir in 1903. This photo provides evidence of their meeting.

Language Arts (Grades 9-12): Creates persuasive compositions addressing problems/solutions or causes/effects.

Our increasingly complex society generates enormous amounts of data. Edward Tufte in **Beautiful Evidence** states that "the most common data display is a noun accompanied by a number... placed in the relevant context, a single number gains meaning." (p 48) Tufte identified these "data-intense, design-simple, word sized graphics" as sparklines.

Sparklines help people reason about visual evidence, see distinctions, and make comparisons.

I created sparklines for my favorite hikes. I want to quickly show people the difference in elevation gain among popular hikes.

Aquarius Pass Trail (640 elevation gain)
Coleman Creek Trail (198 elevation gain)
Donkey Ridge Trail (120 elevation gain)

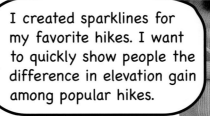

Language Arts (Grades 9-12): Creates persuasive compositions addressing problems/solutions or causes/effects.

Health Education (Grades 9-12): Traces the history and trends related to health care.

Describes health risk factors and techniques individuals can use to manage and reduce those risks.

Creates informational and persuasive communications associated with health care and reducing health risks.

SCORE IT: Inference

Inference is the reasoning involved in drawing conclusions based on evidence and prior knowledge rather than observation. While some students may be able to practice this critical skill with abstract examples, others may need concrete examples. They bring personal meaning to the situation by connecting it with prior knowledge. Students must use hints or clues in the text, visuals, or data to figure out the best solution to the problem or make a decision. They must dig deeper than the surface detail to get to other meanings that are suggested or implied but not stated directly.

Science (All Grades): Describes the relationships among organisms and their physical environment.

How cattails disperse seeds

dry air

wind

water

How do cattails disperse their seeds? Why? What conditions are needed?

My students are encouraged to ask questions and become Science Sleuths. I use photos to show examples and ask students to create graphics to visualize their inferences.

Students must combine the information provided with previous knowledge, experience, and beliefs to come up with the answer. In other words, they make a guess or prediction. As a result, not everyone may draw the same conclusion.

A person's experience impacts their perspective. As a result, it's important that students get multiple opportunities to gain experiences through face-to-face and virtual sharing with others inside and outside the school setting. For instance, students living in different parts of the country could share photos and graphics showing how seeds are dispersed in the place where they live.

Young people need to be able to plan, predict, forecast, influence, and infer. Students are always asking for "the" answer. However when addressing higher order thinking, young people must often "read between the lines" and use logic to draw conclusions. This can be frustrating for students who lack problem solving skills and a deep understanding of content. Design scaffolding to help students develop skills in inferential thinking across the curriculum.

Language Arts (Grades 3-5): Applies skills and strategies related to the reading process. Creates, revises, and confirms predictions based on information found in text including the use of prior knowledge, cues found in illustrations, and foreshadowing.

When making inferences, students must choose among possible explanations. Mystery reading is a popular way to promote inferential thinking.

Our students read "Chasing Vermeer" by Blue Balliett, a mystery about a piece of stolen artwork. Students analyze paintings and collect information to solve the mystery.

We read "Who Sank the Boat?" and made a chart about who we thought would sink the boat. We played the **Blues Clues Sink or Float** game at the **Nick Jr.** website.

We predicted what we thought would sink and float, then did an experiment.

Object	Guess	Try 1	Try 2
	sink	sink	sink
	(float)	(float)	(float)
	(sink)	sink	sink
	float	(float)	(float)
	(sink)	(sink)	(sink)
	float	float	float

Mathematics (Grades K-2): Applies concepts of data analysis and statistics to solve real-world problems. Applies the concept of studying a subset of a population to learn about the group.
Science (Grades K-2): Describes how careful observations and simple experiments can answer questions.

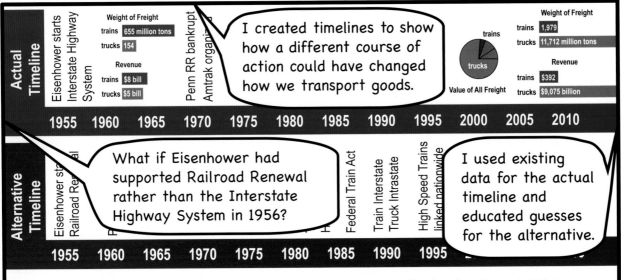

History (Grades 6-8): Uses historical perspective to analyze how specific decisions impacted history. Speculates on how history might have been different in the absence of particular events. Creates and interprets multi-tiered timelines.

An inference involves developing insight and helping students "see the light". Inferring involves many skills: asking questions, collecting and analyzing evidence, making connections between prior knowledge and new information, predicting, making informed decisions and drawing conclusions.

Science (Grades 3-5): Describes the properties and structure of matter. Provides examples of matters that are too small to be seen without magnification.

World History (Grades 6-8): Describes how the transoceanic interconnection of the world led to global change. Traces the impact of the exchange of pathogens, flora, and fauna on the global population.

Describes long-term changes and recurring patterns in world history as a result of global exchange.

Language Arts (Grades 6-8): Applies reading skills and strategies to comprehension of literary passages. Applies writing skills and strategies to the creation of effective communications.

SCORE IT: Teaching

In addition to understanding concepts, it's useful for students to be able to help others learn by creating instructions, conducting demonstrations, and presenting ideas. Involve young people in tutoring, mentoring, and activities that encourage cooperation, collaboration, and sharing. Design projects that ask students to create effective learning environments for others as a way of addressing standards across the curriculum.

Visual Arts (Grades 9-12): Applies techniques and processes related to the visual arts.

It's difficult to make a clay pot, but it's much harder to create an effective photo tutorial to teach others. I really have to think about each step and key techniques.

To be a good Reading Buddy, I need to think about the needs of my young partner and ask good questions.

What do the pictures tell you about the story?

Language Arts (All Grades): Applies skills and strategies of the reading process.

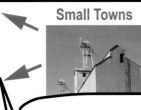
Small Towns

Location

Breadbasket Region

Harvesting

Our team created a virtual tour to teach classmates about a perceptual region of the U.S.

We used a visual to represent each idea on our concept map.

Geography (Grades 6-8): Defines the concept of region and describes types of regions.
Language Arts (Grades 6-8): Creates and conducts oral presentations to a class or other audience incorporating technologies such as presentation tools and electronic whiteboards.

Young people need to be able to present information effectively. Think about how standards support the use of graphics to model, tutor, guide, and review. Involve young people in using visual communications in demonstrations and presentations.

Family/Consumer Science (Grades 9-12): Describes skills and strategies related to careers in early childhood education and services. Applies appropriate instructional methods to meet children's developmental needs and interests.

Movement Skills (Grades 9-12): Demonstrates movement elements and skills in performing dance.

Someday I want to be a professional dance instructor. I've been studying dancing techniques for kids. I created a bulletin board to show young children how to stretch before dancing.

A WebQuest is an inquiry-based approach to learning that asks students to connect their understanding of information to meaningful situations and create original products for authentic audiences. WebQuests provide an environment for problem solving, information processing, and collaboration.

We're creating a WebQuest to help others learn about the Spanish language and also have some fun.

After reading the **Learn Spanish with Superman** comics, we thought it would be fun to incorporate comics into the project.

The mission is to create a Spanish language comic to teach basic vocabulary to people traveling to Spanish-speaking countries. We're making a comic example for the Mexican Marketplace.

Foreign Language (Grades 9-12): Creates communications that express information, concepts, and ideas to a specific audience. Uses language, content, and style of speech appropriate for a business environment. Gives and follows simple written and oral instructions in the language.

Mathematics (Grades 3-5): Applies concepts of data analysis and statistics. Provides examples of how data represent information about real-world things, ideas, or events.

Language Arts (Grades 3-5): Creates and conducts oral presentations to a class incorporating technology tools.

> Students need experiences creating presentations and conducting demonstrations for a variety of audiences. Our kids are showing another class how to make different types of graphs.

> Our class is creating an interactive museum exhibit to teach people about the history of tool making. Our team is investigating how stone tools were made. I'm showing the steps in knapping to make arrows.

World History (Grades 6-8): Traces and describes the significance of advancements in tool and weapon technology through human history.

Language Arts (Grades 6-8): Identifies the features of various types of nonfiction text in providing different kinds of information for specific purposes.

> Each team adopted a non-profit organization. We updated their publications including posters, brochures, and the website. We used lots of photographs. Our team presented our materials to our real-world clients!

Business Education (Grades 9-12): Applies presentation, desktop publishing, and multimedia software to design and develop professional-quality communications.

Family/Consumer Science (Grades 9-12): Applies skills and strategies related to careers in nutrition and food science industries. Describes the purpose of nutritional therapy and creates examples.

Language Arts (Grades 9-12): Designs, develops, and delivers formal presentations to the class incorporating multimedia elements including text, sound, and motion.

Skills and Strategies

Children learn to read pictures before they read words. Unfortunately, we often stop visual teaching once children can read. In this information age, it's important to continue to help people interpret the visual world around them. From books and television to billboards and animation, students are bombarded with graphic images.

Just as children learn how to read text, young people need to understand visual images. They need skills and strategies for reading and comprehending, analyzing and interpreting, using and applying, designing and creating graphics that can be applied to inquiry experiences.

In **A Primer of Visual Literacy**, Donis Dondis states that "seeing is a direct experience and the use of visual data to report information is the closest we can get to the true nature of reality." (p. 2)

Throughout history, people have created visual recordings and communications.

Use old photos to bring history alive for young people. Ask questions that will stimulate discussion and inquiry. Involve students in carefully analyzing the people, places, objects, and events presented in the images.

How is this kitchen like and unlike yours?
How does her life differ from yours, your parents, and grandparents?

Mature information scientists apply graphic skills and strategies throughout the inquiry process. In this section of the book, we'll explore the range of knowledge, skills, and dispositions necessary to conduct graphic inquiry.

After reading Nancy Farmer's fantasy novel **Sea of Trolls**, I began thinking about my Danish heritage. Critiques have praised the blend of fantasy, myth, humor, and history. What's the fact and fiction of the people, places, events, and mythology described in the book?

Read and Comprehend

The ships described in the book match photos of excavated ships and drawings of Viking longships.

Analyze and Interpret

After examining maps, charts, and documents, the events and movements of Vikings seemed to be accurately portrayed.

Graphic Inquiry

Use and Apply

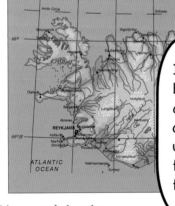

I chose one book character and wrote my own story. I used maps to find the setting for my story.

Design and Create

Yggdrasil by Erkadio

The many representations of Yggdrasil were fascinating. I made a multimedia project comparing the works of art. I end with my own visual.

Reading and Comprehending Graphics

The master student information scientist is able to effectively read and comprehend a wide range of graphic materials.

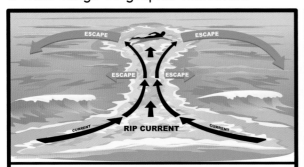

Whether reading an amusement park map to determine the location of a roller coaster or understanding the safety symbols at the beach, reading and comprehending graphics is an essential skill.

Start by getting young people to carefully examine graphics and discuss what they see.

They drive an expensive car. They must be rich.

In **Psychology of Learning for Instruction** Marcy Driscoll states that graphics can facilitate encoding and memory storage of information.

Visuals can help students identify key steps in a process or a cycle.

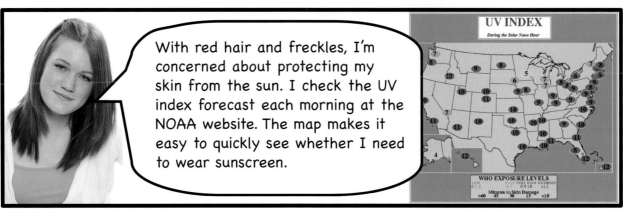

With red hair and freckles, I'm concerned about protecting my skin from the sun. I check the UV index forecast each morning at the NOAA website. The map makes it easy to quickly see whether I need to wear sunscreen.

Like reading a book, students need to be able to translate the visual symbols and images in a graphic. They look for clues in the parts and whole of the picture looking for the main idea and supporting information. When reading a visual, ask questions such as:

What is the main subject?

If there are people,
can they be identified?
What is their appearance
(i.e., age, gender, race)?
What are they wearing?
What are they doing?
What does their expression tell you?
What do you think their lives are like?
How are the people in the visual connected?

What is the setting? Is it inside or outside?
What's the climate, weather, and season?
How do you think the subject got into
this situation?

If there are objects, can they be identified?
What's the purpose of these artifacts?

What's in the background?
Is it real or artificial?
How do the background objects
contribute to the overall setting?

If you divide the image into nine visual sections, can you see any additional details when you look close-up?

Do you know the age of the photograph? If not, what visual elements provide clues about the age?

What might be happening beyond the scope of the camera?

Why do you think the photographer chose this pose or action to photograph? What's the purpose of this visual?

Thousands of photographs at the **Library of Congress** can be used for graphic inquiry. Examine the photo of three women. When could the photo have been taken?
What clues in the photo help you identify the time period?
Look at each person individually. If you were writing an historical fiction novel based on this image, describe each character. This photo was titled **First Vote in New York**. Were these women involved with the Women's Suffrage Movement?

Often young people are shown the well-known photos from popular locations. However for students to gain a deep understanding, they also need to make comparisons. For instance, how is the life of Iowa farmer Hazel Bolger different from the three women in New York? How was rural and urban life different for women in the early 1900s? Compare the Women's Movement in Iowa with that of other places.

Once you've compared two photographs, look for others that might provide additional detail or different perspectives on historical events or time periods. How was the life of a rich person different from a poor person? Compare the experiences of people from different backgrounds, races, religions, and areas of the world.

Be sure to examine other types of visuals that reflect the time period such as posters, advertisements, and paintings.

Comprehension of graphics goes beyond description to involve explanation and understanding. Use picture books to practice comprehension.

Right Here on This Spot by Sharon Hart Addy is told visually by examining the changes that take place in a single location over thousands of years.

Seek out wordless books such as **Sector 7** by David Wiesner and ask students to write the story.

Use picture books with elaborate borders that tell stories or provide information. For example, many of the books by Jan Brett such as **The Mitten** provide visual clues that anticipate later events in the book.

Increasingly, text resources are being presented using graphics. An inquirer might start with a question about the difference between responsibility and obligation. A series of clicks on the visual map may help refine their question and lead them to the words duty and liability.

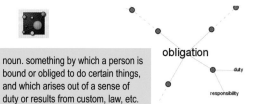

noun. something by which a person is bound or obliged to do certain things, and which arises out of a sense of duty or results from custom, law, etc.

obligation

duty

responsibility

The **Visual Thesaurus** (http://www.visualthesaurus.com/) is an interactive dictionary and thesaurus displayed in a visual way to promote exploration. By illustrating the meaning and relationship between words in a graphic format, students can easily identify words to meet their needs.

Similar visual tools are being introduced for Internet search engines. They can help students quickly identify visual associations and narrow a topic.
Search Cube (http://www.search-cube.com) searches Google and is viewed as a cube made of web pages and images.

I'm doing a project for my psychology class on hallucinations.

Quintura for Kids (http://kids.quintura.com/) provides word clouds for young searchers.

Analyzing and Interpreting Graphics

The mature student information scientist carefully examines the evidence presented in a graphic, then determines fact, value, and intent.

As students gain experience reading graphics, they become increasingly confident in retelling, describing, explaining, and critiquing visuals.

> An elementary student might describe the relationships they see in a photo showing life on a coral reef.

Visual Messages in WWII Posters

Bandana symbol of patriotism for women

Working women are still attractive

We Can Do It!

Rallying call for women

Women are serious and competent

Become part of our group

Women are strong; you can be strong too

Clownfish and sea anenome have a symbiotic relationship.

> A teenager might identify the persuasive techniques used in a World War II propaganda poster.

Graphics provide a great starting point for inquiry-based projects. Students brainstorm questions based on artwork found at the **Picturing America** website (http://picturingamerica.neh.gov/), investigate the origin of well-known historical photos from the **Library of Congress** or trace the origin of data presented in a chart found in an **USA Today** newspaper article.

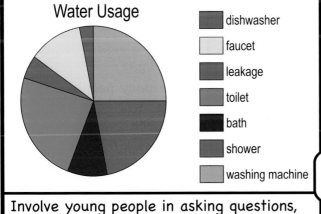

Water Usage

- dishwasher
- faucet
- leakage
- toilet
- bath
- shower
- washing machine

Involve young people in asking questions, evaluating information, collecting evidence, and drawing conclusions using graphics.

40 FE

41

> Recycling involves much more than simply placing junk into the correct bin. I'm learning the metal symbols.

WE RECYCLE

Analysis of graphics involves determining the meaning and quality of the visual presentation or argument. In addition, analysis involves seeking out hidden assumptions, unstated facts, and misleading information that reflect the motives of a creator.

Many images created in the 1800s glamorized the adventures and achievements of Columbus.

Since Christopher Columbus lived before the time of photographs, no one really knows what he looked like. Instead artists have created their own interpretations of the person and events surrounding his voyages.

Edward Tufte stresses the need to test the integrity of content displayed. In **Visual Explanations** he uses the following questions (p. 70):

Is the display revealing the truth?
Is the representation accurate?
Are the data carefully documented?
Do the methods of display avoid spurious readings of the data?
Are appropriate comparisons and contests shown?

What's the Truth?

☐ normal
■ birth defects

Uranium Medical Research Center   New England Journal of Medicine

When comparing the data regarding birth defects as a result of Gulf War Syndrome, I had lots of questions: How is "birth detect" defined? Was the research peer reviewed? How many people were involved in the research?

In **Beautiful Evidence**, Edward Tufte notes that "despite the threat of corruption, a consumer of presentations should try to be hopeful and curious, avoid premature skepticism, and maintain an open mind but not an empty head." (p. 141)

Let's say you're exploring questions related to respiratory health and illnesses. Examine the following questions, criteria, and activities related to analyzing graphic materials.

Authority

What expertise does the author have in the area represented by the graphic? What resources did the author use to draw the conclusions reflected in the graphic?

Rate* of tuberculosis cases, by state/area - United States, 2007†

When examining a map showing tuberculosis cases, I noticed that it was produced by the United States Center for Disease Control using data collected from each state during the past year. After reading about the CDC and their data collection methods, I concluded that the CDC is an authoritative agency.

Sources

How was this graphic distributed? What individuals or group support the communication of this information?

Fifty Facts
Health Issues
Take Action

Fight Smoking

As I examined a graph showing rates of lung cancer, asthma, tuberculosis, and sleep apnea, I noticed that the chart is posted at an anti-smoking website but the data comes from the Canadian Lung Association. I concluded that even though the website may contain biased information in support of anti-smoking legislation, the content of the chart comes from a respected authority.

When I do research for my health class, I look carefully at the authority, sources, context, currency, methodology, and assumptions of the graphic data I use.

Context

In what setting is this graphic presented? Is it shown with other data representing a particular viewpoint or context? Are particular social, economic, or political agendas associated with the information?

Estimated TB Deaths 1996-2006

	1996	1997	1998	1999	2000	2001	2002	2003	2004	2005	2006
Algeria	452	471	491	511	532	554	577	601	626	652	679
Angola	7,896	5,959	7,069	6,889	9,669	6,577	4,494	4,151	5,337	5,838	4,854
Benin	1,055	1,133	1,209	1,188	1,235	1,293	1,447	1,563	1,545	1,587	1,584
Botswana	963	1,147	1,273	1,279	1,347	1,471	1,424	1,553	1,500	1,383	1,696

I noticed that the chart showing rates of tuberculosis discussed in an article called "Health Issues in Africa" was attributed to the World Health Organization.

Currency
Is the information in the graphic timely?
When was the data collected?

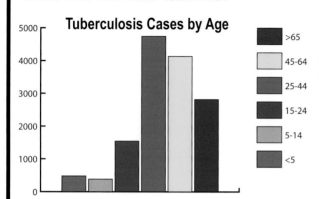

When I analyzed a graphic on the rate of tuberculosis I found in an article, I noticed that no date was provided. I wondered whether this was historical or current information. I compared this data to another source to determine that the data was from 2007.

Methodology
How was the data for the visual collected?
Was a systematic approach taken to experimentation?
Were observations or eye witness reports used?
Is the information valid and reliable?

As I examined a pie graph, I noticed an accompanying note indicating that the study tracked 1000 teenagers during a six-month period to determine their smoking habits. The study was conducted by a well-known agency.

Assumptions
What are the hidden assumptions and unstated facts about the content of this graphic?
Is misleading information conveyed in a visual?

In my search for information about smoking, I was surprised to find a website called "The Dining Experience" on my search results. After examining the home page photograph of a group of people smiling and smoking at a restaurant with the caption "Enjoy Fine Dining", I realized the website was sponsored by a group opposed to legislation banning smoking in restaurants.

Using and Applying Graphics

The mature inquirer looks beyond the easy solution, common examples, and stereotypes to locate, integrate, or create unique ways for using graphics to represent ideas.

Students should carefully select, use, and apply graphics that best reflect their information need. To do this, students must be aware of the bias found in both the presentation and content of graphics.

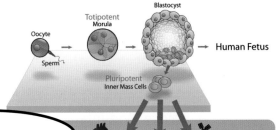

Because of the sensitive nature of the stem cell research topic, I carefully selected the scientific visuals used as evidence in my class debate.

It's also important to consider alternative approaches to the same information. While students may use graphics found in print and electronic sources, they may also create original works and designs to meet a particular need.

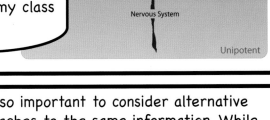

After reading the book **Bud Not Buddy** I created a scrapbook of Bud's adventure. I used historical photographs of real Hoovervilles to show what his experience might have been like.

Students can waste lots of time searching for quality images to use in projects. It's useful to provide students with prompts, templates, and resources to jumpstart inquiry projects. Consider using the Speaker Notes in PowerPoint to provide students with directions and to cite resources.

I provide students with a PowerPoint document with a collection of clip art or photographs to stimulate thinking.

In **Beautiful Evidence**, Edward Tufte identifies six principles for the analysis and presentation of data (p. 122-137).

1. Show comparisons, contrasts, differences
2. Show causality, mechanism, explanation, systematic structure
3. Show multivariate data; that is, show more than 1 or 2 variables
4. Completely integrate words, numbers, images, and diagrams
5. Thoroughly describe the evidence. Provide a detailed title, indicate the authors and sponsors, document the data sources, show complete measurement scales, point out relevant issues.
6. Analytical presentations ultimately stand or fall depending on the quality, relevance, and integrity of their content.

Even young inquirers can create sophisticated projects and proposals. The key is providing a meaningful context for inquiry. For instance, rather than writing traditional animal reports, we encourage children to identify information about an animal that will help them solve a problem or address a question. Students are encouraged to incorporate photographs, maps, charts, and drawings to communicate their arguments or answers to others.

I like to read the **Adventures of Riley** books. They mix cartoon characters and stories with facts and photographs.

After reading **Project Panda**, I used a website simulation to create a panda habitat. Then, I made a presentation to persuade our local zoo to adopt a panda. I included convincing arguments showing that other zoos our size have pandas and we have a place for the pandas.

Explore questions, criteria, and activities for integrating graphic materials into projects focusing on emphasis, selection, proportion, perspective, comparison, and connections.

Emphasis

Ask yourself: What's the central idea represented?
Is this a good choice for emphasis?
What are the extraneous elements?
What are the dominant and subordinate ideas?
Highlighting essential features is an effective way to focus in on the key ideas, but it's possible to leave out important elements. Think about both examples and non-examples when selecting elements for emphasis.

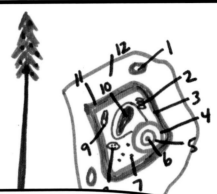

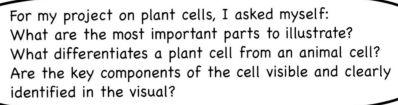

For my project on plant cells, I asked myself:
What are the most important parts to illustrate?
What differentiates a plant cell from an animal cell?
Are the key components of the cell visible and clearly identified in the visual?

Selection

Ask yourself: Does the data chosen for a graphic represent the entire population? Or, is it clear that only a particular group is represented? Is criteria provided for the selection of a subset of data?
When selecting data for comparison, it's possible to leave out important examples. Be sure you have the information you need.

When creating a graph showing the fat content found in meals at various restaurants, I made a list of all the restaurants within 20 miles and the most popular menu items. Then, I narrowed my focus to the restaurants within 10 miles of the school. I selected burgers and fries since they are the most popular with teens.

Proportion

Ask yourself: Is all information equally represented?
Do visuals accurately reflect the data?

I'm selecting images to include in my brochure promoting tourism in Arizona. I noticed that the images in the foreground of a photo may look larger than those in the background. A simple mountain icon may not adequately represent the difference between a mountain range at 5000 feet and 10,000 feet. I need to carefully select the best images to represent this beautiful place.

Perspective

Ask yourself: What facts and opinions are represented in this visual?

Is a particular point of view most often represented? When you see an illustration of a globe, the image generally shows North America although there are many other views that could be presented.

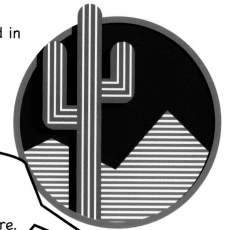

> When you see a visual representing Arizona, it often includes a Saguaro cactus even though this plant doesn't grow in all parts of the state. I want to think of a different visual for my brochure.

Comparison

Ask yourself: How does this graphic compare to other information that's been examined? Was the same or different data used? How do similarities and differences impact overall understandings? How does the method of presentation impact understanding? Which best reflects your intent?

> There's only room for one diagram comparing cactus and non-cactus plants. Would a Venn Diagram, concept map, or labeled photo comparison be more effective? They each provide similar information presented in different ways.

Connections

Ask yourself: How do the ideas in the graphic relate to each other? How do they relate to other ideas being presented? How do they address original questions posed by the inquiry? How do they support the conclusions being drawn in the communication?

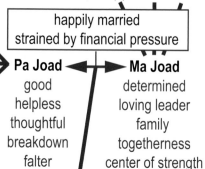

happily married
strained by financial pressure

Pa Joad ◄──► Ma Joad
good   determined
helpless   loving leader
thoughtful   family
breakdown   togetherness
falter   center of strength

> After examining many options, a concept map seems to do the best job showing the relationships among the characters in the novel I'm reading called **Grapes of Wrath**. I used key words to describe the characters and their relationships.

Designing and Creating Graphics

The mature student information scientist creates effective, efficient, and appealing graphics during both the process of inquiry and as a product to communicate results.

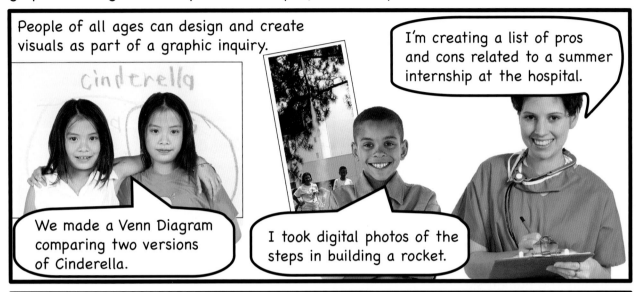

People of all ages can design and create visuals as part of a graphic inquiry.

I'm creating a list of pros and cons related to a summer internship at the hospital.

We made a Venn Diagram comparing two versions of Cinderella.

I took digital photos of the steps in building a rocket.

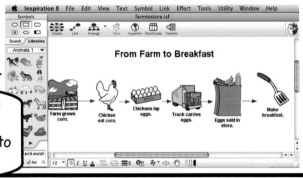

While some projects involve creating graphics from scratch, it's often useful to provide young people with visual resources they can use in building projects.

I provide students with an Inspiration template containing directions and a collection of clipart they might wish to use in building concept maps.

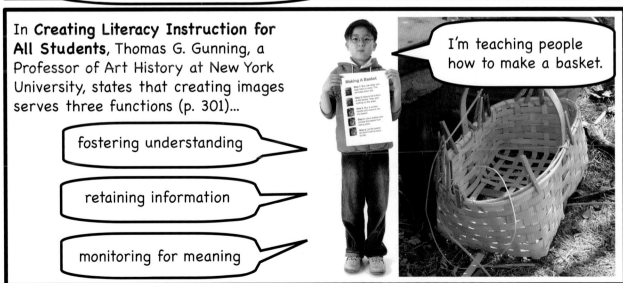

In **Creating Literacy Instruction for All Students**, Thomas G. Gunning, a Professor of Art History at New York University, states that creating images serves three functions (p. 301)...

fostering understanding

retaining information

monitoring for meaning

I'm teaching people how to make a basket.

Robert Marzano, Debra Pickering, and Jane E. Pollock have found that drawing pictures to represent knowledge is a powerful way to generate nonlinguistic representations in the mind. In **Classroom Instruction that Works**, they use the example of students drawing the human skeletal system or the solar system as a way to share understandings.

In an article titled **Cheating the Kids**, Bonnie Meltzer stresses her concern about the use of clip art over other types of graphics. She points out that young people learn important lessons by creating their own graphics...

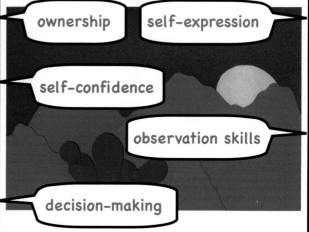

...using simple tools such as ripped pieces of construction paper and adding glue.

Graphics don't need to be exact to convey meaning. **Rapid Visualization** was developed by Kurt Hanks as the process of quickly generating ideas, organizing information, and communicating understandings and meanings through quick drawings.

Hanks' Scale of Refinement ranges from simple sketches created in a few minutes to complex drawings requiring hours to complete.

In **Say It with Charts**, Gene Zelazny identified a few simple commandments for effective media.

Keep visuals simple.

Ensure legibility.

Keep special effects to a minimum.

Use color with purpose, not for decoration.

From markers and post-it notes to computer software and digital cameras, a wide range of tools are available to student information scientists. Help students make good choices about the best tool for a particular project.

Draw circuit with markers

Inspiration concept map of sources ← **Electricity** → **Digital photo of experiment**

Create symbols in Paint software

A piece of flip chart paper and colored markers would work fine for creating a concept map as part of an idea generation session...

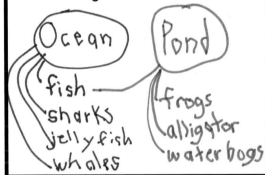

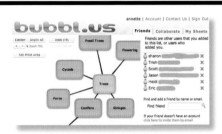

However if students from different classes are collaborating on an inquiry project, it might be more convenient to use an online tool like **Gliffy** (gliffy.com) or **Bubbl** (bubbl.us). These websites allow users in remote locations to collaborate on building a concept map.

In Robert Jacobson's book **Information Design**, Yvonne Hansen identified six Graphic Tools that serve as building blocks for graphical displays (p. 210).

Circle or Curvoid
Enclose area
Set boundary
Locate elements

Square - square corner
Contain text
Describe relationship
Between elements

Triangle
Compare entities
Analysis structure
Hierarchy

Line
Connect entities
Show feedback
before | after   Separate or emphasize

Point
Point in time
Focus attention
Emphasize

Fuzz or Fuzzy Idea
Unknown entity
Emergent entity
Undeveloped

Like writing a poem, students need skills in composing visual communications. When using a digital camera, a student needs to consider the lighting, camera angle, depth of field, context, and other elements of composition.

As students edit their photographs, they may be cropping, extracting, or modifying the visual to best represent their idea for a particular audience.

Basic skills in graphic design and development are essential. Regardless of whether the student is building a timeline of events while reading a biography or creating a visual poem on a bookmark to reflect their own life, student inquirers need to understand the function and creation of effective graphics.

In some cases, graphics are created as part of the inquiry process such as during brainstorming or organization of evidence...

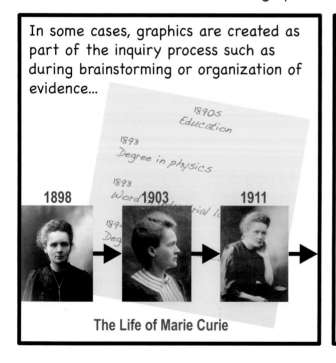

The Life of Marie Curie

At other times, graphics are used as the final product or as part of a culminating communication such as a report or poster.

Interdisciplinary Approaches and Individual Differences

As you match information and content-area standards with the types of graphics that young people may use as part of an inquiry, consider activities that will address individual differences.

A learner who has difficulty with a traditional written science log assignment may be more successful photographing the procedure.

While some students studied a map to better understand the relationship between weather patterns and acid rain, others used historical photographs to see how smoke and acid rain impact local cars.

A Venn diagram was used to compare sources of pollution in two counties, while a timeline documented changes in the air quality regulations over time.

I always wear my goggles.

Acid Rain and Plant Growth

1967	1970	1976	1977	1983	1990
Air Quality Act of 1967	Clean Air Act	Lead Out of Gas	Clean Air Act Amendments	Lead Levels Drop	Clean Air

Drawing on science, technology, geography, and history related to acid rain, each student found graphic resources and approaches to meet their learning needs.

Each child is different. As you design learning environments, consider the learning needs of each student.

Developmental Level. While some children may be ready to understand abstract representations, others may not. It's easy to assume that children can read and understand comics, maps, or photographs, but don't make assumptions.

 Airport    Train

Before beginning an inquiry involving graphics, assess the development levels of your children. Are they ready to handle a visual that involves scale or symbols? Can they follow the sequence of a comic strip or the elements of a diagram?

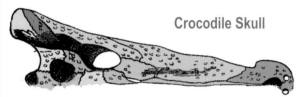
Crocodile Skull

Context. For some children, context is critical for understanding. Use scenarios, a series of photos, diagrams, field trips, maps, and related content to bring meaning to a learning experience.

Varied Resources. If you're working with visually impaired children, provide tactile presentations. Also consider issues such as color blindness.

Experiences. While some children have had lots of experience with graphics, others may not. For instance, some children have grown up in homes with road maps and GPS devices. Consider basic experiences. Children who have not seen a mountain or the ocean may have a difficult time understanding these features on maps.

Tactile graphics are images that use raised surfaces so that blind and visually impaired inquirers can feel and read them. Keep in mind that tactile perception is different from visual perception. While sighted readers can quickly gain an understanding of the "big picture" of a graphic, the visually impaired reader will acquire information from a tactile graphic by gradually building a mental image from the components presented. When designing graphics for the visually impaired, think about ways that points, lines, textures, and labels can be incorporated into graphics. Maps, pie charts, bar charts, and Venn diagrams are a few examples.

Tactile graphics are particularly useful for showing relationships, processes, and concepts that would be difficult to share in other ways. Vacuum forming, paper collage, microcapsule, and embossing are a few of the techniques for creating tactile graphics.

Lois Harrell, in **Teaching Touch: Helping Children Become Active Explorers of Tactile Materials**, pointed out it's easier for visually impaired students to begin learning to use tactile graphic with familiar objects and shapes such as interpreting a map of a familiar location.

Technology tools such as the Talking Tactile Tablet from Touch Graphics also make graphics more accessible.

In the book **Tactile Graphics**, Polly Edman notes that tactile graphics aren't just duplicates of a visual, instead they are interpretations containing the essential elements of the image. She asks people to put themselves in the blind person's shoes. "How would you know what you were looking at if you had never seen the object portrayed, never felt it or read a description of it? What would you have as a base of reference?" (p. 4)

In this section, we'll look for ways to combine content from different subject areas such as language arts, science, and math with information and technology skills and strategies to meet diverse learning needs.

The book **Uno's Garden** by Graeme Base combines the science themes of balance in nature and biodiversity with math topics including subtraction, multiplication, and prime numbers. Icons are used to represent animals, plants, and buildings in Uno's world.

Enature's ZipGuides (http://enature.com/zipguides/) can be used to help learners identify the birds, butterflies, mammals, reptiles and amphibians, trees, and wildflowers found in their region.

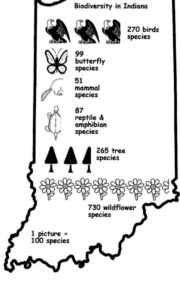

Biodiversity in Indiana

270 birds species

99 butterfly species

51 mammal species

87 reptile & amphibian species

265 tree species

730 wildflower species

1 picture = 100 species

Students can explore their local natural world and represent their findings through their own biodiversity visuals including photos, diagram, and charts.

Mathematics (Grades 3-5): Applies number operations including addition, subtraction, multiplication, and division to solve real-world problems. Applies number theory concepts. Demonstrates how mathematical concepts can be represented visually using graphics and symbols.

Science (Grades 3-5): Describes the diversity of life through the use of examples showing relationships among organisms and their physical environment. Describes the life cycles of various plants and animals.

Language Arts (Grades 3-5): Identifies literacy themes. Connects the characters and plot in a literary work to his or her own life.

Primary Sources in Learning

A primary source is a piece of information created close to an event from direct experience such as actual records and artifacts that have survived from the past.

Primary sources are often used to make comparisons between different time periods such as the use, purpose, design, and construction of tools such as weapons. They might be used in addressing the question: How was the use of wood for shields different than the bronze used in the sketch?

In **Internet Primary Resources to Teach Critical Thinking Skills in History**, Kathleen Craver notes that primary sources enable students "to establish fact, make inferences, and formulate opinions." (p. 8) Craver states that primary sources:

provide an instantaneous representation of events

do not interpret evidence after the fact

furnish information not found in other sources

assist in the discovery of truth about persons, events, and issues

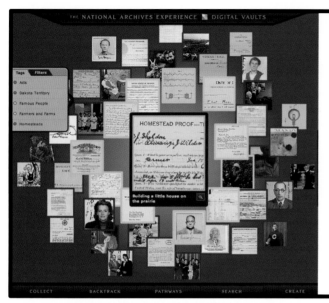

The **Digital Vault from the National Archives** provides access to thousands of documents, maps, photos, and other visual materials.

Understanding and using these materials requires careful observation and interpretation. A primary source may only provide part of a larger story. Examine and compare many resources to gain insights into the people, places, and technologies of the past.

As you analyze primary source materials, think about their origins and purposes:

Was the visual created based on first-hand knowledge (such as a photograph taken during an event) or through reports by others (such as drawings or paintings created many years after the event)?

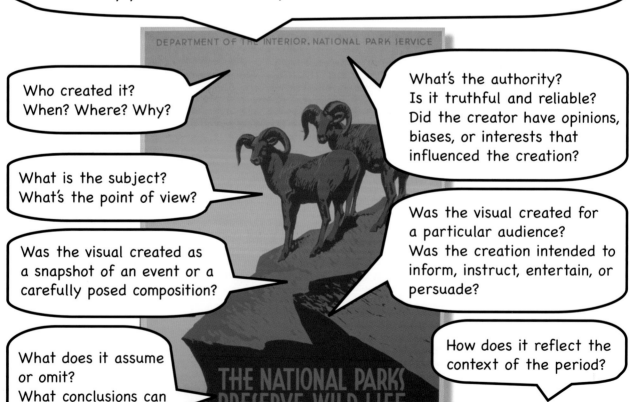

Who created it?
When? Where? Why?

What's the authority?
Is it truthful and reliable?
Did the creator have opinions, biases, or interests that influenced the creation?

What is the subject?
What's the point of view?

Was the visual created as a snapshot of an event or a carefully posed composition?

Was the visual created for a particular audience?
Was the creation intended to inform, instruct, entertain, or persuade?

What does it assume or omit?
What conclusions can be drawn?

How does it reflect the context of the period?

WPA Poster, Aug. 23 1939
Artwork by J. Hirt

Political cartoons exaggerate the features of persons and events to elicit a reaction.

The **National Archives** provides worksheets for analyzing primary sources such as cartoons, maps, and photographs.

In **Teaching Visual Literacy**, Thomas DeVere Wolsey stresses the importance of integrating all types of primary source materials including political cartoons into the classroom.
As you design instructional materials, Wolsey suggests you ask:

Does the use of the visual lead to larger issues or concepts of study?

Does the visual have relevance for students?

Do students have the background to interpret and understand the visual?

Linda Levstik and Keith Barton stress that using multiple sources provides a fuller picture of the past than relying on a single source. Consider using collections of photographs, maps, graphs, and other images to provide multiple perspectives.

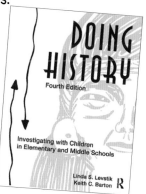

Primary source materials can be incorporated into many different types of graphic inquiries. For instance, they might be woven into a timeline showing a sequence of events in aviation history or connecting world events to the history of aviation.

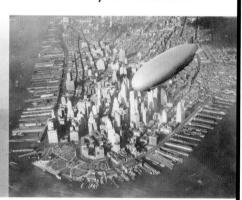

DOG IN SPUTNIK II

Using graphics in activities that require sequencing of events, summarizing facts in chronological order, tracing growth and change, making comparisons, and finding patterns are all particularly useful for young people who have difficulty with reading comprehension.

It's the welcoming committee.

One pipes and it's dog rus!

Whenever there's some new ...

I learned about the space race. Did you know that the Soviets put a dog in space? I read about Laika in a graphic novel then learned more about the history of the animals in space using primary sources.

In **America's History Through Young Voices: Using Primary Sources in the K–12 Social Studies Classroom**, Richard Wyman notes that "visual artifacts add an exciting dimension to the study of any historical period." (p. 5). He suggests combining photographs, diaries, and other sources to add depth to an investigation.

Works of art are another interesting way to integrate primary sources into classroom activities.

In the book **Masterpiece,** a young artist solves a mystery involving works of art. Provide access to the images as the story unfolds.

Escrapbooking involves putting images and ideas together to tell a story. Scraps are pieces of information, insights, emotions, thoughts, memories, and understandings. These elements can be combined into a visual, digital story. Explore escrapbooking.com

Our class read the book **Bread and Roses, Too**. Then, we learned more about the labor strikes of 1912. I created a scrapbook page comparing life "then and now".

A confection does the work of scrapbooking in a single image that represents an idea. In **Visual Explanations**, Edward Tufte states that "confections place selected, diverse images into the narrative context of a coherent argument." (p. 151)

Many campaign posters from the 1800s use the confection approach to represent a position on political issues.

How will I explain the concept of slavery in a single visual? What historical and contemporary images will I select? How will I develop a unifying theme?

"Unlike maps or photographs, confections are not direct representations of preexisting scenes, nor are they the result of placing data into conventional formats such as statistical charts, tables, or maps. Instead, two general strategies are used to arrange and organize the various images gathered together in confections: compartments and imagined scenes." (p. 127)

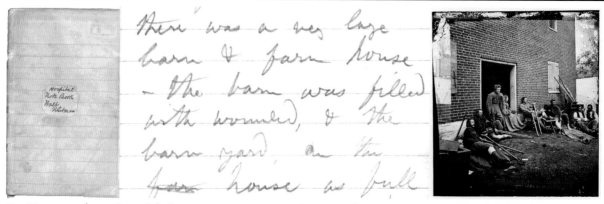

In **Uncovering Our History**, Susan H. Veccia has found that students who use primary sources begin thinking like historians and enjoy the discovery process. The key is building personal interest. Veccia notes that when students read about Walt Whitman's experiences as a nurse in the Civil War, read handwritten notes from the hospital, and also see images of the actual locations, the time period comes to life.

In **Using Internet Primary Resources to Teach Critical Thinking Skills in History**, Kathleen Craver notes that primary source documents are effective in presenting a puzzle, challenging a stereotype, presenting a contradiction, offering an insight, promoting empathy, and presenting generalizations.

I was shocked when the teacher described the Jim Crow system.

I didn't really believe it until I started examining photographs from the early and mid-1900s and saw the signs enforcing racial discrimination.

Examine the curriculum looking for places where visual elements might contribute to understanding. For instance, the English and Communication curriculum explores figurative language that could be associated with visual representations of slogans.

During World War II a series of posters stressed the concern that unguarded talk might be useful to the enemy. It become known as the "loose lips" campaign.

Try the following primary source collections:

Ad Access	http://library.duke.edu/digitalcollections/adaccess/
America on the Move	http://americanhistory.si.edu/onthemove/collection/
Avalon Project	http://avalon.law.yale.edu/default.asp
Cartoon America	http://www.loc.gov/exhibits/cartoonamerica/cartoon-political.html
Great Chicago Fire	http://www.chicagohistory.org/fire/
Great Depression	http://www.english.uiuc.edu/maps/depression/depression.htm
History Matters	http://historymatters.gmu.edu/
Library of Congress	http://memory.loc.gov/
National Archives	http://www.digitalvaults.org/
National Center	http://www.nationalcenter.org/HistoricalDocuments.html
National Park Service	http://www.nps.gov/history/history/
New Deal Network	http://newdeal.feri.org/
NY Public Library	http://digitalgallery.nypl.org/
Repositories	http://www.uiweb.uidaho.edu/special-collections/Other.Repositories.html
U.S. Holocaust Museum	http://www.ushmm.org/
Western Trails	http://www.bcr.org/cdp/exhibits/westerntrails/index.html

Explore the following lessons for additional ideas:

American Revolution	http://edsitement.neh.gov/view_lesson_plan.asp?id=423
American South	http://docsouth.unc.edu/classroom/lessonplans/lessonplan_titles.html
Bio-Graph	http://www.readwritethink.org/lessons/lesson_view.asp?id=1021
Campaign of 1840	http://edsitement.neh.gov/view_lesson_plan.asp?id=556
Case Study	http://www.econedlink.org/lessons/index.php?lesson=EM219&page=teacher
Childhood	http://edsitement.neh.gov/view_lesson_plan.asp?id=286
Colonial Broadsides	http://edsitement.neh.gov/view_lesson_plan.asp?id=390
Decades Mural	http://artsedge.kennedy-center.org/content/2057/
Dust Bowl Days	http://edsitement.neh.gov/view_lesson_plan.asp?id=300
Family Timelines	http://www.readwritethink.org/lessons/lesson_view.asp?id=870
Geo Generations	http://www.nationalgeographic.com/xpeditions/activities/17/geogen.html
Graffiti Wall	http://www.readwritethink.org/lessons/lesson_view.asp?id=208
Harlem	http://artsedge.kennedy-center.org/content/3268/
Historical Treasure	http://www.k12science.org/curriculum/treasure/index.html
Images of New World	http://edsitement.neh.gov/view_lesson_plan.asp?id=714
Interviews, Memoirs...	http://www.readwritethink.org/lessons/lesson_view.asp?id=17
Inventions	http://edsitement.neh.gov/view_lesson_plan.asp?id=408
Japan's Merchant Class	http://edsitement.neh.gov/view_lesson_plan.asp?id=611
Library of Congress	http://memory.loc.gov/learn/lessons/fw.html
Metaphorical Gold	http://edsitement.neh.gov/view_lesson_plan.asp?id=433
Mexican Culture	http://edsitement.neh.gov/view_lesson_plan.asp?id=740
Migration Stories	http://www.nationalgeographic.com/xpeditions/activities/09/interviewing.html
National Archives	http://www.archives.gov/education/lessons/
Native Americans	http://edsitement.neh.gov/view_lesson_plan.asp?id=324
Political Cartoons	http://memory.loc.gov/learn/features/political_cartoon/
Primary Resources	http://memory.loc.gov/learn/start/prim_sources.html
Slave Narratives	http://edsitement.neh.gov/view_lesson_plan.asp?id=364
Social Studies	http://www.readwritethink.org/lessons/lesson_view.asp?id=1059
Sources in History	http://www.americanhistory.si.edu/starspangledbanner/pdf/SSB_Sources_6_8.pdf
What Do You See?	http://memory.loc.gov/ammem/ndlpedu/lessons/97/civilwar/hinesday.html
What is History?	http://edsitement.neh.gov/view_lesson_plan.asp?id=406
What Portraits Reveal	http://edsitement.neh.gov/view_lesson_plan.asp?id=255
What's in a Picture?	http://edsitement.neh.gov/view_lesson_plan.asp?id=621

Data Collection and Use in Learning

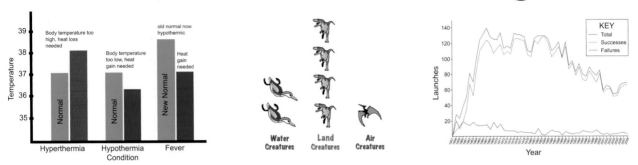

Data is a collection of facts such as numbers, characters, or images. This information is the result of observation, experience, or experiments and can tell us about our past, present, and future. Charts, graphs, and other visuals can help people visualize data.

In **The First Measured Century Book** from PBS, data are used to show trends. Through charts and graphs viewers and readers learn about American history.

Graphics can be used to visualize all kinds of data.

Download the book for free at http://www.pbs.org/fmc/downloadbook.htm.

Data is often numerical such as weights, temperatures, and dollars. Data becomes information when it is organized in a framework that is useful.

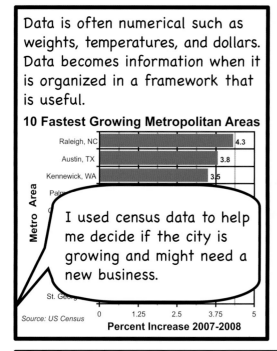

I used census data to help me decide if the city is growing and might need a new business.

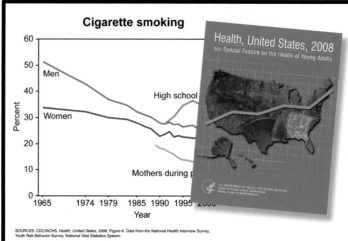

Statistics is a type of information derived from mathematical operations applied to numeric data. Statistics can be used to address questions and provide evidence to make informed decisions.

Young people need to be able to use existing data as well as conduct their own investigations. Use data sets including databases, charts and graphs, GIS/maps, and polls and surveys to jumpstart thinking.

The **USA Today's Snapshots** website http://usatoday.com/news/snapshot.htm provides many examples of their popular graphs. Involve young people in collecting their own data, choosing a graphic type, and making comparisons with the USA Today graphics.

Our group chose to explore the age of the oldest food in our kitchens. We decided that a pie chart was better than a bar chart for showing our data since the total was 100%.

In **How to Interpret Visual Resources**, Harry Stein identifies rules for the statistically literate student to apply to all graphs, charts, and statistical tables.

1. Where did the information originate?
2. Do the sources of the data have biases or special motives?
3. Does any information seem to be missing from the graph or chart?
4. Does the graph indicate one conclusion but project a different one?
5. Finally, do the statistics make sense in light of what you know about the topic?

> **United States Census 2010**
> http://2010.census.gov/ contains lots of data about my state and our country.

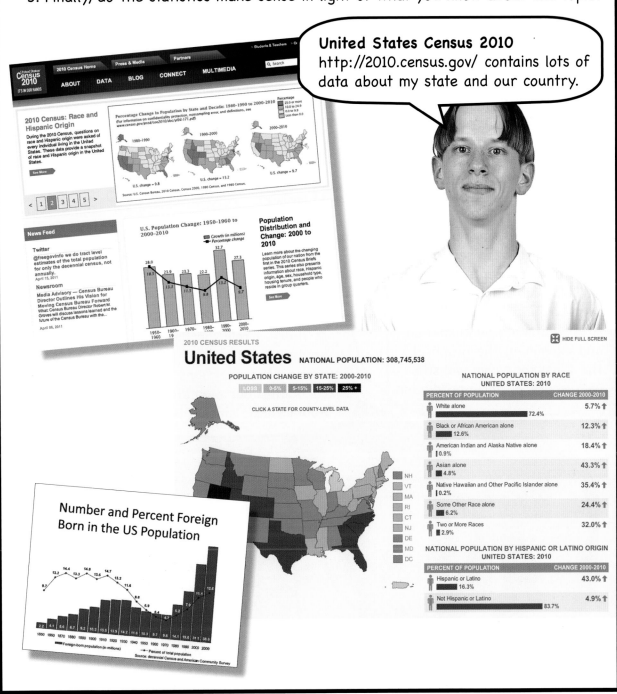

We're comparing the weather we see through our window with the weather forecast.

In **Nurturing Inquiry: Real Science for the Elementary Classroom**, Charles Pearce asks students to differentiate questions that involve research (read-to-find-out) and testable questions that students can answer on their own through direct observation, data collection, or by manipulating variables in an experimental setting. He encourages students to ask "how" and "why" questions.

To develop testable questions, Pearce asks:
Is it possible to...?
When comparing X with Y, which ....?
What if...?
How can we...?
What is...?
If I had..., how could I...?
How can I improve...?
What will happen if...?
Suppose I could...?

We wanted to know if the weather prediction would match the actual weather outside our window.

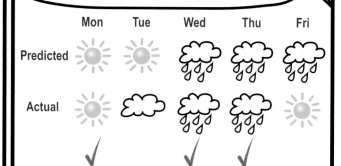

After watching an animation and examining the graph at the **Classzone.com** website, we discussed storm prediction.

Is there a relationship between barometric pressure and storms? Rather than simply writing the questions and answers, we conducted our own study and created a HyperStudio stack sharing our results.

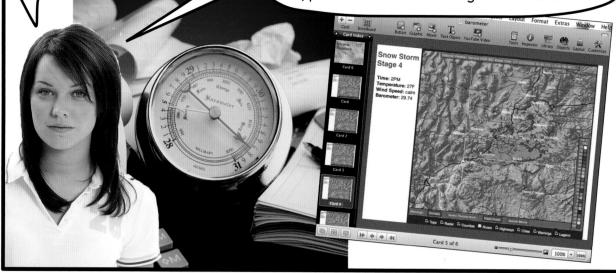

The **FedStats** website http://www.fedstats.gov/ provides easy access to US government data and statistics that can be used in projects across the curriculum. The Kid's Pages are useful for young students.

Graphs provide a more efficient and flexible means for comparing and highlighting trends in sets of data. This is particularly important for students who have difficulty interpreting information.

In the **Journal of Reading** article **Understand Documents**, Peter B. Mosenthal and Irwin S. Kirsch note that there are certain advantages to displaying information visually in graphs over sharing data numerically in tables.

Create a Graph
http://nces.ed.gov/nceskids/createAgraph/ allows students to view data on many different types of graphs. It even includes a tutorial to help young people decide what type of graph would work best for their data.

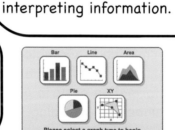

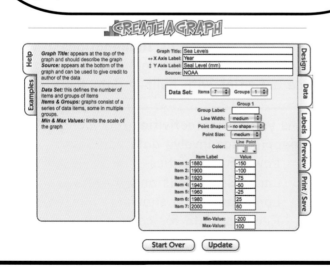

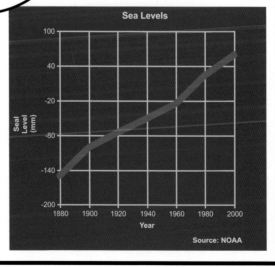

In **Visual Explanations**, Edward Tufte states "When we reason about quantitative evidence, certain methods for displaying and analyzing data are better than others. Superior methods are more likely to produce truthful, credible, and precise findings." (p. 27)

Hours Babysitting Per Week

In an average week, how many hours do you spend babysitting?

○ 0-5 hours
◉ 6-10 hours
○ 11-20 hours
○ More than 20 hours

View Results

Powered by **ZOHO** Polls

Have you ever taken a babysitting class?

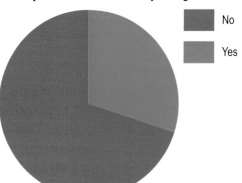

■ No

■ Yes

I found lots of websites for conducting online polls and surveys. I built an online survey for our Babysitting Club blog. Then, I made pie charts of the results for my Child Development class.

In **Visual Literacy: How to Read and Use Information in Graphic Form**, Marcia Weaver notes that a pie chart makes information easy to understand and remember by providing a simple to understand format for displaying data.

We used the **Free Ride** tool to explore gear ratios. We made charts to go along with our bike routes.

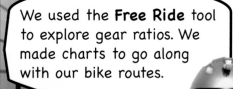

National projects such as **Illuminations** http://illuminations.nctm.org/ provide activities with built-in data tools.

As you design activities for young people that involve data, look for:
    Powerful statistics
    Large-scale polls and surveys
    Long-term data showing changes/trends
    Regional data for comparisons
    Surprising/interesting information

Rather than providing specific problems for students to solve, ask students to explore areas of interest and identify their own questions based on data sets.

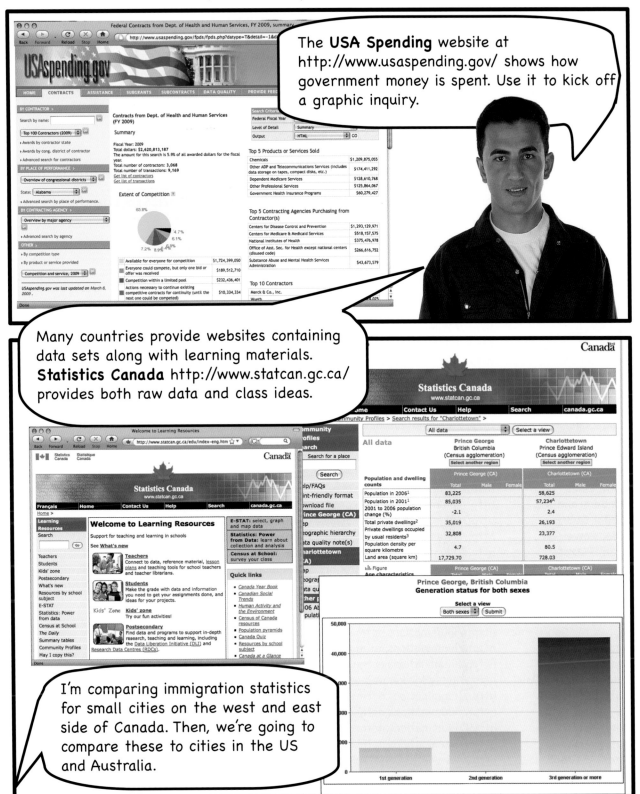

The **USA Spending** website at http://www.usaspending.gov/ shows how government money is spent. Use it to kick off a graphic inquiry.

Many countries provide websites containing data sets along with learning materials. **Statistics Canada** http://www.statcan.gc.ca/ provides both raw data and class ideas.

I'm comparing immigration statistics for small cities on the west and east side of Canada. Then, we're going to compare these to cities in the US and Australia.

Try the following tools:

Bar Grapher	http://illuminations.nctm.org/ActivityDetail.aspx?ID=63
Create a Graph	http://nces.ed.gov/nceskids/createagraph/default.aspx
Grapher	http://www.amblesideprimary.com/ambleweb/mentalmaths/grapher.html
Graphic Map	http://www.readwritethink.org/materials/graphicmap/

Explore the following lessons for additional ideas:

All in the Family	http://illuminations.nctm.org/LessonDetail.aspx?ID=L619
Apple Adjectives	http://www.education-world.com/a_tsl/archives/99-1/lesson0002.shtml
Bar Graph	http://illuminations.nctm.org/LessonDetail.aspx?ID=L42
Bar Graphs	http://illuminations.nctm.org/LessonDetail.aspx?ID=L79
Begin with Buttons	http://illuminations.nctm.org/LessonDetail.aspx?ID=U31
Bio-Graph	http://www.readwritethink.org/beyondtheclassroom/summer/grades9_12/BioGraph/
Cardiac Output	http://illuminations.nctm.org/LessonDetail.aspx?ID=U136
Careers	http://www.econedlink.org/lessons/index.php?lesson=EM212&page=teacher
Categorical Data	http://illuminations.nctm.org/LessonDetail.aspx?ID=U116
Dealing With Data	http://illuminations.nctm.org/LessonDetail.aspx?ID=L297
Dirt Bike Dilemma	http://illuminations.nctm.org/LessonDetail.aspx?ID=L685
Do I Have to Mow..	http://illuminations.nctm.org/LessonDetail.aspx?ID=L729
Eat Your Veggies	http://illuminations.nctm.org/LessonDetail.aspx?ID=U114
Food Court	http://illuminations.nctm.org/LessonDetail.aspx?ID=U149
A Global Perspective	http://www.rpcv.org/lessons/AIDS.doc
Graphically	http://illuminations.nctm.org/LessonDetail.aspx?ID=U82
Graphing	http://illuminations.nctm.org/LessonDetail.aspx?ID=U124
Graphing Plot	http://www.readwritethink.org/lessons/lesson_view.asp?id=869
Graphing Trash	http://illuminations.nctm.org/LessonDetail.aspx?ID=L206
How Many Steps?	http://illuminations.nctm.org/LessonDetail.aspx?ID=L187
Junior Architects	http://illuminations.nctm.org/LessonDetail.aspx?ID=U172
Least Squares	http://illuminations.nctm.org/LessonDetail.aspx?ID=U117
Look at Me	http://illuminations.nctm.org/LessonDetail.aspx?ID=U64
Mathematics	http://illuminations.nctm.org/LessonDetail.aspx?ID=L375
Medicine & the Body	http://illuminations.nctm.org/LessonDetail.aspx?ID=U145
Movie Lines	http://illuminations.nctm.org/LessonDetail.aspx?ID=L629
Numbers and Me	http://illuminations.nctm.org/LessonDetail.aspx?ID=L229
Orbital Debris	http://illuminations.nctm.org/LessonDetail.aspx?ID=L376
Pedal Power	http://illuminations.nctm.org/LessonDetail.aspx?ID=L586
Pizza, Pizza!	http://illuminations.nctm.org/LessonDetail.aspx?ID=U87
Population Pyramids	http://www.nationalgeographic.com/xpeditions/lessons/09/g68/pyramids.html
Population Statistics	http://www.nationalgeographic.com/xpeditions/lessons/09/g68/statistics.html
Rate of Change	http://illuminations.nctm.org/LessonDetail.aspx?ID=U132
Representing Data	http://illuminations.nctm.org/LessonDetail.aspx?ID=U73
Rescue Mission Game	http://illuminations.nctm.org/LessonDetail.aspx?ID=L296
Running Races	http://illuminations.nctm.org/LessonDetail.aspx?ID=U162
Smokey Bear	http://illuminations.nctm.org/LessonDetail.aspx?ID=L381
Songs from the Past	http://artsedge.kennedy-center.org/content/2293/
State Population	http://illuminations.nctm.org/LessonDetail.aspx?ID=L239
Top Speed	http://illuminations.nctm.org/LessonDetail.aspx?ID=L254
Trout Pond	http://illuminations.nctm.org/LessonDetail.aspx?ID=U142
Water, Water	http://illuminations.nctm.org/LessonDetail.aspx?ID=L289
What's a Graph	http://www.sciencenetlinks.com/lessons.cfm?BenchmarkID=12&DocID=37
What's in a Name?	http://illuminations.nctm.org/LessonDetail.aspx?ID=U151
Whelk	http://illuminations.nctm.org/LessonDetail.aspx?ID=U143

Photos in Learning

Photography is an effective method of sharing visual information. While photos can be used to accurately record events, they can also be manipulated for use in advertising or propaganda. Young people need to learn to evaluate, use and create photos in learning.

In the past, lectures and texts were often the primary method of conveying information to students. However images can provide content-area insights and emotions that would be difficult to convey using other methods.

Infuse famous photographs into learning and discuss how they've influenced how we think about particular topics.

For many students, the visual channel of communication is a strength. Use NASA's photos of Mars expeditions to provide an exciting way to explore science.

In **How to Interpret Visual Resources**, Harry Stein uses the following questions when examining people in historic photos: (p. 61)

1. **First Impressions:** Whom do you see? What are they doing? Why are they doing this? Where is this happening?
2. **Your Feelings About What You See:** Examine their faces, arms, hands, fingers. Do they seem proud, bored, happy or scared? Are they posed or natural?
3. **Connecting What You See and Feel with Your Memory:** Have you ever seen similar people before? Do you personally know anyone like this?
4. **Look Again at the Person:** Follow the face from chin to hairline and then from ear to ear. Describe this face to yourself.

Stein suggests that viewers look at the photograph as if it were a clock. To gain a general impression of the picture, move your eyes clockwise around the picture and then counterclockwise.

After learning about the Women's Suffrage Movement, I began to wonder about the Equal Rights Movement. Why was the right to vote a success, but the ERA failed to gather enough support to pass the amendment?

Although it's sometimes difficult to know the motives of a photographer, it's important in understanding an image.

Pearl Harbor Dec. 1941

Was the photographer simply recording the event or trying to create an image that might elicit an emotion?

Some photos are composed so you can easily follow the steps in a procedure or view specific detail.

Posed photos are designed to create an impression or specific idea.

NASA uses photographs to document the growth of plants in space. Did you know they can grow seedless tomatoes with pollination?

Images are often used to record people, places, and events at a particular point in time. These documentary photos may be used to teach a process, document a tragedy, or record a scientific experiment.

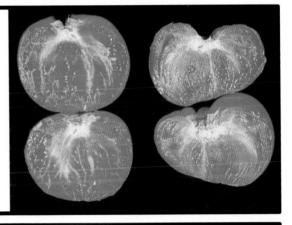

In **Constructing Credible Images: Documentary Studies, Social Research, and Visual Studies,** Jon Wagner notes that collecting visual information is similar to gathering numeric data. He notes that people find images more credible when they are based on observation in a natural setting. He's found three challenges (p. 1477):
1) creating empirically credible images of culture and social life
2) framing empirical observations to highlight new knowledge
3) challenging existing social theory

In the article **Visual Information Literacy,** Debbie Abilock points out that "a documentary photograph may have been created to represent reality, but it is also a vehicle for conveying ideas and a medium for personal expression... even when photographs are unretouched, there is an eye behind the lens." (p. 10)

Ask students to become documentary photographers. Use local events such as building construction, sporting events, or festivals to provide authentic experiences.

Sometimes the photographer sets up a situation to create an image that will convey a particular attitude or emotion. These are known as posed photos.

A politician may be seeking to convey wisdom and intelligence...

...while a cosmetics model may be appealing to young women who want to look beautiful.

Posed images can easily encourage stereotypes. Even the well-known photographs of Edward Curtis were taken by an outsider looking into the culture.

Although it may seem that a photograph is an exact replica of a person, place, or event, the choice of setting, perspective, camera angle, and cropping of the photo can change the impact. Imaging software such as Adobe **Photoshop** or the open source software **GIMP** can be used to edit and enhance images.

Students must consider the ethics and implications of editing images.

Was this photo taken in a zoo or out in the wild?

From historical photos to satellite imagery, software can be used to enhance a photo and discover new information. However, these tools can also hide elements that can change the impact of the visual.

Jamie Lee Curtis is famous for her statements about the fraudulence of magazines that retouch photos to make models look thin. She stressed that perfection is being happy with who you are rather than how you look.

Professional journalists follow a Code of Ethics (The National Press Photographers Association). Documentary photographs should focus on:
- accurate representations
- neutral point of view
- comprehensive view
- avoid influencing subject
- avoid setting up situations

U.S. Air Force photographers documented a flood in North Dakota.

When working with young photographers, it's important to teach good composition. Look for action, light, view, and interest. Ask the following four questions (Lamb 2006).

Where's the Action?
The following photo is okay, but where are they? What are they doing? Why are they smiling? What's happening?

Show movement.
Visualize the context.
Show the emotion.
Make a memory.
Use a series of photos to tell a story.

Where's the Light?
The following photo is pretty, but it's difficult to see the bird with the bright light behind it. Think about the location of the light source.

Put your back to the light source.
Look for interesting reflections.
Be sure you can see details.

Where's the View?
The following photo is okay, but you've seen it many times. Can you think of a different picture that will provide a fresh look?

Shoot up or down.
Zoom in or out.
Look for interesting angles.
Take multiple shots.

Where's the Interest?
The following photo is fine, but where is she? Why is she dressed like that? Take multiple shots to tell the story.

Visually divide the photo into nine parts.
Put interesting elements around the image rather than in the center.

See It - Keep your eyes open for photographic moments.
Log It - Write down the story so you remember later.
Take It - Take a bunch of shots.
Share It - Be sure to share your stories with others!

When using photographs in teaching and learning, seek ways to engage students in high level thinking. The photos below show two photographs from the same location in the Black Hills of South Dakota. Can you see signs of drought? How much time do you think passed between the two photos? What long term impact could a drought have on this area? Can you predict what a future photo might look like?

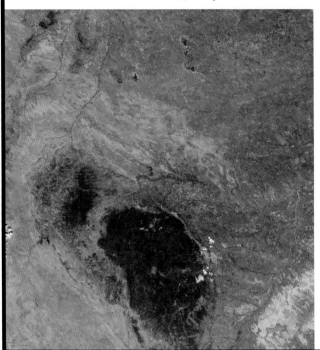 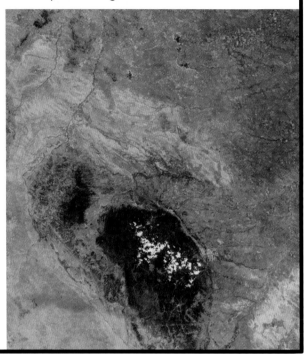

Technology can be used to enhance photos. In the edited version, the drought becomes even more apparent.

Technology tools can enhance learning across the curriculum. For instance, **Piclits.com** provides photos and suggests words for creative writing activities.

Try the following photography resources:

American Masters	http://www.pbs.org/wnet/americanmasters/education/lesson27_overview.html
American Photography	http://www.pbs.org/ktca/americanphotography
Art & 21st Century	http://www.pbs.org/art21/education/teachingmaterials/index.html
Civil War Photos	http://www.archives.gov/research/civil-war/photos/
Documenting America	http://memory.loc.gov/ammem/fsowhome.html
Earth Observatory	http://earthobservatory.nasa.gov/IOTD/
GRIN from NASA	http://grin.hq.nasa.gov/
People at War	http://www.archives.gov/exhibits/a_people_at_war/a_people_at_war.html
Presidential Portraits	http://memory.loc.gov/ammem/odmdhtml/preshome.html
Understanding Photos	http://www.americanhistory.si.edu/polio/historicalphotos/index.htm
Veteran's Project	http://www.loc.gov/vets/
World War II Photos	http://www.archives.gov/research/ww2/photos/images/thumbnails/index.html

Try the following photography guides:

Photojournalism Guide Grades K-2 (PDF)
http://www.nationalgeographic.com/xpeditions/lessons/09/gk2/photographyguidestudent.pdf

Photojournalism Guide Grades 3-5 (PDF)
http://www.nationalgeographic.com/xpeditions/lessons/09/g35/photographyguidestudent.pdf

Photojournalism Guide Grades 6-8 (PDF)
http://www.nationalgeographic.com/xpeditions/lessons/09/g68/photographyguidestudent.pdf

Photojournalism Guide Grades 9-12 (PDF)
http://www.nationalgeographic.com/xpeditions/lessons/09/g912/photographyguidestudent.pdf

Explore the following lessons for additional ideas:

Characters	http://www.readwritethink.org/lessons/lesson_view.asp?id=986
Courage Using Photos	http://www.readwritethink.org/beyondtheclassroom/summer/grades9_12/BlogPhotos/
Culture	http://www.nationalgeographic.com/xpeditions/lessons/04/g68/picture.html
Depression-Era Photos	http://edsitement.neh.gov/view_lesson_plan.asp?id=304
Documentary Photos	http://interactives.mped.org/preview_mg.aspx?id=560
Geography Detective	http://www.nationalgeographic.com/xpeditions/lessons/02/g35/detective.html
Images at War	http://edsitement.neh.gov/view_lesson_plan.asp?id=273
Insect Models	http://www.sciencenetlinks.com/lessons.cfm?DocID=210
Jimmy Chin	http://www.nationalgeographic.com/xpeditions/lessons/06/g35/jchin.html
Life, In Focus	http://artsedge.kennedy-center.org/content/3526/
Native American	http://edsitement.neh.gov/view_lesson_plan.asp?id=324
On the Oregon Trail	http://edsitement.neh.gov/view_lesson_plan.asp?id=323
Personal Connections	http://www.readwritethink.org/lessons/lesson_view.asp?id=782
Photography	http://artsedge.kennedy-center.org/content/3531/
Picture This	http://artsedge.kennedy-center.org/content/2131/
Rondal Partridge	http://newdeal.feri.org/classrm/partrid.htm
Rummaging for Fiction	http://www.readwritethink.org/lessons/lesson_view.asp?id=1108
Tell a Migration Story	http://www.nationalgeographic.com/xpeditions/activities/09/photography.html
Your Changing Town	http://www.nationalgeographic.com/xpeditions/lessons/18/gk2/changingtown.html

Maps in Learning

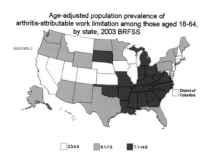

Age-adjusted population prevalence of arthritis-attributable work limitation among those aged 18-64, by state, 2003 BRFSS

From enthusiastic tourists to serious treasurer seekers, maps help people visualize places and mark locations. However, maps can do much more than simply get you from point A to point B. They can help students visualize changes in places over time, compare different regions, and see patterns such as weather systems.

Maps are useful in a wide range of situations:
  Show routes (hurricane evacuation, parade route)
  Show locations (restaurants, sports stadiums)
  Show trails (historical trails, hiking, animal trails)
  Show movements (migration, crime spree)
  Show close-ups of an area (fire area, mines)

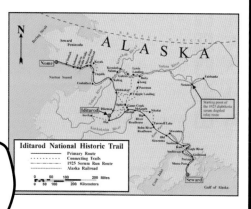

Iditarod National Historic Trail
  Primary Route
  Connecting Trails
  1925 Serum Run Route
  Alaska Railroad

Each year our class follows the Iditarod Sled Dog Race. We've been learning about the history of the Iditarod Historic Trail and Alaska history.

I find that maps are useful across the curriculum. A "bird's eye view" can help students understand spatial relationships, while flow maps can assist students in visualizing historic trade routes.

Maps place information in a spatial context:
  Locate a subject in place
  Define territories
  Show processes, trails, migration
  Show changes over time
  Record movement of people & products

Land Recreation

- Archery
- All-terrain trail
- Baseball
- Climbing
- Driving tour
- Exercise/Fitness
- Hang gliding
- In-line skating
- Playground
- Rock collecting
- Skateboarding
- Spelunking/Caves
- Technical rock climb
- Tennis
- Wildlife viewing

Symbols play an important role in map activities. Keep in mind that some students may have difficulty interpreting these images. Provide opportunities for young people to practice interpreting standard icons as well as creating their own symbol systems.

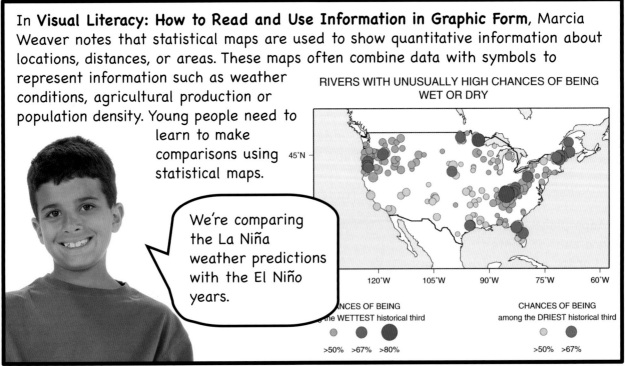

In **Visual Literacy: How to Read and Use Information in Graphic Form**, Marcia Weaver notes that statistical maps are used to show quantitative information about locations, distances, or areas. These maps often combine data with symbols to represent information such as weather conditions, agricultural production or population density. Young people need to learn to make comparisons using statistical maps.

We're comparing the La Niña weather predictions with the El Niño years.

RIVERS WITH UNUSUALLY HIGH CHANCES OF BEING WET OR DRY

CHANCES OF BEING among the WETTEST historical third

>50% >67% >80%

CHANCES OF BEING among the DRIEST historical third

>50% >67%

The Development of Manhattan Island

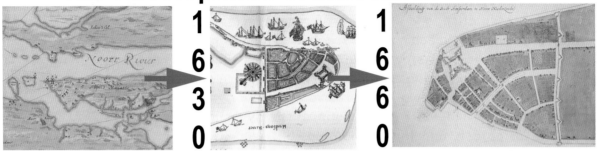

1630   1660

Maps are useful in showing changes over time. When examining maps it's helpful to have multiple maps for comparison and to provide a context.

Identify Place.

Where am I? Where do I want to go?
What does this place look like?
What are the key elements of this place?
How is this place like and unlike other places? Why?
How does this place compare?

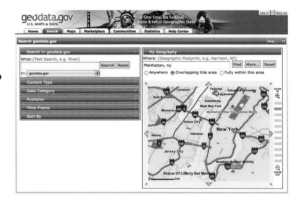

Identify Changes.

What happened here?
What changes do you see over time?
What's the rate of change?
How is the speed of change like and unlike other places?
How has it changed for each generation?

> I'm examining the history of Manhattan Island from the 1600s to the present.

Interpret Change.

What will happen in the future at this location?
What's the cause of the change (human or natural forces)?
How have factors such as population and land use impacted this place?
How will changes impact me?

> I'm not just reading about the history. I can actually see the changes!

Make Predictions.

What changes do you anticipate in the future?
What do you think this area will look like...
five, ten, one hundred years into the future?

Big Questions

Can maps illustrate my literary experience?
Can maps enhance my artistic experience?
Can maps help me visualize complex problems?

In **Learning to Think Spatially**, spatial thinking is described as a "constructive amalgam of three elements: concepts of space, tools of representation, and processes of reasoning... It depends on understanding the meaning of space and using the properties of space as a vehicle for structuring problems, for finding answers, and for expressing solutions. By visualizing relationships within spatial structures, we can perceive, remember, and analyze the static and, via transformations, the dynamic properties of objects and the relationships between objects."

This map shows vegetation around the world. I've been thinking about the distances between areas with high and low vegetation, projecting the future by comparing this map to climate change data, and drawing conclusions about areas that are the most threatened. The map helps to visualize the information and issues.

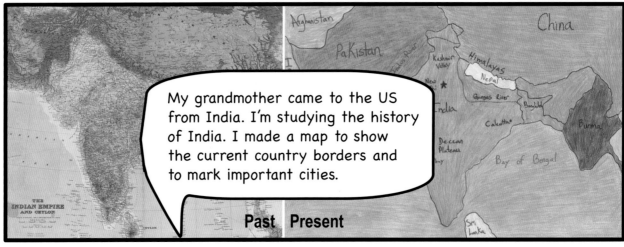

My grandmother came to the US from India. I'm studying the history of India. I made a map to show the current country borders and to mark important cities.

Past   Present

Maps have many practical uses in teaching and learning. Think about ways they can help young people visualize geographic information across the curriculum.

Communicate – express data when verbal language might be a barrier

Compare – highlight differences or similarities in data

Explain – show data in a meaningful context

Persuade – show convincing evidence to change attitudes or sell products

Present – quickly and efficiently display volumes of data

Track – show trends or changes over time

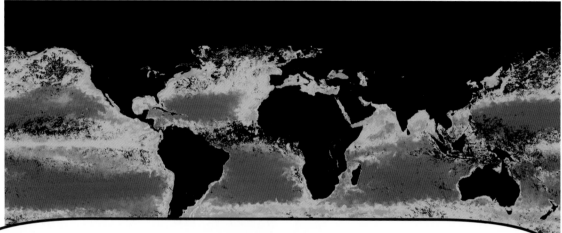

NASA has been following the concentration of chlorophyll for many years. These measurements provide scientists with information about the health of the ocean and the ocean carbon cycle.

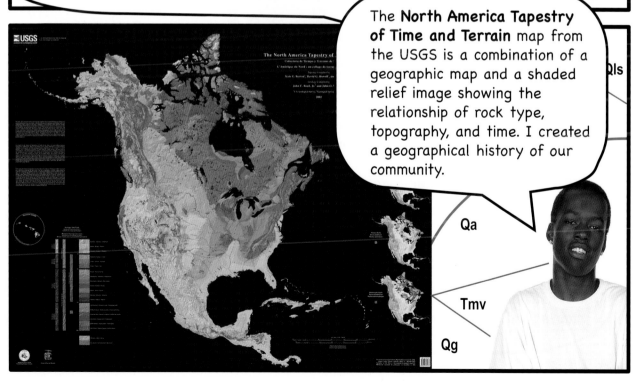

The **North America Tapestry of Time and Terrain** map from the USGS is a combination of a geographic map and a shaded relief image showing the relationship of rock type, topography, and time. I created a geographical history of our community.

In **Making Maps: A Visual Guide to Map Design for GIS**, John Krygier and Denis Wood stress that there is more to a map than the map itself. The titles, legend, explanatory text, scale and directional indicators, sources, credits, border, and insets are all pieces that must be placed carefully for an effective map.

When creating a map, Krygier and Wood suggest three aspects to evaluation:
Documentation - keep records of progress
Formative - process checks of the design
Impact - critique of the final product

My grandfather was in the Vietnam War. To understand military movement in the conflict, it's essential to explore the Ho Chi Minh trail. Rather than writing a traditional report, I'm combining photos, interviews, and maps to tell the story of this complex maze of paths that played a central role in this complex war. I'm creating a log of the data and conferencing with my teacher about my progress. We'll be sharing our projects at a family night!

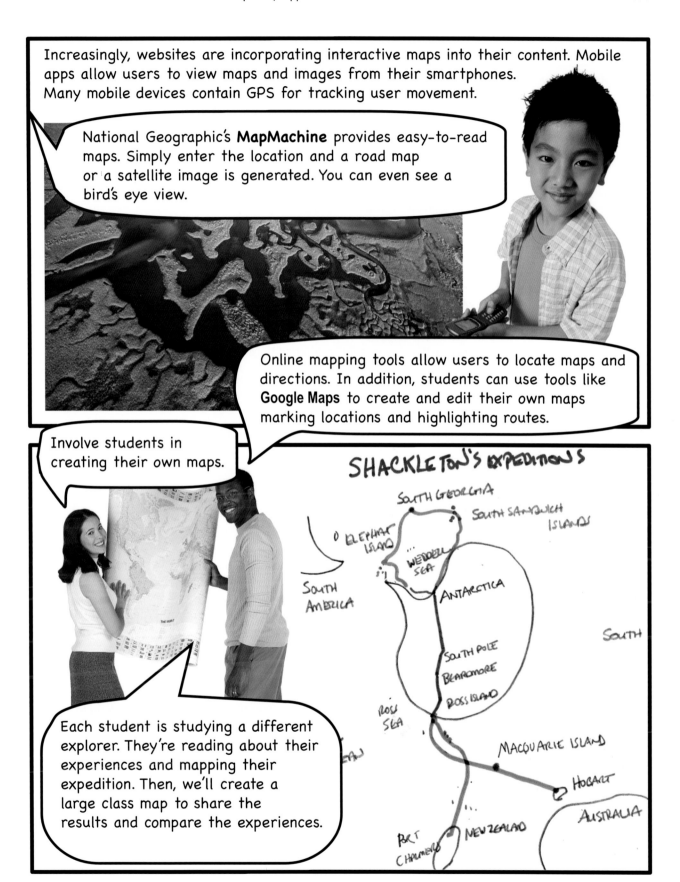

Increasingly, websites are incorporating interactive maps into their content. Mobile apps allow users to view maps and images from their smartphones. Many mobile devices contain GPS for tracking user movement.

National Geographic's **MapMachine** provides easy-to-read maps. Simply enter the location and a road map or a satellite image is generated. You can even see a bird's eye view.

Online mapping tools allow users to locate maps and directions. In addition, students can use tools like **Google Maps** to create and edit their own maps marking locations and highlighting routes.

Involve students in creating their own maps.

Each student is studying a different explorer. They're reading about their experiences and mapping their expedition. Then, we'll create a large class map to share the results and compare the experiences.

SHACKLETON'S EXPEDITIONS

Try mapping tools and resources:

Earth Observatory	http://earthobservatory.nasa.gov/GlobalMaps/
EarthShots	http://earthshots.usgs.gov/
EnviroMapper	http://www.epa.gov/enviro/html/em/index.html
Geography and Maps	http://www.loc.gov/rr/geogmap/guide/gmilltoc.html
Geospatial One Stop	http://geodata.gov
Google Earth	http://earth.google.com/
Google Maps	http://maps.google.com/
Highways	http://www.fhwa.dot.gov/planning/nhs/
Map Blog	http://strangemaps.wordpress.com/
Map Machine	http://maps.nationalgeographic.com/map-machine
Mapping Our World	http://www.oxfam.org.uk/education/resources/mapping_our_world/
Naming the West	http://www.galileo.org/initiatives/ntw/index.html
National Atlas	http://www.nationalatlas.gov/
Perry-Castañeda Maps	http://www.lib.utexas.edu/maps/index.html
Place In the World	http://www.fieldmuseum.org/maps/highlights.asp
Tapestry	http://tapestry.usgs.gov/default.html
US Neutrality	http://teachingamericanhistory.org/neh/interactives/neutrality/
Xpeditions	http://www.nationalgeographic.com/xpeditions/hall/

Explore mapmaking guides:

Mapmaking Guide Grades 3-5 (PDF)
http://www.nationalgeographic.com/xpeditions/lessons/09/g35/cartographyguidestudent.pdf

Mapmaking Guide Grades 6-8 (PDF)
http://www.nationalgeographic.com/xpeditions/lessons/09/g68/cartographyguidestudent.pdf

Explore the following lessons for additional ideas:

Black Death	http://edsitement.neh.gov/view_lesson_plan.asp?id=675
Caribou Migration	http://www.nationalgeographic.com/xpeditions/lessons/09/gk2/migrationcaribou.html
Explorer's Experience	http://www.artsedge.kennedy-center.org/content/2365/
Genographic	http://www.nationalgeographic.com/xpeditions/lessons/09/g912/genographic1.html
Great Plains	http://edsitement.neh.gov/view_lesson_plan.asp?id=265
Handy Map	http://illuminations.nctm.org/LessonDetail.aspx?ID=L71
Human Migration	http://www.nationalgeographic.com/xpeditions/lessons/09/g35/humanmigration.html
Japan, 1940-1941	http://edsitement.neh.gov/view_lesson_plan.asp?id=751
Make State Maps	http://www.nationalgeographic.com/xpeditions/lessons/03/g35/exploremaps.html
Mapmaking	http://www.nationalgeographic.com/xpeditions/lessons/01/g68/mapmaking.html
Mapping Change	http://www.eduplace.com/activity/mapping.html
Mapping Colonial...	http://edsitement.neh.gov/view_lesson_plan.asp?id=716
Mapping Our Worlds	http://edsitement.neh.gov/view_lesson_plan.asp?id=329
Mapping the Past	http://edsitement.neh.gov/view_lesson_plan.asp?id=328
Mapping Your State	http://www.nationalgeographic.com/xpeditions/lessons/10/g35/tgmapping.html
Over the River...	http://www.nationalgeographic.com/xpeditions/lessons/02/gk2/riverwoods.html
Sprawl	http://www.nationalgeographic.com/xpeditions/lessons/12/g912/sprawlnational.html
Trekking to Timbuktu	http://edsitement.neh.gov/view_lesson_plan.asp?id=508
Which Way?	http://www.nationalgeographic.com/xpeditions/lessons/17/g68/whichway.html

Info Graphics and Organizers in Learning

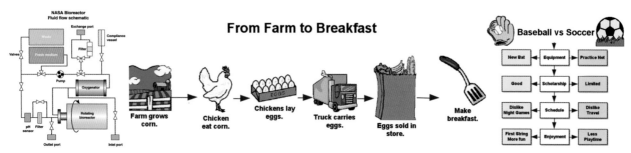

Because information graphics and graphic organizers can incorporate many formats of information, they appeal to all learning styles and intelligences. For example, young people with strengths in verbal-linguistic intelligence would be drawn to charts and graphs emphasizing key words and lists of text, while those with logical-mathematical intelligence would likely choose bar graphs, timelines, logic maps, and other numeric visuals. Maps, sketches, and photographs would suit those with visual-spatial intelligence. The classification aspects of diagrams and comparison charts would appeal to those with naturalistic intelligence. The use of graphics for goal setting and meta-cognitive activities is associated with the intrapersonal intelligence, while the social aspects of collaborative planning for graphics is related to the interpersonal intelligence.

In **Webbing with Literature: Creating Story Maps with Children's Books**, Karen D'Angelo Bromley states that webbing is a visual display of categories of information and their relationship. She notes that webbing encourages responses, extends comprehension, builds literacy, and enhances learning. It can be used in teaching, learning, and assessment.

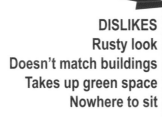

DISLIKES
Rusty look
Doesn't match buildings
Takes up green space
Nowhere to sit

LIKES
Geometric shapes
Simple design
Outside
Blows in wind

Alexander Calder Sculptures

I'm reading Blue Balliett's book **The Calder Game**. I like making concept maps to show what I'm thinking and learning as I read. I use words, images, and lines to help me organize my thoughts.

In the article **Learning with Concept and Knowledge Maps: A Meta-Analysis**, Nesbit and Adesope found that "across several instructional conditions, settings, and methodological features, the use of concept maps was associated with increased knowledge retention."

In their article **Eight Types of Graphic Organizers for Empowering Social Studies Students and Teachers**, Nancy Gallavan and Ellen Kottler stress the importance of identifying the purpose of the graphic organizer, using the vocabulary associated with each visual, and selecting the best tool to represent the data before, during, and after reading and discussion. Let's explore their eight categories based on purpose:

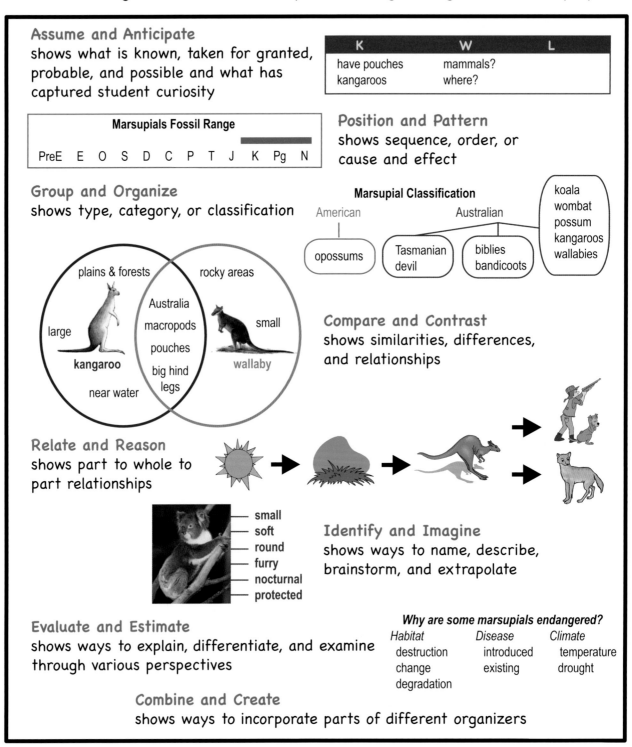

Assume and Anticipate
shows what is known, taken for granted, probable, and possible and what has captured student curiosity

K	W	L
have pouches	mammals?	
kangaroos	where?	

Marsupials Fossil Range

PreE   E   O   S   D   C   P   T   J   K   Pg   N

Position and Pattern
shows sequence, order, or cause and effect

Group and Organize
shows type, category, or classification

Marsupial Classification

American — opossums

Australian — Tasmanian devil — biblies bandicoots

koala
wombat
possum
kangaroos
wallabies

plains & forests | Australia macropods pouches big hind legs | rocky areas

large

kangaroo

near water

small

wallaby

Compare and Contrast
shows similarities, differences, and relationships

Relate and Reason
shows part to whole to part relationships

— small
— soft
— round
— furry
— nocturnal
— protected

Identify and Imagine
shows ways to name, describe, brainstorm, and extrapolate

Evaluate and Estimate
shows ways to explain, differentiate, and examine through various perspectives

Why are some marsupials endangered?

Habitat
destruction
change
degradation

Disease
introduced
existing

Climate
temperature
drought

Combine and Create
shows ways to incorporate parts of different organizers

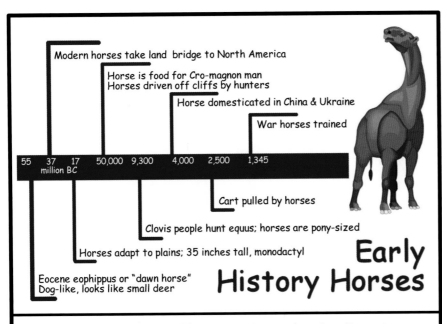

Modern horses take land bridge to North America

Horse is food for Cro-magnon man
Horses driven off cliffs by hunters

Horse domesticated in China & Ukraine

War horses trained

| 55 | 37 | 17 | 50,000 | 9,300 | 4,000 | 2,500 | 1,345 |
million BC

Cart pulled by horses

Clovis people hunt equus; horses are pony-sized

Horses adapt to plains; 35 inches tall, monodactyl

Eocene eophippus or "dawn horse"
Dog-like, looks like small deer

Early History Horses

Illustrate timelines photos and artwork.

Try activities such as following the life cycle of a bird in a nest.

Many students have difficulty with understanding changes over time. Use timelines as a way for students to show their understanding of migration stories, the evolution of inventions, or changes through a lifetime.

I'm doing a project on the post-election crisis in Kenya. I used a web to show the key issues and concerns.

I'm doing a presentation comparing cars powered by gas versus hydrogen fuel cells. First, I identified the key issues, then I made my comparison. I think clipart makes my graphic organizer more understandable.

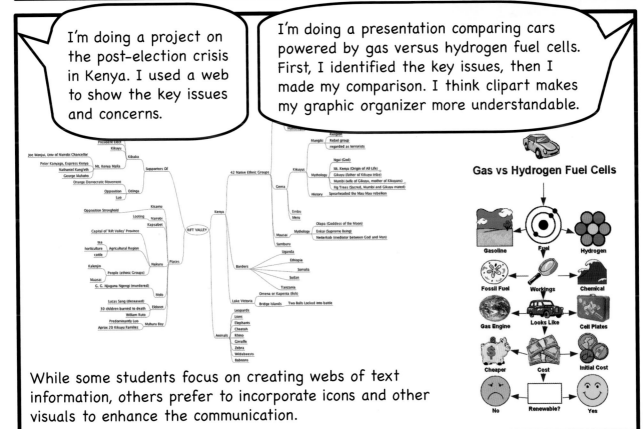

Gas vs Hydrogen Fuel Cells

While some students focus on creating webs of text information, others prefer to incorporate icons and other visuals to enhance the communication.

When communicating complex ideas and relationships, it's sometimes useful to combine elements of diagrams, illustrations, maps, and graphic organizers to create information graphics.

Online tools can help students create graphic organizers. The **ReadWriteThink** website at http://www.readwritethink.org/ provides dozens of tools to help with reading and writing activities.

We used the Animal Study, Story Map, and Plot Diagram **ReadWriteThink** tools to help us write our own Mercy Watson story.

The **Titanic in the Classroom** project at http://connections.smsd.org/titanic/ is a great example of incorporating graphic activities into a project-based learning approach.

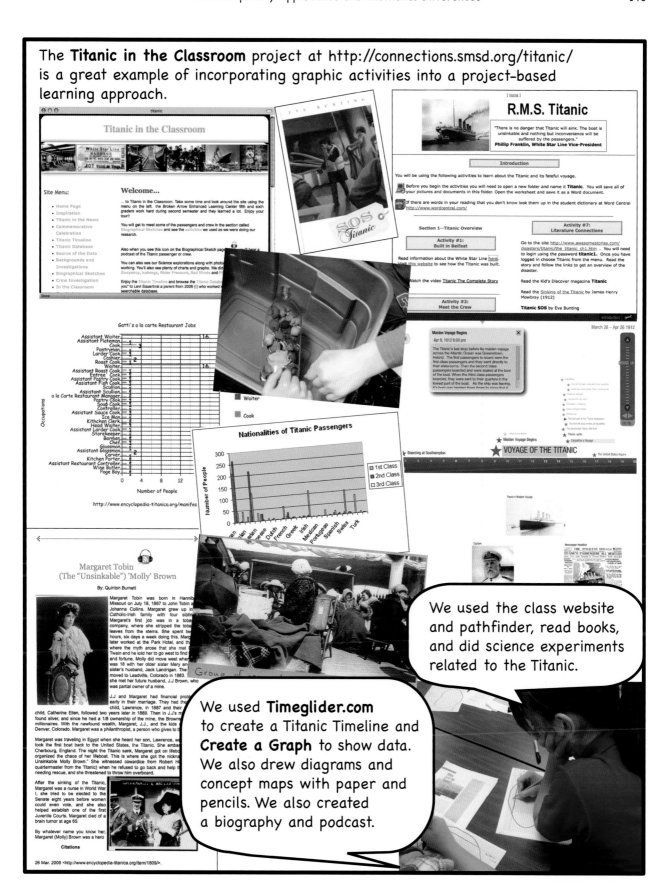

We used the class website and pathfinder, read books, and did science experiments related to the Titanic.

We used **Timeglider.com** to create a Titanic Timeline and **Create a Graph** to show data. We also drew diagrams and concept maps with paper and pencils. We also created a biography and podcast.

Try online tools:

2-Circle Venn Diagram	http://www.readwritethink.org/materials/venn/
3-Circle Venn Diagram	http://interactives.mped.org/venn28.aspx
Animal Inquiry	http://www.readwritethink.org/materials/animal-inquiry/
Circle Plot Diagram	http://www.readwritethink.org/materials/circle-plot/
Compare and Contrast	http://www.readwritethink.org/materials/compcontrast/map/
Drama Map	http://www.readwritethink.org/materials/dramamap/
Essay Map	http://www.readwritethink.org/materials/essaymap/
Gliffy	http://www.gliffy.com/
Graphic Map	http://www.readwritethink.org/materials/graphicmap/
Literary Elements Map	http://www.readwritethink.org/materials/lit-elements/
Plot Diagram	http://www.readwritethink.org/materials/plot-diagram/
Story Map	http://www.readwritethink.org/materials/storymap/
Timeline	http://www.readwritethink.org/materials/timeline/
Webbing Tool	http://interactives.mped.org/view_interactive.aspx?id=127
My webspiration	http://www.mywebspiration.com/

Explore the following lessons for additional ideas:

2-Circle Venn Diagram	http://www.readwritethink.org/student_mat/student_material.asp?id=6
3-Circle Venn Diagram	http://www.readwritethink.org/student_mat/student_material.asp?id=32
Allegory in Painting	http://edsitement.neh.gov/view_lesson_plan.asp?id=643
Antarctic Food Chain	http://www.nationalgeographic.com/xpeditions/lessons/08/gk2/antarcticfood.html
Are the von Trapps...	http://artsedge.kennedy-center.org/content/2385/
Ballads	http://www.readwritethink.org/lessons/lesson_view.asp?id=1097
Biography Project	http://www.readwritethink.org/lessons/lesson_view.asp?id=243
Biomagnification	http://www.nationalgeographic.com/xpeditions/lessons/08/g912/greatlakes.html
Building a Matrix	http://www.readwritethink.org/lessons/lesson_view.asp?id=263
Can We Keep...	http://www.nationalgeographic.com/xpeditions/lessons/14/gk2/clean.html
Capturing History	http://artsedge.kennedy-center.org/content/2368/
Castles & Cornerstones	http://www.artsedge.kennedy-center.org/content/3701/
Charting Characters	http://www.readwritethink.org/lessons/lesson_view.asp?id=267
Charting Countries	http://www.nationalgeographic.com/xpeditions/lessons/13/g35/countries.html
Circle Plot Diagram	http://www.readwritethink.org/student_mat/student_material.asp?id=26
Circular Plot	http://www.readwritethink.org/lessons/lesson_view.asp?id=292
Classifying Numbers	http://illuminations.nctm.org/LessonDetail.aspx?ID=L274
Compare & Contrast	http://www.readwritethink.org/student_mat/student_material.asp?id=66
Comparing Tales	http://artsedge.kennedy-center.org/content/2343/
Completing the Circle	http://www.readwritethink.org/lessons/lesson_view.asp?id=827
Contaminants	http://www.nationalgeographic.com/xpeditions/lessons/14/g912/tgsouhegan.html
Correspondence	http://www.readwritethink.org/lessons/lesson_view.asp?id=1083
Creative Communication	http://www.readwritethink.org/lessons/lesson_view.asp?id=10
Crocs, Then and Now	http://www.nationalgeographic.com/xpeditions/lessons/08/g68/crocsthennow.html
Cultural Myths	http://artsedge.kennedy-center.org/content/2298/
Diagram It!	http://www.readwritethink.org/lessons/lesson_view.asp?id=781
Don't Freeze	http://illuminations.nctm.org/LessonDetail.aspx?ID=L649
Drama Map	http://www.readwritethink.org/student_mat/student_material.asp?id=12
Essay Map	http://www.readwritethink.org/student_mat/student_material.asp?id=63
Explorations	http://illuminations.nctm.org/LessonDetail.aspx?ID=L290

Exploring Change	http://www.readwritethink.org/lessons/lesson_view.asp?id=1082
Exploring Comparison	http://www.readwritethink.org/lessons/lesson_view.asp?id=54
Exploring Cross-Age	http://www.readwritethink.org/lessons/lesson_view.asp?id=215
Expository Texts	http://www.readwritethink.org/lessons/lesson_view.asp?id=925
Eye on Idioms	http://www.readwritethink.org/student_mat/student_material.asp?id=30
Family Message	http://www.readwritethink.org/lessons/lesson_view.asp?id=82
Get the Reel Scoop	http://www.readwritethink.org/lessons/lesson_view.asp?id=46
Graphic Map Lessons	http://www.readwritethink.org/student_mat/student_material.asp?id=39
Graphic Organizers	http://www.readwritethink.org/lessons/lesson_view.asp?id=95
Grand Canyon	http://www.nationalgeographic.com/xpeditions/lessons/07/g68/canyon68.html
Guantanamera	http://artsedge.kennedy-center.org/content/2323/
Guided Comprehension	http://www.readwritethink.org/lessons/lesson_view.asp?id=229
Happily Ever After?	http://www.readwritethink.org/lessons/lesson_view.asp?id=374
He Said/She Said	http://www.readwritethink.org/lessons/lesson_view.asp?id=287
Heroes	http://www.readwritethink.org/lessons/lesson_view.asp?id=784
High Temperature	http://illuminations.nctm.org/LessonDetail.aspx?ID=L171
How Do ...	http://www.nationalgeographic.com/xpeditions/lessons/08/g35/seasseal.html
How Much...	http://www.econedlink.org/lessons/index.php?lesson=EM456&page=teacher
Jelly Belly Jam	http://www.econedlink.org/lessons/index.php?lesson=EM365&page=teacher
Leopard Seals	http://www.nationalgeographic.com/xpeditions/lessons/08/g68/seasseal.html
Let's Build a Snowman	http://www.readwritethink.org/lessons/lesson_view.asp?id=239
Literacy Blues	http://www.readwritethink.org/lessons/lesson_view.asp?id=266
Literary Elements Map	http://www.readwritethink.org/student_mat/student_material.asp?id=11
Magazine Redux	http://www.readwritethink.org/lessons/lesson_view.asp?id=214
Many Sets of Buttons	http://illuminations.nctm.org/LessonDetail.aspx?ID=L24
Mapping Characters	http://www.readwritethink.org/lessons/lesson_view.asp?id=409
Maria von Trapp	http://artsedge.kennedy-center.org/content/2382/
Native Americans	http://www.readwritethink.org/lessons/lesson_view.asp?id=63
Neighborly Interests	http://www.nytimes.com/learning/teachers/lessons/20031203wednesday.html
Once Upon a Time	http://www.readwritethink.org/lessons/lesson_view.asp?id=853
Plot Diagram Lessons	http://www.readwritethink.org/student_mat/student_material.asp?id=40
Plot Structure	http://www.readwritethink.org/lessons/lesson_view.asp?id=904
Plot Structure	http://www.readwritethink.org/lessons/lesson_view.asp?id=401
Pollution: Cause/Effect	http://www.readwritethink.org/lessons/lesson_view.asp?id=1035
Powerful Patterns	http://illuminations.nctm.org/LessonDetail.aspx?ID=U69
Ramp Builder	http://www.sciencenetlinks.com/lessons.cfm?DocID=20
Read-Alouds	http://www.readwritethink.org/lessons/lesson_view.asp?id=1077
Reluctant Writer	http://www.readwritethink.org/lessons/lesson_view.asp?id=217
Scratch Dance	http://artsedge.kennedy-center.org/content/3687/
Shaping the View	http://edsitement.neh.gov/view_lesson_plan.asp?id=635
Sizing Up	http://illuminations.nctm.org/LessonDetail.aspx?ID=L593
Sky and Artist	http://artsedge.kennedy-center.org/content/2366/
Sky Watching	http://www.sciencenetlinks.com/lessons.cfm?DocID=321
Sorting Time	http://illuminations.nctm.org/LessonDetail.aspx?ID=L138
Splish, Splash	http://www.nationalgeographic.com/xpeditions/lessons/07/gk2/water.html
Story Map Lessons	http://www.readwritethink.org/student_mat/student_material.asp?id=8
Street Games	http://artsedge.kennedy-center.org/content/2249/
Sun and the Earth	http://www.nationalgeographic.com/xpeditions/lessons/07/g35/seasons.html
Teaching the Epic	http://www.readwritethink.org/lessons/lesson_view.asp?id=225
Timeline Lessons	http://www.readwritethink.org/student_mat/student_material.asp?id=7
Using Venn Diagrams	http://www.nationalgeographic.com/xpeditions/lessons/08/g68/venn.html
Utopian Visions	http://artsedge.kennedy-center.org/content/2345/

Comics in Learning

From comic strips and political cartoons to graphic novels and webcomics, sequential art has become a popular resource for educators and visual learners.

Graphic novels and comics are popular with visual readers. In **Going Graphic: Comics at Work in the Multilingual Classroom**, Stephen Cary states that "Superman made me a reader. Dick and Jane tried their best, but they couldn't give me what The Man of Steel offered: a good reason to read... Reading became a deadly bore and, by extension, school too, since reading was such a large part of what went on in school... I devoured every comic book I could get my hands on including all the Classics Illustrated like The Three Musketeers... Most teachers banned them from the classroom, believing them frivolous and educationally bankrupt at best, lurid and morally unhealthy at worst." (p. 1-2)

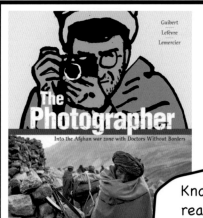

In recent years, the views of educators and librarians have changed tremendously. Critically acclaimed graphic novels like **The Photographer** have increased interest and provided credibility for this type of literature.

Known for his research on reading, Stephen Krashen has found that comics are a great example of how free voluntary reading can improve comprehension, increase vocabulary, develop effective writing style, increase competence in grammar, and encourage other reading.

James Bucky Carter notes that librarians have lead the way in making the case for graphic novels as exciting reading for adolescents.

A growing body of evidence asserts that graphic novels benefit young people across the curriculum from hesitant readers to gifted students.

An increasing number of comics are designed specifically for learning about a particular topic such as copyright law.

In **Graphic Storytelling and Visual Narrative**, Will Eisner states that "the reading process in comics is an extension of text. In text alone the process of reading involves word-to-image conversion. Comics accelerate that by providing the image." (p. 5)

According to Rocco Versaci (2008), a comic book panel contains a variety of information that must be processed... the visual narrative involves understanding pictures in the context of those around it.

Young people need skills in learning to interpret comics and cartoons. Wolsey (p. 117) suggests a series of steps in thinking about cartoons:
- Observe the document's features
- Use prior knowledge
- Speculate about causes and consequences
- Make personal connections
- Use evidence to support speculation

In **How to Interpret Visual Resources,** Harry Stein states that "a good cartoon rockets an opinion or problem to the viewer, causes a reaction or even a laugh, and then stretches the viewer's imagination and mind to new thinking." (p. 46)

Increasingly, comics are used to address serious issues.

What's a "happy cow"?

In **Understanding Comics**, Scott McCloud explains that digital comics can take any size or shape. No longer are they restricted to a particular genre.

Even established magazines like the journal **Nature**, have published comics as a way to communicate ideas and information on topics such as synthetic biology at http://www.nature.com/nature/comics/syntheticbiologycomic/.

Web comics often contain a directory showing thumbnails (small versions) of the comic pages. Users can also use the arrows for navigation.

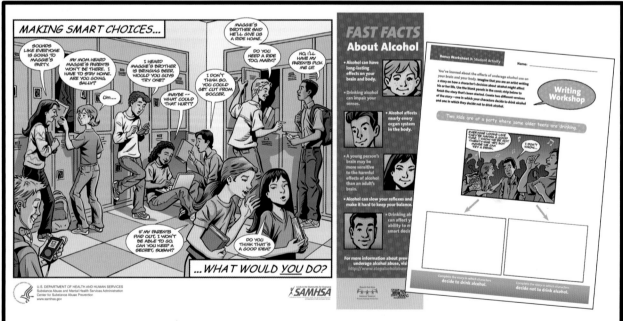

Government agencies have a long tradition of using comics for educational outreach. The **Too Smart to Start** project focuses on preventing underage drinking. In addition to the website at http://www.toosmarttostart.samhsa.gov/, activities involve young people in creating their own comics about alcohol safety.

Some students have a difficult time acquiring information from textbooks and nonfiction materials. Graphic texts provide a way for these students to access and assimilate information in an appealing and non-threatening environment.

The Vietnam War: A Graphic History provides an outstanding balance of concise text with rich visual elements that bring the Vietnam era to life for readers of all ages.

When seeking graphic histories, look for the clarity of information presentation and the depth of historical content.

When designing a recent assignment for my psychology class dealing with the relationship between mental and physical illness, I gave students a wide range of reading choices. While some students selected traditional texts, others chose graphic materials.

In their article **Let's Create a Comic Strip**, Wright and Sherman (1999) advocate student-made comic strips for building literacy and critical thinking skills. They describe an interdisciplinary approach combining language and art where students are involved in all aspects of comic strip production. A three-panel format can help students learn basic story structure (beginning, middle, and end) as well as the essential elements of setting, character, dialogue, and action.

What Did You Say?

Many people aren't aware that using headphones and earbuds can cause life-long hearing loss. My comic helps people learn about the issue.

Free online tools such as **http://makebeliefscomix.com/** make the process of building comics easy for children. Or, use free clipart from **http://openclipart.org/** and build your panels from scratch.

I've always been a comic fan, so I was thrilled when Mr. Pace said we could read a graphic novel-style history book.

After reading **Journey into Mohawk Country** by George O'Connor, I wanted to learn more about the history reflected in the book and how much of the book was true. I used Comic Life software to share my results. I brought in images from the book as well as primary source materials I found.

From writing original narratives to creating illuminated term papers, software such as Comic Life can be integrated across the curriculum. While some young people enjoy creating their own artwork, others prefer to use existing, documents, photographs, artwork, and other visuals in their comic projects.

Try online tools:

Build Your Own Comic	http://www.childrensmuseum.org/special_exhibits/comics/games.html
Cartoon Creator	http://www.readwritethink.org/materials/comic/
ComicArt School	http://comicartschool.ning.com/
Comiqs	http://comiqs.com/
Disney's Comic Creator	http://disney.go.com/surfswell/comiccreator.html
Garfield's Comic Creator	http://www.nhlbi.nih.gov/health/public/sleep/starslp/missionz/comic.htm
HyperComics	http://www.hypercomics.com/
Kabam! Comic Creator	http://www.bam.gov/sub_yourlife/yourlife_comiccreator.html#
Make Your Own Graphix	http://www.scholastic.com/goosebumpsgraphix/makeyourown/index.htm
MakeBeliefsComix	http://www.makebeliefscomix.com/
Pixton	http://pixton.com/
Sam & Max	http://www.telltalegames.com/samandmax/comics/create
Toondoo	http://www.toondoo.com/

Explore online resources:

Amazing Kids	http://www.amazing-kids.org/akcomics.htm
The Comic Book Project	http://www.comicbookproject.org/
Daryl Cagle's Index	http://www.cagle.com/
Fun Brain's Web Comics	http://www.funbrain.com/brain/ReadingBrain/ReadingBrain.html
Graphic Novels from ALA	http://wikis.ala.org/professionaltips/index.php/Graphic_novels
Graphic Novels Guide	http://library.buffalo.edu/libraries/asl/guides/graphicnovels/index.php
Herblock's History	http://www.loc.gov/rr/print/swann/herblock/cartoon.html
No Flying, No Tights	http://www.noflyingnotights.com
Parent Guide	http://www2.scholastic.com/browse/article.jsp?id=3745810
Using Graphic Novels	http://www2.scholastic.com/browse/article.jsp?id=7582

Explore the following lessons for additional ideas:

Book Report Alternative	http://www.readwritethink.org/lessons/lesson_view.asp?id=236
Book Report Alternative	http://www.readwritethink.org/lessons/lesson_view.asp?id=195
Buzz! Whiz! Bang!	http://www.readwritethink.org/lessons/lesson_view.asp?id=867
Change Happens	http://www.eduplace.com/activity/change.html
Comic Creator Lessons	http://www.readwritethink.org/student_mat/student_material.asp?id=21
Comic Makeovers	http://www.readwritethink.org/lessons/lesson_view.asp?id=207
Comics in the Classroom 1	http://www.readwritethink.org/lessons/lesson_view.asp?id=188
Comics in the Classroom 2	http://www.readwritethink.org/lessons/lesson_view.asp?id=223
Creating Comic Strips	http://www.artsedge.kennedy-center.org/content/2126/
Daryl Cagle's Teachers Guide	http://www.cagle.com/teacher/
Draw a Math Story	http://www.readwritethink.org/lessons/lesson_view.asp?id=144
Draw a Story	http://www.readwritethink.org/lessons/lesson_view.asp?id=45
Drawing Political Cartoons	http://www.artsedge.kennedy-center.org/content/2100/
Election Process	http://artsedge.kennedy-center.org/content/3775/
Family Comic Strips	http://www.eduplace.com/activity/2_5_act2.html
Modern Culture	http://www.nationalgeographic.com/xpeditions/lessons/10/gk2/fairytale.html
Picture Perfect Facts	http://artsedge.kennedy-center.org/content/2089/
Rhythm and Art	http://artsedge.kennedy-center.org/content/2051/
Russian Fairy Tales	http://edsitement.neh.gov/view_lesson_plan.asp?id=590
Story Switch Comics	http://www.eduplace.com/activity/1_7_act3.html
To, Too, or Two	http://www.readwritethink.org/lessons/lesson_view.asp?id=284
Wanted: A New Friend	http://artsedge.kennedy-center.org/content/2361/

Literature and Visual Thinking

    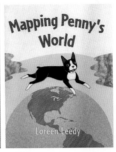  

Regardless of whether a story is told through illustrations or readers are asked to create their own mental images, literature is directly connected with visual thinking.

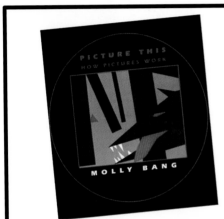

Molly Bang, Istavan Banyai, and Lucy Micklethwait are well-known for designing picture books that teach visual thinking.

In **Getting Graphic**, Michele Gorman explains that visual messages alongside minimal print help ease frustrations of beginning or struggling readers.

Visually-rich literature can draw in reluctant readers.

A growing number of nonfiction authors are creating graphic treatments of their content.

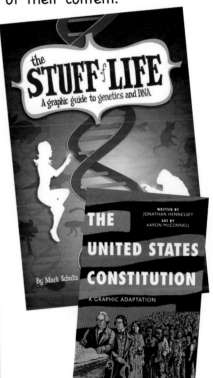

Graphic novels are one of the few types of texts that consistently engage male readers. Edgy, engaging, and different, graphic novels satisfy boys' overwhelmingly clear urge to explore visual texts (Smith & Wilheim, 2002).

Candace Fleming uses a scrapbooking approach to writing about historical figures such as Ben Franklin, Abraham Lincoln, and Eleanor Roosevelt.

After reading the historical fiction book titled **Uprising**, I wanted to learn more about the horrific 1911 fire that killed 146 women.

I used historical photos and drawings to retell the story of the Triangle Shirtwaist Factory Fire. I identified maps to show the location. I also shared how fire regulations have changed as a result of this disaster.

Using Fleming's nonfiction history books as inspiration, I created a multimedia scrapbook using historical images in Microsoft PowerPoint.

Strikes & Safety

In the years leading up to the fire, there were a number of labor strikes. Most famous was the New York shirtwaist strike of 1909 (Uprising of the 20,000). Primarily involving Jewish young women, it was led by Clara Lemlich and supported by the National Women's Trade Union. In addition to concerns about low wages and long hours, there were safety issues.

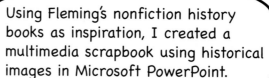

1 2 3 4 5 6 7 8 9 10 11 12 13 14 15 16 17

Use picture books to encourage young children to think visually and create their own.

In the **Great Graph Contest**, Loreen Leedy introduces students to bar graphs, pie charts, Venn diagrams, and other visual representations through a contest between two amphibian friends who both try to make the best graph.

Favorite American Symbol

First graders created class bar graphs on symbols and cookies.

Third graders created photo comics about animal features.

Books on science topics such as **What Do You Do with a Tail Like This?** provide visual clues that encourage children to to seek evidence, make comparisons, and draw conclusions.

WHAT DO YOU DO WITH A BEAK LIKE THAT?

BY KAYLEE R.

Birds have beaks. They are used for eating, grooming, and feeding babies.

My beak is good for eating fruit.

My beak is sharp so I can kill rabbits.

I scoop up shrimp with my beak.

I use my beak to get bugs from trees.

I can dig for food underwater with my beak.

Many children's books have roots in historical events.

When reading the award-winning picture book **Henry's Freedom Box**, make comparisons with historical drawings of the event.

The **Pride of Baghdad** is a high school level graphic novel by Brian K. Vaughan focusing on the impact of the War in Iraq on zoo animals. The graphic novel may inspire teens to create their own visual story focusing on the consequences of war.

I chose to use black and white images to show the stark reality of war. I used close-up photos and interesting angles to draw attention to the specific settings.

Use book and author websites to stimulate student thinking about their own writing.

The **Mouse Guard** website http://www.mouseguard.net/ shows the characters and settings used in the book series. Involve students in creating their own story-planning pages.

Many books share fantasy or futuristic worlds. Involve young people in visualizing these places.

Students might create cartoon images to represent the characters in **The Uglies** by Scott Westerfeld.

While reading **Tuck Everlasting**, learners might collect photos that reflect their thoughts on the setting of the book.

Maps might be used to show the world of Orwell's **1984**.

Literature is no longer confined to traditional print media. Instead, an increasing number of publishers are providing multi-platform experiences.

> Some publishers provide a companion website with maps, games, clues, extra content, and activities. Young people reading the **Septimus Heap** books use a website map to explore the online materials.

> In addition to websites, some books provide other types of materials such as card packs for **The 39 Clues** series, ephemera for the **Cathy** series, and personal effects for the book **Dark Art**. These visual materials can provide clues to help readers solve mysteries.

> In the novel **Trackers**, the story is told through an interview along with images taken using secret cameras.

> In the book **Skeleton Creek**, the print journal and online videos are interconnected. Young people use both resources to solve a mystery.

These transmedia stories often connect to social technologies such as Facebook pages, Flickr images, and Twitter messages. Readers of the book **The Amanda Project** are encouraged to build characters and post art at http://theamandaproject.com/.

When designing learning experiences, seek out lesser used images to connect with literature. The **Civil War Literature Wiki** at http://civilwarlit.wikispaces.com/ encourages students to share information about the historical fiction and nonfiction books they are reading. Rather than incorporating well-known photographs, consider exploring the drawings available at the Library of Congress.

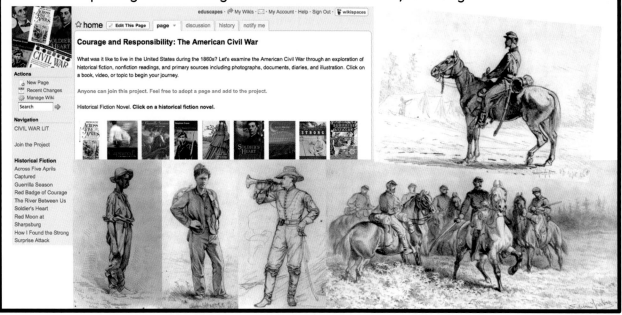

As you think about literature, interdisciplinary approaches and individual differences, consider three areas:
(1) visual narratives that convey information in nontraditional ways.
(2) images that enhance a traditional reading experience.
(3) graphic organizers and visual tools that help organize findings.

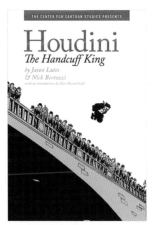

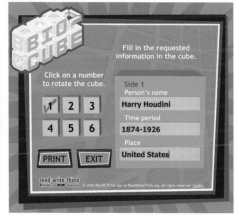

Combining a graphic biography with historical photos and the **BioCube** organizer at http://readwritethink.org/materials/bio_cube/ provides a unique environment to address standards related to Language Arts, History, and 21st Century Learners.

Try online tools:

BioCube	http://readwritethink.org/materials/bio_cube/
Book Cover Creator	http://www.readwritethink.org/materials/bookcover/
Character Scrapbook	http://teacher.scholastic.com/activities/scrapbook/
Character Trading	http://readwritethink.org/materials/trading_cards/
Doodle Splash	http://www.readwritethink.org/materials/doodle/
Flashlight Readers	http://teacher.scholastic.com/activities/flashlightreaders/
Literary Graffiti	http://www.readwritethink.org/materials/graffiti/
MysteryCube	http://readwritethink.org/materials/mystery_cube/

Explore the following lessons for additional ideas:

BioCube Lessons	http://www.readwritethink.org/student_mat/student_material.asp?id=57
Book Cover Creator	http://www.readwritethink.org/student_mat/student_material.asp?id=58
Book Report	http://www.readwritethink.org/lessons/lesson_view.asp?id=972
Bridging Literature	http://www.readwritethink.org/lessons/lesson_view.asp?id=822
Character Trading	http://www.readwritethink.org/student_mat/student_material.asp?id=56
Children's Picture Book	http://www.readwritethink.org/lessons/lesson_view.asp?id=1022
Doodle Splash	http://www.readwritethink.org/student_mat/student_material.asp?id=22
Escaping Slavery	http://www.readwritethink.org/lessons/lesson_view.asp?id=127
Every Picture Tells...	http://artsedge.kennedy-center.org/content/2471/
Fact or Fiction	http://www.readwritethink.org/lessons/lesson_view.asp?id=778
Fiction	http://artsedge.kennedy-center.org/content/2235/
From Fact to Fiction	http://www.readwritethink.org/lessons/lesson_view.asp?id=111
Go West	http://edsitement.neh.gov/view_lesson_plan.asp?id=277
Literary Graffiti	http://www.readwritethink.org/student_mat/student_material.asp?id=23
Looking at Landmarks	http://www.readwritethink.org/lessons/lesson_view.asp?id=841
Make a Splash	http://www.readwritethink.org/lessons/lesson_view.asp?id=1128
Mind Pictures	http://www.readwritethink.org/lessons/lesson_view.asp?id=792
Mystery Cube	http://www.readwritethink.org/student_mat/student_material.asp?id=59
Multigenre Texts	http://www.readwritethink.org/lessons/lesson_view.asp?id=293
A Tale of Two Stories	http://illuminations.nctm.org/LessonDetail.aspx?ID=L295
Teaching Shapes	http://www.readwritethink.org/lessons/lesson_view.asp?id=797
Telling a Story	http://www.readwritethink.org/lessons/lesson_view.asp?id=421
Unicorns	http://edsitement.neh.gov/view_lesson_plan.asp?id=244
Using Pictures	http://www.ncrtec.org/tl/camp/lessons.htm
What's in a Mystery?	http://www.readwritethink.org/lessons/lesson_view.asp?id=865

Graphic Inquiry and the 21st Century Learner

Inquiry is a process that involves asking questions and searching for evidence that can be used to design arguments, make decisions and draw conclusions. Daniel Callison (2002) identified five components of information inquiry: questioning and exploration, assimilation and inference, and reflection.

Graphic inquiries weave visual tools, materials, resources, and thinking throughout the inquiry process.

Graphic inquiry is much more than supplementing text with visuals. Instead, visuals are infused into all aspects of inquiry from questioning to reflection. According to Stephen Cary (2004, p. 23), visuals can increase the number of concepts learned and the length of time those concepts are remembered.

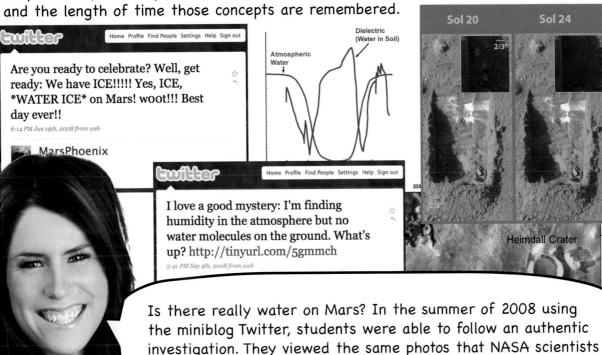

twitter   Home Profile Find People Settings Help Sign out

Are you ready to celebrate? Well, get ready: We have ICE!!!!! Yes, ICE, *WATER ICE* on Mars! woot!!! Best day ever!!

6:14 PM Jun 19th, 2008 from web

MarsPhoenix

twitter   Home Profile Find People Settings Help Sign out

I love a good mystery: I'm finding humidity in the atmosphere but no water molecules on the ground. What's up? http://tinyurl.com/5gmmch

5:41 PM Sep 4th, 2008 from web

Atmospheric Water

Dielectric (Water in Soil)

Sol 20   Sol 24

Heimdall Crater

Is there really water on Mars? In the summer of 2008 using the miniblog Twitter, students were able to follow an authentic investigation. They viewed the same photos that NASA scientists saw and had access to some of the same data. Through this visual communication, they felt part of a great discovery!

Graphic inquiry is woven throughout the American Association of School Librarians **Standards for the 21st-Century Learner**.
1. Inquire, think critically, and gain knowledge.
2. Draw conclusions, make informed decisions, apply knowledge to new situations, and create new knowledge.
3. Share knowledge and participate ethically and productively as members of our democratic society.
4. Pursue personal and aesthetic growth.

Graphic inquiry is closely connected to other types of inquiry. In **Constructing Credible Images: Documentary Studies, Social Research, and Visual Studies,** Jon Wagner defines social inquiry as "an effort to generate new knowledge of culture and social life through the systematic collection and analysis of sensory evidence and other forms of real-world data." (2004, p. 1479)

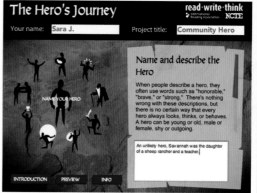

The interactive tool called **The Hero's Journey** http://readwritethink.org/materials/herosjourney/ uses icons to help young people explore the characteristics of a local or legendary person.

Photographs, sketches, and other graphics can expand on these notes to create a visual story about the hero's journey.

In **The Natural Investigator** (2000), Michael Bentley, Christine Ebert and Edward Ebert identified different types of inquiries across subject areas:
- **Trial and error** – arbitrary search for solutions
- **Documenting** – making and recording observations
- **Prediction testing** – making and testing predictions
- **Product testing** – identifying and using criteria
- **Experimenting** – identifying and controlling variables
- **Reflecting** – contemplating ideas
- **Generating models** – creating constructs
- **Inventing** – selecting and combining ideas and objects

Any of these types could incorporate elements of graphic inquiry.

In **Education for Thinking**, Deanna Kuhn (2005, p. 57) notes that "the skills of inquiry are not intuitively given and cannot be assumed to be in place among middle-school students. Nor do they develop on their own, as an outgrowth of young children's 'natural' curiosity.

The nature and sequence of development of inquiry skills need to be identified in careful detail, and the conditions established that will support this development."

Graphics are often overlooked when designing inquiry-based learning experiences.

In the **National Science Education Standards**, the National Research Council states that "inquiry into authentic questions generated from student experiences is the central strategy for teaching science."

The trash matches the main idea.

Explain these words

Show the whole net so you can see it.

Show a picture of the scientist

I think the book will be about water pollution because I see trash on the beach. I also see the words trash and ocean in the title. I don't know what flotsam and jetsam mean.

The book is about oceanographer across the oce... cover shows th... trash. The sea... left by a boat.

The Smithsonian series **Scientists in the Field** explores the activities and contributions made by today's scientists. We started by analyzing book covers in the series and chose an image we wanted to explore through the book. Next, we created our own scientist scrapbooks sharing our experiences and discoveries.

The book **Inquiry and the National Science Education Standards: A Guide for Teaching and Learning** describes features of student inquiry (2000, p. 24-35):

Teachers help students learn how to ask good questions.

Learners attempt to answer these questions through hands-on investigations by analyzing and interpreting data, synthesizing their ideas, making inferences and predictions, building models, and actively creating, modifying, and discarding some explanations or answers. Students work together to compare results and discuss what evidence is the best.

Learners communicate and justify their proposed explanations to classmates and teachers by presenting their reasoning and evidence.

Learners evaluate their explanations in light of alternative explanations, particularly those reflecting scientific understanding. They clarify concepts and explanations with teachers and other expert sources of scientific knowledge.

Learners extend their new understanding and abilities and apply what they have learned to new situations.

Learners, with the teacher, review and assess what they have learned and how they have learned it.

In **Guided Inquiry: Learning in the 21st Century**, Carol Kuhlthau, Leslie Maniotes, and Ann Caspari identify six principles of guided inquiry (2007, p. 25):

Children learn by being actively engaged in and reflecting on an experience.
Children learn by building on what they already know.
Children develop higher-order thinking through guidance at critical points in the learning process.
Children have different ways and modes of learning.
Children learn through social interaction with others.
Children learn through instruction and experience in accord with their cognitive development.

Kuhlthau, Maniotes, and Caspari stress the importance of intervention at critical points during the inquiry process.

I've picked the berries, but I'm not sure whether to make jam or jelly. Which is faster? Which would be easier?

The diagram of anaphase in my textbook is slightly different from what I see in the microscope. Once I started comparing different representations, I began to see the features that make each phase unique. I also have a better understanding of mitosis as a process with a series of fluid rather than discrete stages.

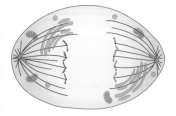
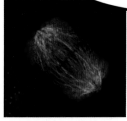
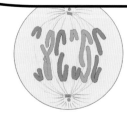
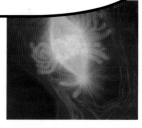

The goal of inquiry is not to simply answer questions. It's to explore alternative perspectives, collect data from a variety of resources, and examine different viewpoints in order to gather evidence that can be used to make decisions, invent new strategies, or convince others.

When designing graphic inquiry-based learning environments, seek out effective instructional approaches. In **Classroom Instruction that Works: Research-Based Strategies for Increasing Student Achievement**, Robert Marzano, Debra Pickering, and Jane Pollock identified instructional strategies in nine areas:

THE HUMAN HEART

Setting objectives and providing feedback

The heart is the organ that pumps blood to the whole human body. Without the heart, we would die. The heart is a muscle that needs exercise to stay healthy.

Generating and testing hypotheses

Cues, questions, and advanced organizers

How does the heart work?

See if you can figure it out yourself.

When the heart beats, it sends blood through the body.

Reinforcing efforts and providing recognition

Identifying similarities and differences

With lungs, it's air. With the heart, it's blood.

Great thinking. Can you show me?

Cooperative learning

We worked together.

Nonlinguistic representations

Summarizing and note taking

We drew a picture of the heart.

Everyone practiced putting the parts of the heart in the correct place.

Homework and practice

Marzano, Pickering, and Pollock point out that nonlinguistic representations are important in constructing knowledge.
   Creating graphic representations
   Making physical models
   Generating mental pictures
   Drawing pictures and pictographs

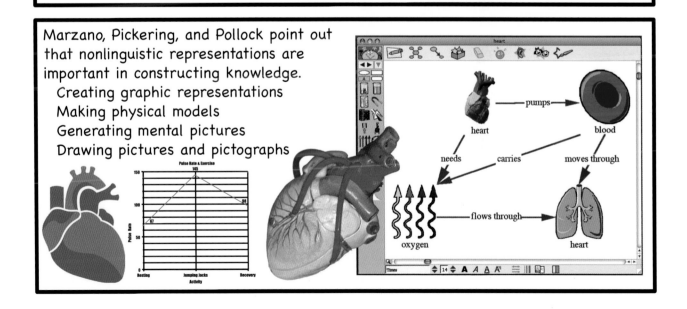

This section of the book explores five elements in the graphic inquiry process. As you examine standards for 21st century learning, think about the many ways that graphics can be infused into the inquiry projects. Also keep in mind that inquiry is a recursive process. Students may revisit elements over and over as they work their way through an inquiry.

Question

"A wise man - he was a jester by trade - once told me that living by answers is a form of death. It's only questions that keep you living."
(Crispin, p. 97-98)

Why would a jester say this?
Are jesters clowns or wise men?

Explore

People didn't have freedom of speech, however the jester often spoke openly about controversial topics.

 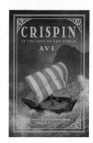  

Assimilate

From ancient China to 14th century Europe, the role of jester can be found in societies throughout history and around the world. Many of them are thinkers.

Infer

Jesters were much more than simply entertainers. Some jesters were very smart and used their role as a fool to talk about issues that would otherwise be off-limits. They used riddles and questions as a way to get people to think.

fool	intelligent
juggler	deep thinker
musician	connector
joker	strategist
buffoon	riddler
colorful	thoughtful

Reflect

I see jesters as wise men who had to walk a dangerous line between comedy and tragedy.

Blake the Jester

I like the idea of keeping an open mind. I'm not a good musician or juggler, but I think it would be fun to use humor as a way to open the minds of others.

Question

Observing clouds, watching a butterfly, or examining a photograph are all ways students might begin a graphic inquiry.

An inquiry begins with an open mind that observes the world and ponders the possibilities.

The Watching phase asks inquirers to become observers of their environment becoming in tune with the world around them from family needs to global concerns.
The Wondering phase focuses on brainstorming options, discussing ideas, identifying problems, and developing questions (Lamb 1997).

In **Education for Thinking**, Deanna Kuhn states that "a cornerstone of inquiry is the idea of a thesis, or question, and potential evidence that bears on it. Entertaining a thesis that is understood as capable of being disconfirmed by evidence sets the stage for the coordination of theory and evidence that lies at the heart of inquiry. Without this capability, there can be little point to the inquiry. At worst, inquiry is reduced to demonstration (of what one already believes to be true) or to the undirected compiling of information toward no particular end." (p. 57)

What is the question I'm trying to answer, the problem I'd liked to solve, or the key issue I need to resolve?

As you design inquiry-based learning environments, consider local expectations along with national standards from AASL, ISTE, and subject area organizations.

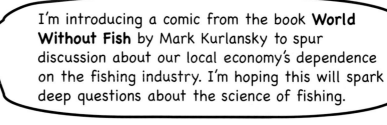

I'm introducing a comic from the book **World Without Fish** by Mark Kurlansky to spur discussion about our local economy's dependence on the fishing industry. I'm hoping this will spark deep questions about the science of fishing.

Applies prior knowledge to generate questions based on a real-world interest.
Frames a range of questions that explore different aspects of a problem.
Refines questions digging beyond superficial facts.
Demonstrates adaptability and flexibility in questioning.

Inquiry begins with an invitation to learn or the desire to discover. Questioning is at the core of information inquiry and drives the teaching and learning process. In an era of "one answer" standardized tests, it's essential that students learn to develop and address questions with many possible answers and problems with multiple solutions.

Inspiration comes from genuine curiosity. Meaningful questions originate in real-world problems and situations. Graphics provide a visual context and shared experience that encourage brainstorming and peer discussions. Invite students to think, then question:

What do I want to know about this?
What do I need to know?
What do I know already and
how do I know it?

I made a list of what I know about Toby, our class turtle. How is the sea turtle we're following online at http://www.greatturtlerace.com/ different from the one in our classroom aquarium?

I want to ask the firefighter why he has stripes on this coat. Why is his helmet yellow? Does he like fire or hate fire?

In information inquiry, questions may range from the most basic, factual reference questions to the most complex puzzles of life for which there are no answers.
Novice inquirers may not be able to verbalize their thoughts on unfamiliar topics and may benefit from the support of visuals. Use photographs to help them brainstorm questions.
Mature inquirers may use visuals to extend their thinking. They may examine images to generate questions from new perspectives.

Visual stories are an effective way to jumpstart an inquiry.
What are the most important ideas in the story?
Could the story be told from a different perspective?
What other types of visuals could be used?
How would the story be different in another setting?
Could you tell the entire story without words? How?
What questions do you have about the story's topic?
What are your questions about the people and place?

For some students, developing questions can be difficult and frustrating. Use graphics to assist in this process. Seek images that elicit an emotional response such as hunger, suffering, love or violence. Ask...

Does this image provoke, agitate, or frustrate you? Does it evoke, kindle, or awaken you?

Dueling images to contrast

Visualizations to spur speculation

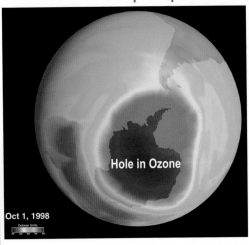

Visual brainstorming to jumpstart ideas

News photos as visual prompts

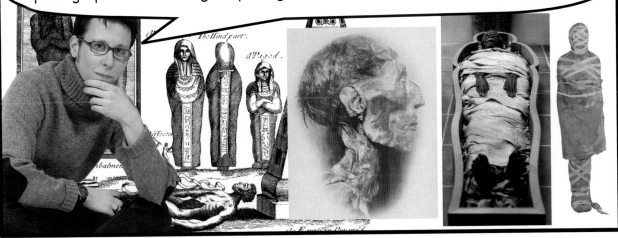

I thought my students would love a mummy inquiry, but I was disappointed that their initial questions were surface level. However after showing them photographs and drawings depicting mummies, they exploded with questions.

Developing questions converts thoughts into opportunities for action.

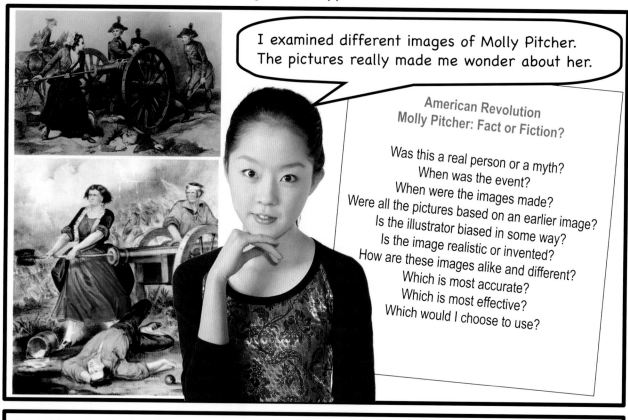

I examined different images of Molly Pitcher. The pictures really made me wonder about her.

American Revolution
Molly Pitcher: Fact or Fiction?

Was this a real person or a myth?
When was the event?
When were the images made?
Were all the pictures based on an earlier image?
Is the illustrator biased in some way?
Is the image realistic or invented?
How are these images alike and different?
Which is most accurate?
Which is most effective?
Which would I choose to use?

Socratic questioning is an approach educators can use to draw out deeper questions. Teachers seek to understand the direction of the student's inquiry and respond with questions that deepen the investigation. Questions help students associate prior knowledge, find connections, and more fully develop thoughts. It's helpful to have a set of questions that can guide the process of questioning. In **Q Tasks** Carol Koechlin and Sandi Zwaan provide questions to get students and teachers started.

What other questions might be useful?
How are the ideas alike or different?
How will this information help me answer my questions?
What would this look like from another perspective?
What are the causes and effects?
What are the consequences of?
What if ..?
What does this imply about...?
What evidence supports this argument?
What do you mean by...?
What do you see?
What objects go together? Why?
Which objects should be separated? Why?
What would you name this group? How would you describe it?
In what other ways could these objects be grouped?

Jamie McKenzie developed the "Questioning Toolkit" to help young people distinguish among different types of questions (1997, p. 1).

Essential Questions are central to our lives and touch our hearts and souls. They probe deep into issues that reflect the complexity of life. They often deal with abstractions and the "how" and "why" of people, places, and things.

Should ATVs be allowed in wilderness areas?

Subsidiary Questions are smaller queries that often lead to larger insights. They're sometimes combined together to ask larger questions.

What's the impact of ATVs on the soil?

Hypothetical Questions explore possibilities and test relationships. They are useful when making decisions and solving problems. They're often "what if" questions.

What if everyone drove off-road with their ATV?

Telling Questions focus an investigation on specific evidence. Information is gathered leading to a specific target.

How long does it take for the soil to recover from "off-road" ATV use?

Planning Questions help students organize their thinking, structure their investigation, and sequence activities.

What source would have the best statistics on ATV use?

Organizing Questions help structure information in meaningful ways.

What patterns can we find in ATV use?

Probing Questions ask students to apply logic, connect to prior knowledge, use intuition, and experiment with data to acquire useful evidence.

What are the fundamental concerns regarding ATVs and the environment?

Sorting & Sifting Questions focus on the relevance of information in addressing a particular need.

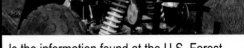

Is the information found at the U.S. Forest Service website regarding ATV use reliable?

Clarification Questions help students define words and concepts, examine the logic of an argument, and identify the underlying assumptions.

What do we mean by "off-road use" and "wilderness area"?

Strategic Questions arise during the inquiry process as students are exploring, assimilating, inferring, and reflecting.

What's the best way to gather information on illegal, off-road ATV use?

Elaborating Questions extend and expand findings by asking students to look for implicit (unstated) meanings.

What if ATV groups and environmental organizations worked together to establish ATV trails in areas adjacent to wilderness areas?

Unanswerable Questions explore those areas where truth may never be found. Students must understand that some problems may not be solved.

If wilderness areas have already been touched by humans, are they truly wild?

Inventive Questions encourage the discovery of new ideas or rethinking of existing approaches.

What if I just concentrated on the impact of illegal ATV use?

Provocative Questions challenge the status quo by promoting doubt and skepticism. They may explore irony, satire, and parody.

How could the ATV craze actually help environmentalists protect more land by illustrating how easily it's destroyed?

Irrelevant Questions distract students from their original questions, but these diversions are sometimes useful in finding new, relevant directions.

What is it about ATVs that get environmentalists so worked up?

Divergence Questions explore topics adjacent to the original questions, but issues that might be connected.

Where do mountain bikes fit into the discussion of wilderness access?

Irreverent Questions challenge students to think outside the box. Although they may seem disrespectful or impolite to some, they may generate important discussions about key issues.

Why not ban all humans from wilderness areas to keep them wild?

Explore

Examining a globe, reading a graph, and photographing an experiment are all ways student information scientists gather information and record ideas as they address their questions.

Exploration involves observing the world, investigating possibilities, collecting resources, interviewing experts, and experimenting with ideas.

The **Webbing** phase involves students in identifying and connecting ideas and information. Data is located and relevant resources are organized into meaningful clusters. One piece of information may lead to new questions and areas of interest (Lamb 1997).

As you design inquiry-based learning environments, consider local expectations along with national standards from AASL, ISTE, and subject area organizations.

I eat fish, but never really thought about the fishing industry, the impact of fishing on ocean life, and how the food choices I make impact the environment. Various resources seem to represent the issue in different ways. I need to explore all the different perspectives.

Should I be eating this?

Displays motivation, curiosity and interest in learning and inquiry.
Connects information based on personal learning and interests.
Uses creative and innovative approaches to locate and organize information.
Identifies the structure of media and how it impacts the subject and perspective.
Selects resources based on characteristics of each in addressing information needs.
Uses multiple representations of information to find information.
Applies evaluation criteria when examining visual information.
Applies knowledge of culture to understanding media messages.
Persists in seeking graphic information to gain a broad perspective.
Displays confidence in the use of graphic materials.

In **How To Use Your Eyes**, James Elkins urges us to "stop and consider things that are absolutely ordinary, things so clearly meaningless that they never seemed worth a second thought. Once you start seeing them, the world – which can look so dull, so empty of interest - will gather before your eyes and become thick with meaning." (p. xi)

Student information scientists explore the world around them seeking answers to their questions. From highly structured database searches to informal library shelf browsing, exploration is a critical component of inquiry. While the goal of exploration may be focused on specific questions, it may also be a more general curiosity about a topic.

Darwin Australia, February 1942

What did Darwin look like before this photo was taken?

Why was Darwin attacked?

How does this event fit on my WWII timeline?

I've seen many images of WWII in Europe, but I never really thought about the war impacting Australia. I'm going to refocus my inquiry.

While some resources may provide background information, others may lead the inquirer to more focused questions or new insights. In order to make effective use of novel ideas and information, inquirers must be aware of their prior kowledge. In his landmark textbook on educational psychology, David Ausubel (1968) stressed that what the learner already knows is the most important factor influencing learning.

Students often begin by exploring library and online resources. When guiding graphic inquiries, remind students about the use of visual resources such as photo collections, atlases, artwork, and illustrated books. Consider the wide range of graphic resources that might provide different perspectives on a subject.

Rocco Versaci suggests using comic books to "quite literally put a face on a given subject; readers "see" the characters through the illustrations." (2008, p. 101)

In addition to gathering information from established resources, young people may also collect their own data through observation, interviews, and experimentation.

Technology tools such as laptops, digital cameras, and audio recorders are useful in recording experiences.

Encourage students to incorporate graphic elements into interviews:
    Use photos to provide a context.
    Use maps to discuss places in time.
    Use objects to jog memories.
Digitally record the interview for later use.
Photograph historical re-enactments, safety procedures, or steps in a process.

Traditionally students take written notes with an emphasis on text. However graphic inquirers record visual notes focusing on graphic clues, annotating images, and arranging materials on bulletin boards or wall charts.

1969 Jordan River - a patrol from the Popular Front for the Liberation of Palestine

Egyptian weapons

head coverings

sturdy boots

I'm exploring the history of guerilla warfare. As I find useful images, I'm putting them on a timeline so I can make visual comparisons over time.

What information will help me answer my question, solve my problem, or resolve my issue?

What are visual ways I can record my findings?

Students need tools to help them record their explorations.

paper scraps
note cards
post-its
checklists
push pins
tape
clips

acid

Particularly for spatial learners, it's important to provide flexible workspaces where records can be physically laid out. These visual notes can then be organized and rearranged on bulletin boards, in scrapbooks, or on wall charts.

In **Visual Thinking**, Rudolf Arnheim states that when "a student is asked to copy what he sees under the microscope, he cannot aim, mechanically, for mere accuracy and neatness. He must decide what matters and what types of relevant shapes are represented in the accidental specimen. Therefore, his drawing cannot possibly be a reproduction; it will be an image of what he sees and understands, more or less actively and intelligently." (p. 307)

Some students may need scaffolding for visual note taking. Use tools such as Microsoft **PowerPoint** to provide prompts, starters, and electronic worksheets for visual information organization.

Kurt Hanks (2003, p. 70) suggests using the word "Capture Cards" to describe the use of cards to store key concepts, and ideas. Put the title in the upper left corner, provide definitions, labels, and a visual. Use the back side for citations or notes. With PowerPoint, 4-12 cards can be printed per page to review vocabulary.

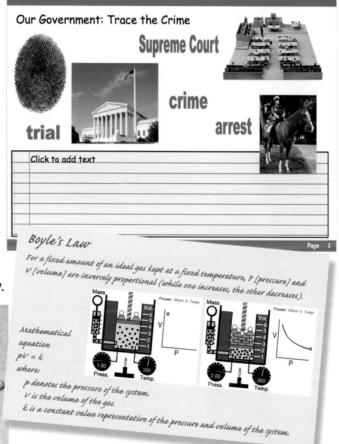

"Drawing, sketching, jotting, mapping, and other artistic and graphic representations are equally valuable – and when combined with words, in strategies like clustering, semantic mapping, or cartooning, they can powerfully leverage students' thinking about the curriculum... As a cognitive tool, learning logs can work for learners in any content field. After all, whatever the subject matter, learners can always jot down their responses, record their own prior knowledge, probe their own thinking patterns, map predictions, diagram connections, or sketch plans for what to do next." (Zemelman, Daniels, & Hyde, 1998, p. 239-240)

Exploring leads back to questioning. Questions may be refined, restated, or new queries may emerge. Encourage inquirers to be risk-takers.
Ask:

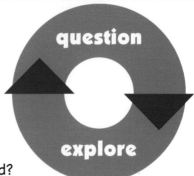

  What can I answer and what new questions do I have?
  How can I focus and narrow my questions?
  Did we miss anything the first time around?
  Are there other ways to think about the same thing?
  Are there other points of view that should be considered?
  Can I think of unusual approaches or different ways of thinking?

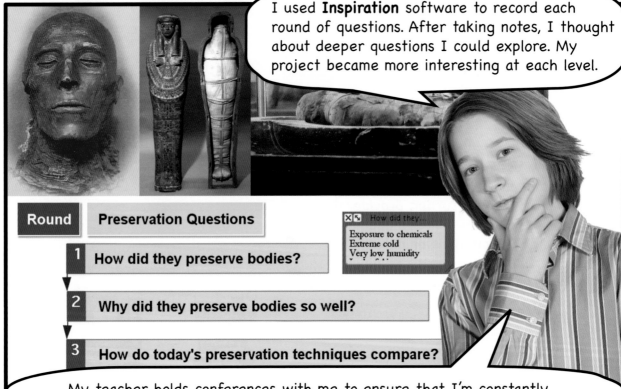

I used **Inspiration** software to record each round of questions. After taking notes, I thought about deeper questions I could explore. My project became more interesting at each level.

Round	Preservation Questions
1	How did they preserve bodies?
2	Why did they preserve bodies so well?
3	How do today's preservation techniques compare?

How did they...
Exposure to chemicals
Extreme cold
Very low humidity

My teacher holds conferences with me to ensure that I'm constantly seeking broad, narrow, and related questions. She gives me feedback and credit for each level of depth to encourage thinking.

Many students are looking for the quick answer. Encourage students to move from the shallow to the deep end of thinking through supporting cycles of questioning and exploring. In **Info Tasks for Successful Learning**, Koechlin and Zwann (2001) suggest evaluating the quality of student research questions by asking:

  Focus - Does your question help to focus your research?
  Interest - Are you excited about your question?
  Knowledge - Will your question help you learn?
  Processing - Will your question help you understand your topic better?

Assimilate

Creating diagrams with chalk, forming mental maps, and incorporating new perspectives into existing thoughts all involve connecting prior knowledge with new information.

> After reading about dinosaurs, we came outside with a measuring tape and chalk to draw them. We used our bodies for comparison. Wow, they were huge!

Assimilation involves processing, associating, and integrating new ideas with already available knowledge in the human mind. The **Wiggling** phase is often the toughest phase for students. They may be uncertain about what they've found and where they are going with a project. Wiggling involves evaluating content, along with twisting and turning information looking for clues, ideas, and perspectives (Lamb 1997).

As you design inquiry-based learning environments, consider local expectations along with national standards from AASL, ISTE, and subject area organizations.

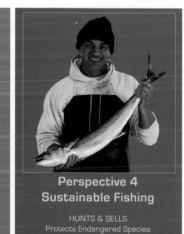

**Perspective 4
Sustainable Fishing**

HUNTS & SELLS
Protects Endangered Species
Hunts Sustainable Fish
Advertises as Sustainable

WORKS WITH
Fed Govt. Organizations

> I'm organizing based on views found in different categories of local people.

Identifies main and supporting ideas.
Identifies new knowledge and connects to existing information.
Connects information to personal experiences.
Adjusts personal knowledge based on new information.
Organizes knowledge in personally meaningful ways.
Makes sense of information by building connections among information.
Acts on information (accept, reject, modify) based on criteria.
Associates prior knowledge with information needs.
Applies criteria to the evaluation of information.
Seeks reasons rather than relying on feelings and peer pressure.
Represents data in a variety of ways to meet particular needs.
Conveys information in ways that support reasons, but don't distort facts.
Identifies bias, misconceptions, and conflicting information.
Applies knowledge of different perspectives to understand facts.
Respects divergent perspectives, differing opinions and viewpoints.
Describes the benefits of diversity.
Demonstrates emotional resilience.
Demonstrates critical and creative thinking in processing information.

The process of assimilation involves reinforcing and confirming information that is known, altering thinking based on new information, or rejecting information that doesn't match the student's belief system. In an inquiry, assimilation leads to consideration of new options and points of view (Callison, 2006, p. 7).

Carol Kuhlthau (1993) notes that conflicts between what is believed and new information that is found can lead to uncertainty and frustration.

Challenging a student's thinking is an effective way to encourge questioning and extend the quest for additional information. School media specialists and classroom teachers should encourage the habit of deliberately seeking information that opposes students' belief (Fitzgerald 1999).

Once I began evaluating and comparing the data, I could start seeing trends. I just needed to keep an open mind.

While some people rarely criticize new information, others see ideas as flexible. Those with an open mind are more likely to challenge their own thinking and try new things. Assimilated information can be accepted as knowledge whether the information is right or wrong. Thus, assimilation should involve not only the actions of reading and listening, but also the processes of critical analysis, debate, and comparison of facts and ideas.

Mary Ann Fitzgerald notes that students have a difficult time evaluating information. However children develop evaluation skills over time. Young children have limited prior knowledge and experience. They tend to believe what they see and are unlikely to question authority. Children need cues and guidance to scaffold their evaluation activities.

I've been reading stories from around the world, examining old and new artwork, and learning about what's real and make believe about dragons. I found a website that said there are dragons in caves, but I didn't believe it. The Komodo Dragon is the only real one.

Evaluation of information resources is an important activity during assimilation. Students must be able to judge the quality of data, sort out information, prioritize the findings and decide what is important. They identify sequences and events that connect noting discrepencies, nuances, and differences in how data is presented. As this happens, ideas begin to coalesce, information is melded, and inquirers begin to develop generalizations. This process of analyzing and interpreting information leads to selection of evidence that can be used to address questions and make inferences.

I'm using the "Trash or Treasure" method of deciding what fits and what doesn't fit with my thinking. I'm not just evaluating resources, I'm also collecting evidence to address questions and begin building arguments. My visual notes contain the most important ideas.

Mature information scientists seek connections through a metacognitive process.

What do I bring to the inquiry process?

How do I assimilate new knowledge?

How do my understandings and insights change as I infuse new ideas?

Discover	Identify new ideas and ways of thinking about the evidence
Discern	Identify the origins of information and underlying thinking
Detect	Seek out fallacies, flaws, and misinformation along with reasons for these errors
Deduce	Identify possible conditions and consequences
Divide	Organize information by comparing how people, places, and events are alike and different. Also, classify information into categories based on commonality
Dictate	Identify themes, patterns, and generalizations
Devise	Build arguments by organizing evidence

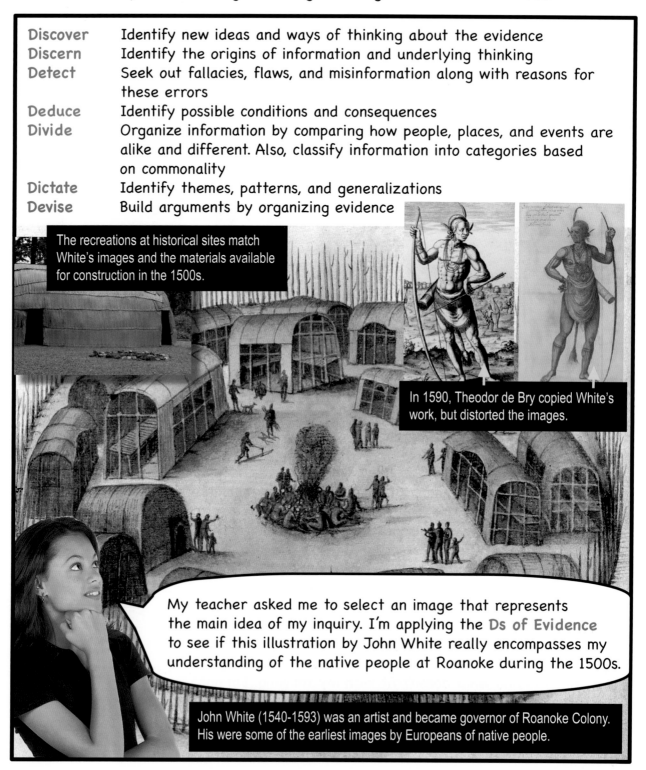

The recreations at historical sites match White's images and the materials available for construction in the 1500s.

In 1590, Theodor de Bry copied White's work, but distorted the images.

My teacher asked me to select an image that represents the main idea of my inquiry. I'm applying the Ds of Evidence to see if this illustration by John White really encompasses my understanding of the native people at Roanoke during the 1500s.

John White (1540-1593) was an artist and became governor of Roanoke Colony. His were some of the earliest images by Europeans of native people.

In **Visual Literacy**, Marcia Weaver notes that "sometimes graphics serve as tools to record and organize information as it is gathered, and for keeping that information organized until decisions are made about it." (1999, p. 53)

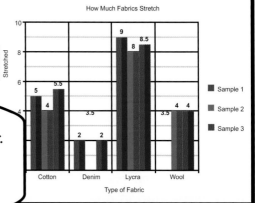

How Much Fabrics Stretch

I'm looking for the best fabrics to use for stretchable sportwear. I'm collecting my own data and charting the results. Next, I'll look at cotton and lycra blends.

Although assimilation occurs deep within our brain, we can use visual activities to build these associations. Marzano, Pickering, and Pollock (1997) identified six graphic organizers that correspond to six common information organization patterns:

Descriptive patterns. Webs are used to represent facts about people, places, things, and events.

Time-sequence patterns. Timelines and cycle diagrams organize events by chronology.

Find Maple Tree   Tap Tree   Collect Syrup   Taste Test   Sell

Process/cause-effect patterns. Fishbone charts and "how to" diagrams organize information into a causal network or into steps leading to products.

Episode patterns. These visuals organize information about specific events including setting, specific people, duration, sequence, and cause and effect.

Generalization/principle patterns. Use hierarchies to organize information into general statements and supporting evidence or examples.

Concept patterns. Use concept maps to organize classes and categories about people, places, things, and events.

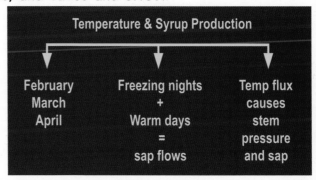

Temperature & Syrup Production

| February March April | Freezing nights + Warm days = sap flows | Temp flux causes stem pressure and sap |

Young people need to question and challenge the adequacy of information in terms of accuracy, meaning, relevance, currency, authority, understanding, and value as convincing evidence. Whether analyzing graphics made by others or evaluating the quality of your own visual, ask yourself:

Purpose – What's your overall impression? What's happening in the visual? Is it intended to inform, instruct, or persuade? Is it effective? Why was it created? What existing knowledge, attitudes, and values do you associate with this visual?

Focus – Does the image represent a particular time, place, or event? If so, is this an accurate portrayal? What is included and excluded? Does this impact effectiveness?

Layout – Is the presentation of the data effective? How would the graphic look if it were presented in a different way or from an alternative viewpoint? What if the scale were changed? Does the layout give you clues about point of view or bias?

Design – Do the elements of design contribute or distract from the effectiveness of the illustration? Why or why not? Does the visual reflect good design practices? How?

Representations – Does the image reflect reality or is it distorted? Is it natural or posed? What symbols are used to represent information or ideas? Are these effective?

Content Source – Where did the information originate? Does this content have an historical foundation or reference? Do these sources have bias or special interests? Are stereotypes or stereotypical thinking reflected in this work? What's the tone, humorous or serious? Does a particular organization support these materials?

Illustrator – Who is the illustrator and why was this visual created? What expertise does this person have in this subject? What other visuals has this person created?

Context – When and where was it composed? Who was the intended audience? Are other materials associated with this graphic? Is there a social or historical reference?

Applications – Does the visual make sense in terms of what you know and need to know about the topic? Does the information have adequate depth?

Conclusions – What conclusions can be drawn from the graphic? Do you agree? Why?

Extension – Can you confirm or refute the graphic contents using other sources?

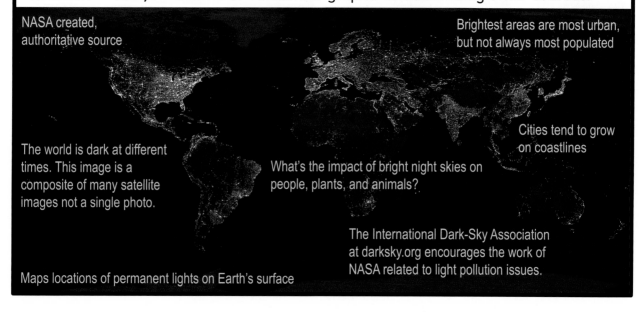

NASA created,
authoritative source

Brightest areas are most urban,
but not always most populated

Cities tend to grow
on coastlines

The world is dark at different
times. This image is a
composite of many satellite
images not a single photo.

What's the impact of bright night skies on
people, plants, and animals?

The International Dark-Sky Association
at darksky.org encourages the work of
NASA related to light pollution issues.

Maps locations of permanent lights on Earth's surface

Infer

Inventing a new way to build a backyard fort, creating an innovative approach to recycling, and building a case against a new coal power plant all involve applying evidence to solve problems and make decisions.

If you can recycle plastic, why not reuse shoes?

The **Weaving** phase consists of organizing ideas, creating models, and formulating plans. It focuses on the application, analysis, and synthesis of information (Lamb 1997).

As you design inquiry-based learning environments, consider local expectations along with national standards from AASL, ISTE, and subject area organizations.

Uses varied strategies to interpret graphic information.

Differentiates fact from opinion in building arguments.

Collaborates with others to analyze information and develop new understandings.

Exchanges ideas to broaden perspectives.

Gathers meaning by synthesizing information from multiple resources.

Draws conclusions from a variety of resources.

Identifies patterns of evidence leading to a decision.

Formulates alternative conclusions based on evidence.

Incorporates diverse and global perspectives into decision-making.

Applies valid information to create reasoned conclusions.

Expresses understandings through meaningful products.

Applies the writing process to the design of graphic communications.

Creates products that accurately reflect findings for an authentic, real-world audience.

Builds communications for specific audiences and particular purposes.

Demonstrates ethical decision-making.

Considers the cultural and social context in making decisions.

Visuals help me see and explain the difference between how the purse seiner and the trawler collect fish.

purse seiner net

trawler net

While assimilation involves accumulation of information, alteration of existing knowledge, and consideration of alternatives, inference attempts to apply this knowledge to address questions. Inquirers must read between the lines and use clues to solve problems. They solve puzzles by applying evidence, unlock mysteries by using evidence as clues and create meaning by organizing evidence in relevant ways.

Evidence is necessary to support a claim, justify change, or make an informed decision. Students must learn to identify, process, and judge evidence. This begins with looking for patterns of evidence. Ask:

What evidence is most useful in addressing my questions?
How does this evidence connect with what I already know?
How is this evidence relevant for my question?
What are my assumptions?
What am I guessing about and what do I know for sure?
What evidence is from primary versus secondary sources?
Which sources are biased and which are credible?
What are all the possible perspectives and viewpoints?
Why would someone consider one viewpoint better/worse?
What pieces of evidence support and refute a perspective?
What are the most important pieces of evidence?
What are the supporting pieces of evidence?
What are the patterns of evidence?
What new questions does this evidence raise?

Our class is comparing two areas of the pond near our school. One area contains an invasive plant called lythrum salicaria. Last year the plant was removed from the second study location. We're looking for convincing evidence showing whether removing the invasive species makes a difference in the habitat.

Site 5

We collected physical and scientific evidence from the pond, along with documentary evidence from government and organization websites. We created photo logs, maps, timelines, diagrams, and charts to organize evidence.

Critical and creative thinking are necessary for inquirers to synthesize information and develop a persuasive set of evidence that can be used to justify a decision or draw a conclusion. Developing a convincing argument is more than simply providing information. Evidence must be organized in a way that supports an argument and also makes sense to the audience.

While reading the historical fiction book, **The Big Burn,** by Jeanette Ingold I became interested in learning the facts behind the role of the Forest Service in managing fires, so I watched documentaries, read books, examined websites, and conducted online interviews to gather information and identify the different perspectives.

Arguments provide evidence to support a claim. To develop useful arguments, inquirers must evaluate evidence, examine different points of view, and determine the most logical approach or meaningful conclusion. Ask:

How does the evidence fit together?
What claims and supporting arguments could be made?
How can the evidence be arranged to support a conclusion?
What's the core of the argument?
What pieces of evidence support what perspectives?
How do the arguments fit with my understandings?
What is the reasoning behind each argument?
What are the limitations of these arguments?
What are the errors in reasoning?
Where are the holes in the evidence?
How could this information be misleading?
What are the problems and barriers?
How could it be corrected or improved?
What are the relationships/causes/effects?

Observe, no action → Arguments

Managed Logging → Argument

I found that there are many different perspectives on how wildfires should be managed. I built a concept map showing the overlap in the perspectives. Then, I created a visual showing the arguments for each approach.

In **Classroom Instruction that Works: Research-Based Strategies for Increasing Student Achievement**, Robert Marzano, Debra Pickering, and Jane Pollock noted that generating and testing hypotheses is one of the most powerful and analytical of cognitive operations. Both inductive and deductive thinking are effective. It's important that students are able to clearly explain their hypotheses and conclusions.

Deductive arguments apply general principles and theories to specific situations. This is the most effective educational technique. Students are asked to explain their hypotheses, experiments, and conclusions.

> I applied four principles of flight to predict which paper airplane would work best.

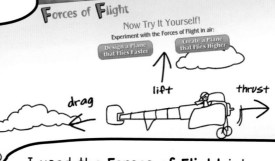

> I used the **Forces of Flight** interactive from the National Air and Space Museum website to figure out how airplanes work. Then, I designed and tested my own online plane.

Inductive arguments move from specifics to generalizations. Thinkers use observations to draw conclusions.

> I'm trying to decide whether we should continue producing the penny. I turn facts and figures into visual data that are easier for me to understand and interpret. Although I really like the penny, it is costly to produce and use. I think the penny should be discontinued.

$80 million $134 million

market value   cost to produce

Richard Paul and Linda Elder (2002, p. 17–18) distinguish between two types of critical thinking. Weak-sense critical thinking defends current beliefs and relies on slick arguments, while strong-sense critical thinking evaluates all claims and beliefs, carefully weighing evidence before coming to a decision.

Arguments use evidence and reason to demonstrate a particular perspective or version of the truth. These arguments may be persuasive if they are presented in a way to convince others to take action. Explanations show why the audience should believe the arguments. Inquirers use graphics to persuade themselves and also others.

The bricklayer game from Colonial Williamsburg at http://www.history.org/kids/games/ deserves the WOW award because it accurately depicts the process of making bricks in Colonial America.

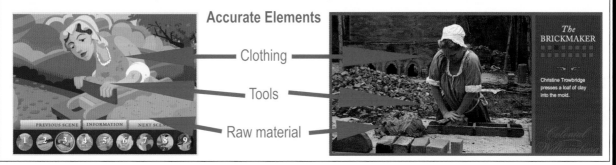

In **Beautiful Evidence**, Edward Tufte states that "the fundamental analytical act in statistical reasoning is to answer the question 'Compared with what?' Whether we are evaluating changes over space or time, searching big data bases, adjusting and controlling for variables, designing experiments, specifying multiple regressions, or doing just about any kind of evidence-based reasoning, the essential point is to make intelligent and appropriate comparisons. Thus visual displays, if they are to assist thinking, should show comparisons." (p. 127)

When designing persuasive messages, ask:
>   Who is my audience and what do they need to know?
>   What are examples and nonexamples?
>   In what ways can the evidence be presented to communicate the argument?
>   How can my messages be shared in an effective, efficient, and appealing way?
>   How can my messages be conveyed in a number of different ways?
>   What parts of the argument are difficult to understand?

According to Callison (1999), "assimilaton and inference are constantly interacting as a decision process to accept or reject new information".

In most academic situations, inquiry involves accumulating evidence that supports inferences that seem reasonable, logical, and persuasive. Students ask:

What inferences can I make based on the evidence?
What conclusions can I draw?
What decisions can I make?

Jamie McKenzie (1994) stresses that it's important for young people to keep an open mind. He notes that the final product of inquiry is built on three elements: assumptions, evidence, and logic.

With each inquiry cycle, inquirers must revisit questions with an open mind.

What evidence do I still need to gather?
What has changed since my last cycle of questioning, exploring, assimilating, and inferring?
Have I visualized the evidence in many different ways?
What pieces of information still need to be connected? What's not obvious?
Are there alternatives I haven't considered? Are there opinions I should seek?
What are the risks and benefits of each approach?
What generalizations can I draw based on the evidence?
Do I have enough information to draw a conclusion or make a decision?
How do I most effectively present arguments and cite evidence?
How can graphics be used to better understand the data and my conclusions?

Reflect

I've figured it out. Who should I tell?

Considering the strengths and weaknesses of the final draft of a bike path proposal, wondering about the impact of a decision not to smoke, and exchanging ideas about future collaborations are metacognitive and social activities for self-evaluation.

The **Wrapping** phase involves creating and packaging ideas and solutions. Why is this important? Who needs to know about it? How can I effectively convey my ideas? The **Waving** phase consists of communicating ideas to others through presenting, publishing, and sharing. How will I market my ideas and who will I ask for feedback? The **Wishing** phase involves assessing, evaluating, and reflecting on the process and product of inquiry. Was the project a success? What will I do next (Lamb 1997)?

As you design inquiry-based learning environments, consider local expectations along with national standards from AASL, ISTE, and subject area organizations.

I've learned a lot during my inquiry. From now on, I'm going to be more careful about the fish I eat, as well as how I fish myself. My guidebook was a great way to share what I learned. But, I wish I had started the project earlier so I could have spent more time at the fish hatchery. I want to extend the experience by learning more about how our local lakes are stocked.

A Guide to Sustainable Fishing

Your choices matter!

By Cameron Campbell

Assesses the inquiry process.
Develops personal criteria for the evaluation of inquiry.
Monitors and adapts the inquiry process to ensure effectiveness.
Demonstrates a systematic process for evaluating the inquiry experience.
Critiques processes and procedures in one's own inquiry.
Connects understandings to both personal interests and larger societal needs.
Develops future directions based on inquiry experiences.
Demonstrates leadership through inquiry.
Shows social responsibility throughout the inquiry process.
Identifies areas of the inquiry to complete, expand, or extend.
Describes the value of examples and need for on-going research.
Participates in the social exchange that reaches beyond the learning community.
Addresses audience questions related to inquiry conclusions and communications.
Applies feedback from teachers, mentors, and peers in revising inquiry skills.
Uses knowledge of inquiry gaps and limitations to improve future inquiries.
Applies strengths and positive outcomes to improve future inquiries.
Applies inquiry experiences to future investigations.

As inquirers draw conclusions and make decisions, they consider ways to share their findings with others.

We want the world to know about the problem of teenage pregnancy, so we combined our research into the medical and psychological aspects with three case studies from our community. We published our findings as a book to be sold online. The proeeds will go to a local non-profit family planning center.

From original works of art to diagrams visualizing innovative products, graphics can play an important role in communicating solutions and conclusions.

Whether presenting to classmates, sharing with family members, or posting to the world on the Web, authentic audiences provide young people with a context for selecting, organizing, and communicating their evidence, arguments, and ideas.

1922: Isiah Cross born , my grandfather (died 1984) (click on picture above)

1930: Lillie Mae born in AR , my grandmother, (click on picture above)

1947: James Cross, my father, born in East Prarire, MO

1930s

I've created both a family timeline and a Civil Rights Movement timeline so we can talk about how each member of the family might have been impacted by what was happening nationally.

1925 Ku Klux Klan marches in Washington DC

1930-1945 World War II 2.5 million black men serve in military and many black women volunteer

Students often think of reflection as summative, however successful inquirers contemplate their progress and make adjustments in their thinking throughout the inquiry process. Reflections that assess questioning, exploring, assimilating, and inferring are formative and make the learner aware of strengths and weaknesses in their thinking at each phase of inquiry.

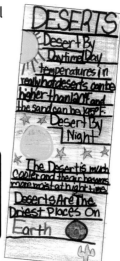

My conferences with Mr. Howell during the inquiry process really helped me think about my progress and create a vision for my project. Rather than just copying from Wikipedia, I thought about what a tourist would really want to know about the desert.

After rounds of questioning and exploring, assimilating and inferring, ask students to revisit the questions and goals of their inquiry. How did the project evolve?

I started my inquiry by exploring sheet music from the 1850s at the Library of Congress. I found a funny song about fashion and was surprised how little the basic idea of fashion has changed in 150 years. Each generation has their own idea about what fashion means.

My inquiry was full of twists and turns. I now have a totally different idea about what the word "fashion" means. I wrote a song in GarageBand and designed a music cover that's intended to persuade, predict, and parody the fashion industry.

Inquiries may go in different directions depending on the questions. While some inquiries look for answers, others seek solutions. The goal may not be apparent in the first round of the cycle. By encouraging inquirers to reflect throughout the process, inquiry becomes a cycle building deep understandings.

Ask: Did my question(s) reflect my need or problem?

Have I been successful in answering my question(s)?
Were my search strategies flawed?
Could my information be biased or incorrect?
Is this the best information to address this question?
Could I have made incorrect connections?
Could the inferences identified be flawed?
Have I addressed the needs of my audience?
What new questions have arisen from the evidence?
Have I chosen the best conclusion or decision?
Am I satisfied with my progress?
What are my strengths and weaknesses in the research processs?

As students reach the end of their inquiry, graphics can be used to visualize reflections.

Although my project began with a single focused question, the ideas spiraled like this Whirlpool Galaxy. Each arm of stars represents an expanded idea.

Young children often use smile faces to reflect their thoughts. After exploring the letter D, children described their favorite activities visually.

Older students may be asked to represent their feelings using more abstract visuals. Teens were asked to select an image from space that reflects their thoughts about an inquiry project.

Encourage metacognitive thinking through the use of graphic organizers. Ask students to trace their thinking through the inquiry process. Then, direct inquirers to reflect on their actions, approaches, resources, and conclusions.

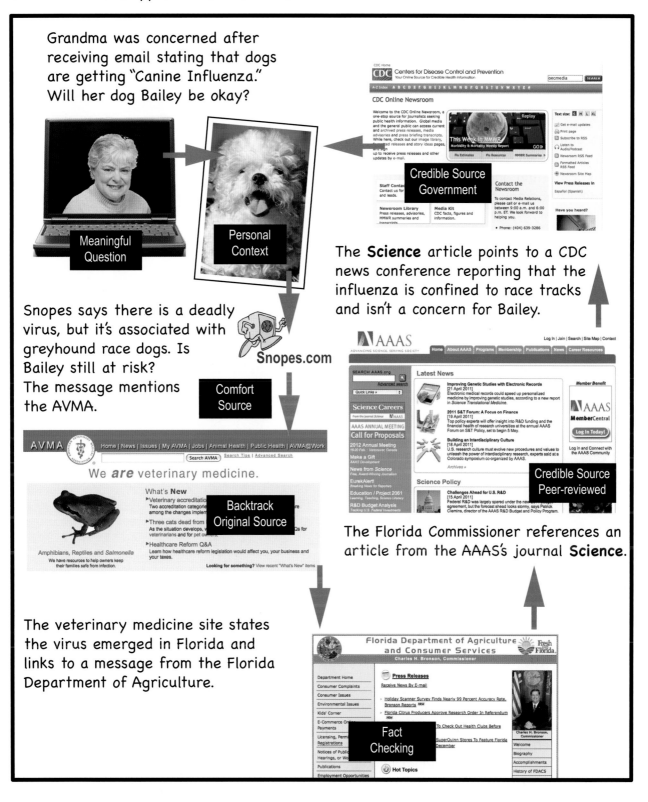

Grandma was concerned after receiving email stating that dogs are getting "Canine Influenza." Will her dog Bailey be okay?

Meaningful Question

Personal Context

Credible Source Government

The **Science** article points to a CDC news conference reporting that the influenza is confined to race tracks and isn't a concern for Bailey.

Snopes says there is a deadly virus, but it's associated with greyhound race dogs. Is Bailey still at risk?
The message mentions the AVMA.

Snopes.com

Comfort Source

Backtrack Original Source

Credible Source Peer-reviewed

The Florida Commissioner references an article from the AAAS's journal **Science**.

The veterinary medicine site states the virus emerged in Florida and links to a message from the Florida Department of Agriculture.

Fact Checking

According to Danny Callison (1999, p. 31), the highest levels of reflection are demonstrated when the inquirer:

"Draws extensively on evidence from multiple resources to support conclusions and the conclusions show a coherent use of evidence."

"Has significant recognition of authority and has shown some attempt to investigate and document the authority's credibility or point of view."

"Recognizes all sides of an issue, is able to weigh the pros and cons of all sides, and recognizes the strengths and limitations of each position in taking a stand."

To reach these high levels of reflection, students need many opportunities to gain experiences. Involve students in selecting images, creating diagrams, and writing statements as part of culminating activities associated with inquiry.

When I was in school back in the 1960s, I learned that Monarch butterflies wintered in California. In the 1970s, scientists discovered wintering spots in Mexico. Since then, they've learned even more about migration patterns. Our class map is much different than the one I made in the '60s. Inquiry never ends.

In addition to new knowledge and skills related to the inquiry topic, students acquire other important life skills from graphic inquiry. They learn that some questions can't be answered and some problems can't be resolved. New evidence is always emerging and theories evolve while understanding grows.

Learning through Graphic Inquiry

Whether selecting existing graphics or using the wide range of devices to create images, graphic inquiry can engage learners in meaningful experiences with authentic resources.

> We use our phones to take photos and videos for class projects.

In **How to Interpret Visual Resources**, Harry Stein notes that knowledge is gained from sight and the other senses. "Scientists believe that only 35 percent of our knowledge is learned from words. You have spent many years learning how to read. Learning to see more, to see differently, and to understand what you have seen is a very important skill that is not often stressed in school." (p. 4)

> I use visually-rich books such as **Nubs** to kickstart inquiry. Students are encouraged to create their own visuals during inquiry. We explore meaningful topics such as pets.

> Publishers of print materials are becoming aware of the need to support the visual interests of young people. Readers of the book **Nubs** can go to the book website to view photos, maps, and videos.

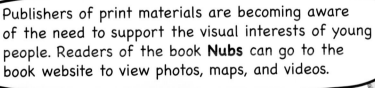

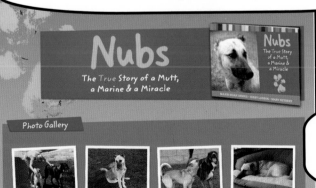

> Visual resources are also integrated at the end of lessons as part of review and follow-through.

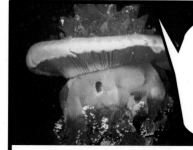

I always thought jellyfish were interesting, but it wasn't until I saw a diagram that I really thought about this creature's anatomy.

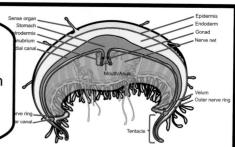

As you design learning environments that promote graphic inquiry, begin by creating an atmosphere that promotes curiosity, free thinking, and questioning. Jamie McKenzie (2004) developed the idea of the "question press" as a way to think about different dimensions of questioning. Consider six areas:

Understanding. Figuring out how and why something works, knowing how ideas are connected, or seeing the "big picture" are examples of activities that focus on developing understanding.

Persuasion. Challenging the thinking of others, convincing a friend to change their actions or inviting people to rethink their behavior involves persuasion.

Invention. Creating a more efficient way of doing a task, building a more effective way of accomplishing a goal, or a more appealing way of conveying an idea are all part of invention.

Prediction. Forecasting events, speculating on the future, and anticipating changes involve young people in making predictions.

Decision. Choosing a course of action, making a judgment based on alternative perspectives, or selecting among choices are examples of decision-making activities.

Solution. Completing a puzzle, solving a mystery, or cracking a code involve gathering clues, developing hypothesizing, and conducting experiments. Students must figure out how things work, gather evidence, and synthesize information to develop an effective solution.

I began with questions about endangered animals and ended with persuasion questions about how best to save animals. As my questions evolved, my inquiry became deeper, more interesting, and more meaningful.

Through a health inquiry, I help children understand the role of medicine in a hospital setting.

As students explore information and work with evidence, look for ways to facilitate learning through use of graphics.

While some students have difficulty synthesizing information and building evidence for arguments, others simply need scaffolding for organizing ideas.

SCAMPER was created by Alex Osborne as an idea-triggering device.
Each letter contains a strategy for synthesizing data (Michalko 1991).

Substitute
Combine
Adapt
Modify, Minify, Magnify
Put to other uses
Eliminate
Reverse, Rearrange

In **Visual Explanations**, Edward Tufte states "visual representation of evidence should be governed by principles of reasoning about quantitative evidence. For information displays, design reasoning must correspond to scientific reasoning. Clear and precise seeing becomes as one with clear and precise thinking" (1997, p. 53). Tufte identified six principles related to evidence and design of information displays. They should:

document sources and characteristics of data

provide appropriate comparisons

demonstrate cause and effect

express mechanisms quantitatively

recognize the multivariate nature of problems

evaluate alternative explanations

Design activities that allow students to work together and contribute to a shared information display.

Young people need guidance in the use and design of graphics. In **Guided Inquiry: Learning in the 21st Century**, Kuhlthau, Manitoes, and Caspari suggest that interventions should be designed to address different kinds of learning (2007, p. 141).

Curriculum Content
help for fact finding, interpreting, and synthesizing

> Shaun Tan's author website http://shauntan.net/ provided insights into the book.

Information Literacy
help for locating, evaluating, and using information

> Historical photos were compared with illustrations from the book.

> Our class is reading **The Arrival** by Shaun Tan and discussing the process of immigration in U.S. history.

Learning How to Learn
help for initiating, selecting, exploring, focusing, collecting, and presenting

> The Library of Congress photo collection was accessed.

Literacy Competence
help for improving reading, writing, speaking, and listening

> Students compared photographic evidence with immigrant interviews.

Social Skills
help for interacting, cooperating, and collaborating

> Students worked as families and contributed comic chapters.

History (Grades 3-6): Identifies immigration patterns of the late 1800s and early 1900s including geographic locations, opportunities, challenges, and contributions by various individuals and groups.

Carol Kuhlthau, Leslie Maniotes, and Ann Caspari identified observation and performance as two ways of determining what children have learned.

Observation. Take field notes based on direct observation of student work. Also hold conferences and take notes about what children are doing, thinking, and feeling.

Performance. Use journals as a way to trace progress. Charts, concept maps, timelines, flowcharts, and other visual organizers can be used to track the process. Use portfolios to gather and artifacts. Rubrics are an effective way to make students aware of the criteria and actively involve them in the process. Ask students to reflect on their inquiry:

> Did I make good observations?
> Did I raise deep questions?
> Did I interpret evidence?
> Did I collect evidence?
> Did I apply this evidence?
> Did I communicate with the group?
> Did I make logical inferences?
> Did I make reasonable predictions?

As you build learning experiences, inform students of the expectations. Use the following list as you design evaluation tools (Craver 1999; Paul 2009):

> Clear/unclear
> Precise/imprecise
> Specific/vague
> Accurate/inaccurate
> Relevant/irrelevant
> Plausible/implausible
> Consistent/inconsistent
> Logical/illogical
> Deep/superficial
> Broad/narrow
> Complete/incomplete
> Significant/trivial
> Adequate/inadequate
> Fair/biased

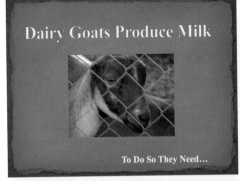

Dairy Goats Produce Milk

To Do So They Need...

Fresh Hay

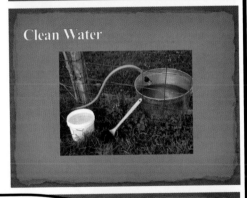

Clean Water

At first I was concerned about teaching graphic inquiry because I wondered how I would assess the nontraditional student products.

However by using a combination of process and produce checks I feel confident in assessing their work.

The final section of this book explores ways that graphic inquiry can be integrated into teaching and learning.

Shark Tooth

Our class inquiry immersed students in the world of sharks. From life-sized shark models and diagrams to drawings and displays, young people used graphics throughout inquiry.

In our object-based and place-based inquiry, each student selected a shark from the aquarium field trip to investigate.

As the school librarian, I worked with pairs of students to create videos to share their inquiry experiences.

Students collaborated on a class project titled **Shark Myths** exploring a dozen misconceptions about sharks.

Students created diagrams and models of their sharks. They made concept maps to organize information and built displays to share their findings.

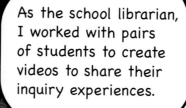

Graphics and Object-based Inquiry

Leaves in the fall.
An old family cedar chest.
A favorite work of art.

Artifacts and objects can serve as inspiration for exciting, inquiry-based learning environments.

Cameras, pencils, markers, and other tools can be used to record observations and experiences with these artifacts and objects.

Objects are living and nonliving natural things.

Why do snakes have scales?

I'm interested in the history of guitars.

Artifacts are things created by humans.

In **Art and Visual Perception**, Rudolf Arnheim states that "visual experience is dynamic." (p. 11) Objects are perceived as having a certain size, level of brightness, and location in space. No object is isolated. What you perceive isn't simply a shape, color, or movement, it's an interplay of forces.

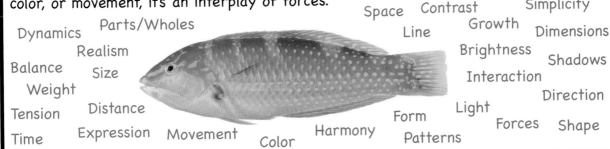

Dynamics   Parts/Wholes   Space   Contrast   Simplicity
Realism   Line   Growth   Dimensions
Balance   Size   Brightness   Shadows
Weight   Interaction
Tension   Distance   Direction
Time   Expression   Movement   Light   Forces   Shape
Color   Harmony   Form   Patterns

In **Inquiry-based Learning Using Everyday Objects**, Amy Alvarado and Patricia Herr note that "in object-based learning, objects themselves become central to developing the concepts which are essential to your unit of study. The objects are not merely an add-on component. They are not just for display. They do not come with a 'no touching' sign attached. The objects are the central component of the lesson and the overall unit of study." (2003, p. 5-6)

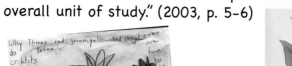

Students use graphics throughout the inquiry process to convey an understanding of objects.

Alvarado and Herr (2003, p. 7) note that object-based learning involves...

Developing lessons focused on objects

Posing and investigating object-based questions

Encouraging questions that stimulate thinking

Using students' natural curiosity

Leading students to knowledge construction

Promoting student-centered activities

Inquirers need a context to make connections. In **Visual Thinking**, Rudolf Arnheim stresses that it's not enough to simply provide photos, drawings, or live exhibits. To ensure understanding, viewers must be able to interpret the relevant features visually (1969, p. 308).

Drawing is an effective tool for observation.
Artists are required to look carefully and observe details.

Just like investigating a real crime, we're analyzing finger prints, hair samples, and other evidence to solve a case using science.

Design activities that ask students to use objects to solve problems or make decisions.

I'm interested in how the objects we use every day have changed since Colonial times. My team took photos of old and new objects, then we made a display.

THEN
NOW
THEN

When selecting objects that might work well for inquiries, consider:
    Will students be able to use all of their senses?
    Are there details, parts/wholes, varied elements that can be observed?
    Is there a set of objects that can be classified or compared?
    Can the object be viewed from different perspectives?
    Will students be able to connect the artifact to
    their experiences or the experiences of others?

Consider the many types of natural and human-made objects that could be used in teaching and learning. Seek out unusual, unexpected, and unique objects.

Lincoln Memorial under construction

Tibetan Buddhist Mandala

Petrified wood

When designing learning environments incorporating objects, consider using a mystery approach. Challenge students to determine the function or time period of an object.

Use the **Smithsonian's History Explorer** at http://historyexplorer.americanhistory.si.edu/artifacts/ to identify thousands of artifacts to use in building your own mystery projects.

First artifical heart

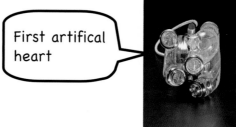

The Smithsonian's **Within These Walls** mystery interactive at http://americanhistory.si.edu/house/ features artifacts from different time periods.

In **Nurturing Inquiry: Real Science for the Elementary Classroom**, Charles Pearce stimulates inquiry through the use of objects by asking students to:

         Describe the object.
         Sketch and label the object.
         Write questions about the object.
         List ways answers could be found.

Although many object-based learning activities may involve students in photographing or drawing objects, consider other ways graphic representations might be incorporated.

In **I See What You Mean**, Steve Moline suggests that in effective diagrams, illustrations and words work together to make meaning.

Picture Glossary – helps the reader to identify, differentiate, or define items within a group or parts of a whole.

Mature Flower

Stigma
Style
Filament

Perianth
Petal:Corolla
Septal : Calyx

Floral axis
Nectary
Articulation
Pedicel

My diagrams will help people understand the difference in size between a human and each kind of dinosaur. I used dinosaur pictures from Wikimedia Commons.

Anchiceratops

Scale Diagram – helps the viewer understand a subject through identifying individual parts using a scale to indicate size, mass, temperature, or distance.

Analytic Diagrams – helps the reader see inside a subject to understand how it works.

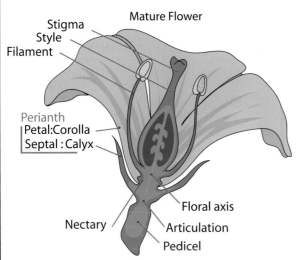

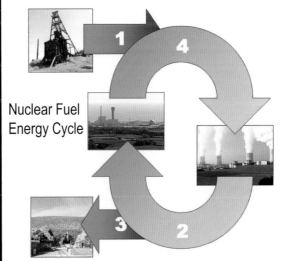

Nuclear Fuel Energy Cycle

Synthetic Diagrams – helps the viewer connect the parts of a sequence or subgroups within a larger group.

In **Classroom Instruction that Works**, Robert Marzano, Debra Pickering, and Jane Pollock note that creating a physical model is an effective approach for learning.

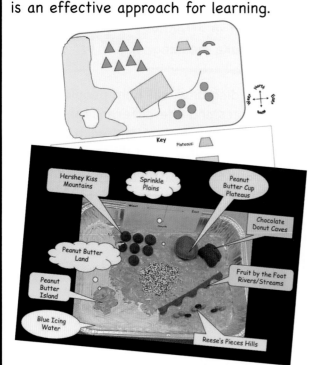

These concrete representations of knowledge may include many of the same elements as a diagram including titles, labels, keys. Digital photos can be used for documentation. Young people can then write or audio record reflections.

Incorporate the following elements into your object-based lessons:
Locate meaningful objects
Focus on essential understandings
Develop open-ended questions
Design guiding questions to refocus
Visualize with all graphics types
Extend and transfer thinking

To elicit inference, provide leading questions about student objects:
Is there a particular place where you find this thing?
Is this thing related to a particular time of day or year?
What is the process for making this or how was it made?
What is larger or smaller than this? Is this part of a whole?
How is this like and unlike other objects?
How is this connected to other things?
Does this object have a particular taste, feel, smell?
Does this thing have a specific color, size, amount?
Does this artifact connect to a particular emotion or value?
How does this thing make you feel?
What's the history of this thing?
How does this object change over time? How does it move?

Graphics and Place-based Inquiry

Why did people settle here?
What plants are native to our area?
How do we prevent water contamination?

Place-based learning connects students with the local community by grounding experiences in local phenomena. Rooted in Dewey's focus on authentic learning, place-based approaches include cultural and historical studies, nature exploration, and real-world problem solving.

In order to share their understanding of place, young people might create maps and brochures of local nature trails using a compass and GPS device.

After reading **Measuring Penny** by Loreen Leedy, students may measure items around the school and create graphs sharing their findings.

I chose this piece of artwork by Scott Patton to show my thoughts about rural Iowa. I'm writing about each person, place, and thing I see in the painting.

Graphics play a significant role in place-based inquiries. Ongoing activities such as the **Montana Heritage Project** at http://www.montanaheritageproject.org/ involve young people in learning about their natural and cultural environment. Students take the role of scientist, archivist, and historian to learn about their heritage. They use primary source documents and design original multimedia presentations.

The National Science Teachers Association (NSTA) stresses that "inquiry into authentic questions generated from student experience is the central strategy for teaching science" (1996, p. 31).

In the article **Place-Based Investigations and Authentic Inquiry**, Somnath Sarkar and Richard Frazier found that place-based inquiry makes hands-on science activities more meaningful because students are involved in solving scientific problems within a realistic, local context.

Each group selected a part of town to investigate the types of pollution that might be present.

We were concerned about pollution from the fertilizer used at the golf course, so we developed a proposal to reduce the nitrogen levels in the groundwater over the next ten years.

We chose the golf course and focused on water pollution. Next, we developed an argument using photographs and water testing data as evidence about the scene.

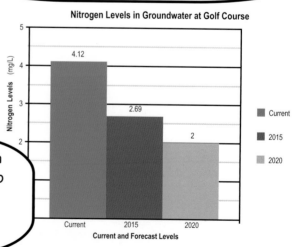

In **Shifting from Activity Mania to Inquiry**, Hedy Moscovici and Tamar Holmlund note that although students may be able to follow the steps of the scientific method, they may find it difficult to actually solve a scientific problem. Moscovici and Holmlund recommend shifting from pre-packaged, hands-on activities toward inquiry-based environments.

From the journals of Lewis and Clark to the pioneer diaries of the westward movement, people have used sketches and diagrams along with words to share their place-based scientific and cultural experiences.

Naturalist Titian Ramsay Pearle's 1938 field journal describes the flora and fauna of the South Seas.

Look for ways to incorporate graphic elements in both the process and product of inquiry.

We created an inventory of the creatures living in the wetlands along a stream. A chart was used for identification, then we created sketches and descriptions of each specimen.

Students used cameras, GPS devices, handheld devices, and field journals to record data for their **CSI: Cemetery Scene Investigation** http://connections.smsd.org/csi/ project.

CSI: Cemetery Scene Investigation

Site Menu:

> Home Page
> Schedule
> History of Cemeteries
> History of Johnson County
> Headstones
> Tombs
> Symbolism
> Epitaphs/Inscriptions
> Burial Customs
> Famous Burial Sites
> Cemetery Horticulture
> Weathering
> Preserving Cemeteries
> Our Rubbings

Introduction

Students at the Nieman Enhanced Learning Center have received a grant from the Shawnee Mission Education Foundation. The funded project, called **CSI: Cemetery Scene Investigations**, invites students to look at cemeteries as primary sources needing to be preserved. Using current technologies students will answer an important question. Why is the preservation of local cemeteries important?

Everything ages, especially monuments built by man! Depending on how long ago it was established, your local cemetery headstones, monuments, and important site buildings are aging. As these primary source documents age important information may be disappearing if no one is maintaining it.

Artwork is an effective way to reflect local culture. Both small towns and major cities have used painted, tile, and mosaic murals as a means of sharing their local heritage, cultural traditions, and societal issues.

Our team is learning about the Latino culture in Chicago. We're designing a mural for our school wall that reflects the cultures represented in our community.

In an article titled **Visual Information Literacy**, Debbie Abilock states that "a documentary photograph is a medicated communication of truthful evidence. When displayed in exhibits or gathered photo essays, these photographs become an argument with evidence for a claim." (2008, p. 10)

I'm documenting the resources we have available for disaster preparation. I want to determine whether our city plan has really been implemented.

Video recording and editing is an effective way to help young people assimilate information. It's a concrete process of associating concepts.

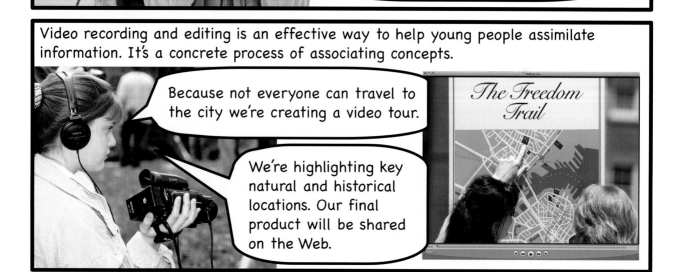

Because not everyone can travel to the city we're creating a video tour.

We're highlighting key natural and historical locations. Our final product will be shared on the Web.

Marzano, Pickering, and Pollock (2001) identified six types of tasks that can be associated with place-basd learning across the curriculum. Consider how graphics could be integrated into:

Systems Analysis. Ask students to generate hypotheses that predict what would happen if some aspect of a system were changed. Test your hypothesis by making this change.

> Predict what would happen to the plants and animals if the pond were changed from spring-fed to local water.

Problem Solving. Ask students to identify and solve a problem containing specific obstacles and constraints. Students must generate and test hypotheses seeking possible solutions.

> What is causing the rapid growth of algae on the school pond?

Historical Investigations. Ask students to construct plausible scenarios for events from the past, about which there is no agreement.

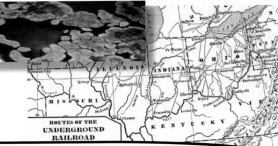

ROUTES OF THE
UNDERGROUND
RAILROAD

> What role did families, the waterway, and local religions in the community play related to the Underground Railroad? How would the abolitionist history of the area have been different if any of these elements didn't exist?

Invention. Ask students to generate and test hypotheses in the process of invention.

PANEL

LEGO
PEOPLE

SIDE

SOLAR BOAT PLAN

> Design a solar boat that will cross the school pond.

Experimental Inquiry. Ask students to develop and test hypotheses across the curriculum.

> Do the teachers at our school drive energy efficient cars or gas hogs?

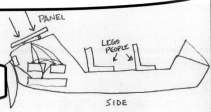

Energy Efficiency of Teacher Cars
■ Gas Hogs ■ Average ■ Efficient

20
45
35

Decision Making. Ask students to apply inquiry to a decision making activity.

leader
thinker
innovator
motivator
nurturer
creator

I nominate
Helen
Cassidy

> In replacing the old brick fountain in the park with a new statue, what local person would best represent the town?

In **Nurturing Inquiry: Real Science for the Elementary Classroom**, Charles Pearce combines literature with inquiry using ecological mysteries. In books by authors such as Jean Craighead George, characters solve mysteries related to the environment. These "ecomysteries help reinforce the importance of questioning, gathering information as part of an investigation, and drawing conclusions in response to data." (p. 71)

We've identified local ecomysteries. Students created storyboards and comics based on their questions.

Why are the fish dying in our tank?
What kinds of seeds are these and where did they come from?
Why are there so many butterflies in our school yard?
Why are there so many spiders around the building?
What are these tracks in the snow?

Our class read **A River Ran Wild** by Lynn Cherry. We compared the river in the story with a river in our town then tracked other changes in our town over many generations.

1917

1941

Graphics are an important element of place-based inquiry. They provide an effective, efficient, and appealing means for communicating information about a location. Charts, diagrams, illustrations, maps, organizers, images, and symbols can all be integrated into an authentic learning experience.

Someday I want to own a flower shop. I'm investigating whether there would be enough customers to justify the store or if I might need to combine it with another business such as wedding planning or a gift shop. I've done a survey, drawn a floorplan of the store, created a logo, and even picked a location and looked at traffic patterns.

Community, Collaboration, and Authentic Learning

What we're doing matters to our community. Real-world activities make learning meaningful. Connecting with students around the world is cool!

Real, genuine, true... these are words associated with authentic learning. Students explore the world around them, ask questions, find resources, discover connections, discuss ideas, and make decisions that have a real-world impact.

Authentic learning is directly connected with 21st-century skills and standards. **AASL 3.3.4** Create products that apply to authentic, real-world contexts.

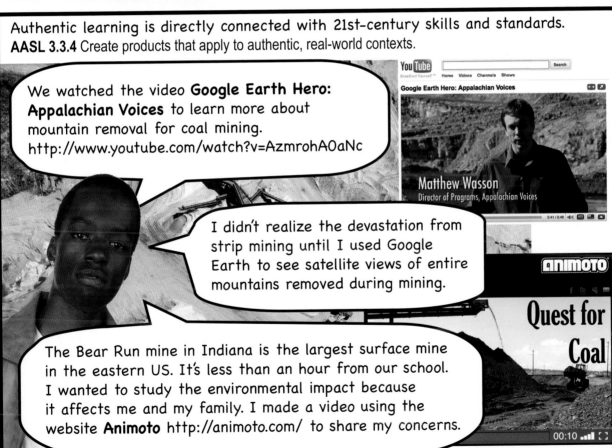

We watched the video **Google Earth Hero: Appalachian Voices** to learn more about mountain removal for coal mining. http://www.youtube.com/watch?v=AzmrohA0aNc

I didn't realize the devastation from strip mining until I used Google Earth to see satellite views of entire mountains removed during mining.

The Bear Run mine in Indiana is the largest surface mine in the eastern US. It's less than an hour from our school. I wanted to study the environmental impact because it affects me and my family. I made a video using the website **Animoto** http://animoto.com/ to share my concerns.

Because the content and context of situations are viewed as relevant by students, authentic learning is engaging and motivating. Graphics play an important role by providing a starting point for questioning, a source for evidence used in arguments, or a means of sharing results.

Educators face a dilemma when trying to create authentic environments for learning. In **Visual Thinking**, Rudolf Arnheim notes that teachers must balance the overwhelming complexity of the real-world with the simplicity of a relevant image. As students move from a novice to expert level, they're better able to grasp closer approximations of intricate real situations.

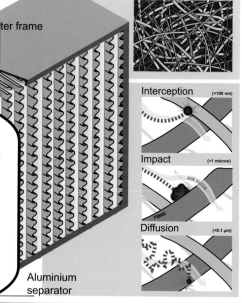

Filter sheet of randomly arranged fibres

ter frame

Interception (<100 nm)

Impact (>1 micron)

AIR FLOW

FIBRE

Diffusion (<0.1 μm)

Aluminium separator

I'm interested in the science behind the HEPA filter. Just examining photos of the filter didn't help me understand how and why it works.

However when I found an illustration that showed the interception, impact, and diffusion, it began to make sense. The diagram helped me focus attention on the key elements. Now, photos of filters make more sense.

Now I understand why it's called the HEPA (high efficiency particulate absorbing). I'm going to design a small one for a baby carriage.

Authentic assignments are grounded in reality, so students create meaning from their experiences.

The key to success is ensuring that students have enough concrete experiences to provide a context for the more abstract learning.

After seeing a live demonstration, I learned how to drape a toga. I hope my diagram will help other people who want to learn how a toga works.

Problem-solving activities with an authentic context, question, task, activity, and assessment are motivating for young people. In **Instructional Message Design**, Richard Mayer (1993, p. 253-304) focuses on instructional design for problem-solving. These approaches can be applied to graphic inquiry:

> Use questions about an image to emphasize relevant information
> Use visual content structures to present ideas
> Visualize a series of events in which one event causes another
> Show differences and similarities between two or more things
> Present a classification system for grouping items
> Provide visuals to clarify, extend, or support an assertion
> Use advanced organizers, analogies to provide context
> Represent problems different ways through visuals
> Help guide selection of relevant and irrelevant information
> Show completed, annotated examples and promote creation of visual summaries

Places & Spaces: Mapping Science at http://scimaps.org/ is a cross-disciplinary project intended to inspire people to talk about human activity and scientific progress. Through illuminated diagrams and maps, young people are invited to manipulate puzzle pieces and solve problems. Young people are invited to think about inventors and inventions relevant to them.

Although students are generally rewarded for their individual efforts, skills in teamwork and collaboration are increasingly important in today's world. Many of the national standards from AASL, ISTE, and content area organizations include outcomes related to the ability to work with others.

We're sharing our projects on the Web with our new buddies.

I'm from California. Our class is learning about celebrations. I'm interested in costumes people wear.

I live in New York. Our class is learning about the history of holidays.

Respects diverse perspectives when interacting both inside and outside the classroom setting.
Demonstrates social responsibility when collaborating with others inside and outside the classroom setting.
Applies technology tools to work collaboratively at a distance.
Works cooperatively and productively with others in pairs and small group settings to create original works.
Connects classroom activities to real-world settings beyond the learning community.
Presents ideas and findings to an audience of peers or members of the larger community.
Promotes global awareness by exchanging ideas and resources with individuals of other cultures.

Collaborative technology tools provide an environment where students can easily collaborate and share their graphic work. According to Bromley, Irwin-De Vitis, and Modlo (1995, p. 31), graphic organizers are great tools when working as a community of learners toward a joint goal. Creating cooperative graphic organizers fosters:
constructive feedback • reasoning • speaking • brainstorming • elaborating • negotiating respecting opinions • turn-taking • listening • categorizing • questioning • brainstorming • problem-solving • constructing shared meanings

In **Thought and Learning**, Vygotsky stresses that learning is social. Move young people from teacher-directed to independent learning situations.

Wikis work well for these types of social and collaborative projects. The sixth grade **Greek Mythology** project at http://mra-ancient-greece.wikispaces.com is a great example. Students worked both independently and interdependently.

Kuhlthau, Maniotes, and Caspari advocate inquiry circles. Like literature circles, Students work independently on tasks that prepare them for a group discussion of a shared topic or theme.

Graphics can play an important role in both the social and individual aspects of inquiry. In **Visual Tools for Constructing Knowledge**, David Hyerle (1996) states that visual tools such as brainstorming webs, task-specific organizers, and thinking-process maps can facilitate the brain's pattern-making activities.

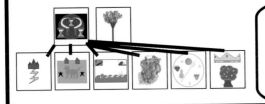

We created a biography related to our own Greek god, but we also made links to our classmates' biographies.

Ares

Ares, the wa
loved war. H
care if he w
being shed.
carrying with
a constant c
was to make
Hephaestus.
parents were
Zeus.

Once in a wh

Multimedia software and collaborative websites create synergy in projects.

I used **HyperStudio** software to share my knowledge of the Nile and ancient Egypt. I was able to share images, make a video, and even link to Google Earth to show the geography of the area.

When community, collaboration, and authentic learning are combined with graphic inquiry, the result is an engaging learning environment. Fifth and sixth graders at School 84 in Indianapolis discovered how almanacs can be a great source of data as well as a wonderful way to share local information.

Students used almanacs as springboards to inquiry.

After identifying the characteristics of almanacs, they decided to make their own school almanac. Students conducted polls and surveys, created charts, and wrote articles.

In addition, they each chose a topic for a personal inquiry and created brochures to organize their thinking and express their understandings about an area of interest.

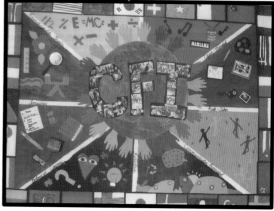

Learn more about this project at http://www.virtualinquiry.com/cases/almanac/

Inquiry, Innovation, and Illuminated Term Papers

I'm tired of assigning five-paragraph essays. Bulleted PowerPoint presentations are boring. I want projects to address multiple intelligences.

Today's teachers are seeking ways to motivate learners, promote high level thinking, and facilitate the creation of products that reflect deep thinking. Graphic inquiry can address these challenging goals.

In **Best Practice: Today's Standards for Teaching & Learning in America's Schools**, Steven Zemelman, Harvey Daniels, and Arthur Hyde (2005) identify activities across the curriculum that can have a positive impact on student achievement. Many of these approaches incorporate the use of graphics.

The Math Adventures picture book series by Cindy Neuschwander is a fun way to review math concepts. I wrote my own picture book combining probability, genetics, and a goofy story about the genetic trait, Hitchhiker's thumb.

In mathematics, children create their own representations of problems and solutions by drawing pictures, diagrams, and graphs.

In social studies, students need opportunities to investigate topics of their choice in depth.

In language arts, students gather, evaluate, and synthesize graphic data and communicate their discoveries through visual channels.

In science, students use a variety of approaches and strategies to address authentic questions.

In art, students need journaling opportunities that include sketching, diagramming, mapping, and other combinations of words and graphic elements.

In order to move away from traditional term papers, provide students with engaging starting points for their inquiry. In **The Back of the Napkins**, Dan Roam identifies six problem "clumps" (2008, p. 15). Let's explore problems that challenge students.

Who & What Problems - qualitative
What made Clara Barton unique?

How Much Problems – quantitative
How much would it cost for new carpet?

7.5 '

75 square feet
8.33 square yards
Add 10%
10 yards of carpet

10 '

Where Problems – spacial positions
Where is the Trail of Tears and where are the ancestors of the survivors?

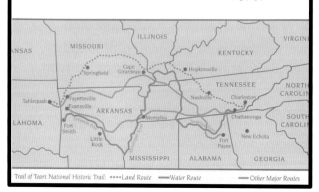

When Problems - time
How long does it take to digest food?

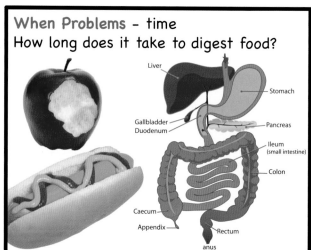

How Problems - how things interconnect
How do nuclear power plants work?

Why Problems - seeing the big picture
Why does a shell sound like the ocean?

Roam (2008, p. 57) identified four rules for dealing with problems. First, collect lots of visual ideas.

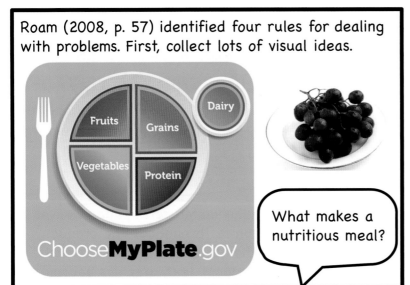

What makes a nutritious meal?

These are all healthy foods.

Second, lay out all the ideas side-by-side.

Third, define a systemic way to organize evidence and ideas.

I'll put them into food groups.

My healthy meal.

Fourth, perform visual triage removing extra visuals and designing a solution.

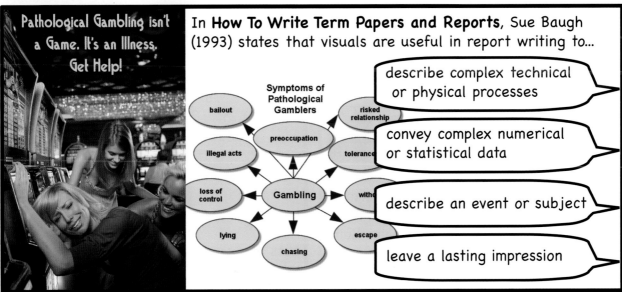

Pathological Gambling isn't a Game. It's an Illness. Get Help!

In **How To Write Term Papers and Reports**, Sue Baugh (1993) states that visuals are useful in report writing to...

describe complex technical or physical processes

convey complex numerical or statistical data

describe an event or subject

leave a lasting impression

For more than a century, reports, essays, and term papers have been a standard product expected of educators. These products can be enhanced through the addition of both hand-made and technology-generated visuals.

An illuminated term paper weaves graphics throughout the product. Rather than simply adding visuals to support text, graphics become a vital element of the communication.

PiXTON
A World of Comics Made by You!
Digital Citizens

Instead of an essay about fire safety, I made a series of comic strips.

Yes, after Atlanta, which we burned to the ground, we came to Savannah. Savannah, because it is right by the ocean, was our last obstacle. Then our campaign through the South would be a success. I knew that the Confederates were weary. Fort McAllister, which lies west of Savannah, only had 150 men defending the bastion. We overran them and continued on toward Savannah. Hardee evacuated his troops, Savannah surrendered and we took the city without burning or bombing it to smithereens.

And we're glad you didn't. Because we were spared destruction, we didn't have to overcome the obstacles of rebuilding during the Reconstruction period.

  If General Sherman and Mayor Johnson had dinner together...

Rather than writing a traditional term paper, design inquiry-based environments that encourage students to explain their thinking, make comparisons, or chronicle experiences visually. Be creative!

Developed by Bernie Dodge, a WebQuest involves students in using web-based resources and tools to transform their learning into meaningful understandings and real-world projects.
WebQuests generally contain:

> an introduction
> a doable, interesting task
> information resources
> a clear process
> guidance and assistance
> closure and reflection

Lots of examples can be found at **WebQuest.org** at http://webquest.org/

WebQuest.Org

Bernie Dodge created **A Taskonomy of Tasks** to share a dozen doable and engaging activities for inquirers. These would work well for graphic inquiries. Explore examples.

Analytical Tasks

Compilation Tasks

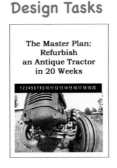

Consensus Building Tasks

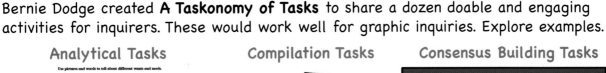

Building Consensus: Four Views on the Proposed Nature Park

Creative Product Tasks

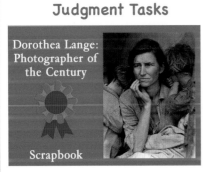

The Endangered Animal Game

Design Tasks

The Master Plan: Refurbish an Antique Tractor in 20 Weeks

Journalistic Tasks

Travel Back in Time to 1776

Founder Interviews

Judgment Tasks

Dorothea Lange: Photographer of the Century

Scrapbook

Mystery Tasks

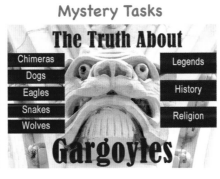

The Truth About Gargoyles

Chimeras
Dogs
Eagles
Snakes
Wolves

Legends
History
Religion

Persuasion Tasks

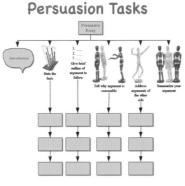

Retelling Tasks

How did place influence Mark Twain's work?

Click each ●

Scientific Tasks

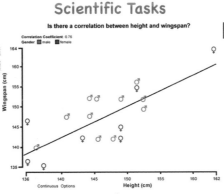

Is there a correlation between height and wingspan?

Self-Knowledge Tasks

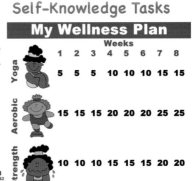

My Wellness Plan

Find more ideas at http://webquest.sdsu.edu/taskonomy.html

Historically, teachers have valued reports and other types of text communications. However whether predicting weather or tracing an epidemic, researchers throughout history have used visuals to analyze and present data.

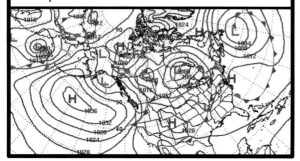

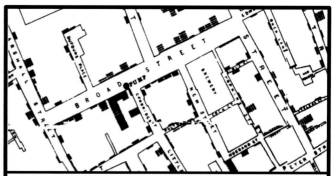

Dr. John Snow was able to discover the cause of the 1854 London cholera epidemic through medical detective work and the shrewd analysis of evidence. His ideas are best understood by examining a map showing the spread of cholera cases.

In **Visual Explanations**, Edward Tufte stresses the importance of using quality methods in displaying and assessing quantitative evidence. Tufte identified four keys to Snow's success with the cholera epidemic:

> Placing the data in an appropriate context for assessing cause and effect
> Making quantitative comparisons
> Considering alternative explanations and contrary cases
> Assessment of possible errors in the numbers reported in graphics (p. 27-37)

Educators concerned about shifting emphasis from a text to a multimedia focus must find ways to design project assignments and assessments that value graphic communication as a core element rather than a supplemental aspect of the inquiry. **Using Pictures in Lessons** at http://www.ncrtec.org/tl/camp/lessons.htm highlights seven strategies in effective graphic use:

Bridge time and space • Simplify complex data • Make abstract ideas concrete •

World War II Uniform

camouflage

Challenge preconceptions • Provide context • Share appreciation • Show identification

In **Using Internet Primary Resources to Teach Critical Thinking Skills in History,** Kathleen Craver suggests seven approaches to the use of primary sources in non-traditional projects:

Thematic. Trace a pattern or compare similar events such as war photos to gain historical perspective.

Database. Organize a collection of materials such as census data and formulate a thesis statement.

Role-playing. Create a "you are there" atmosphere using materials such as historical artifacts to realize the relevance of primary sources.

Class involvement. Conduct debates and mock trials to promote collaborative learning.

Counter-factual. Explore "what if" scenarios to examine historical assumptions and alternatives.

Assignment. Immerse students in specific historical resources and questions.

Simulation. Re-create historical events to explore alternative courses of action.

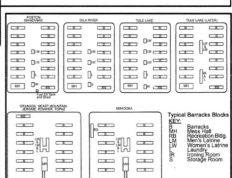

In **Blending Genre, Altering Style: Writing Multigenre Papers**, Tom Romano suggests taking a traditional expository writing assignment and turning it into a multigenre experience where young people "penetrate" a topic and show their understandings.

Tom Romano describes a student who was able to share her themes of Irish culture and family in a multitude of ways. He states that "she moved us through her writing, her voice, her art, her body, her way of perceiving, her very being. We felt her energy, courage, commitment, and passion to express and communicate. The intellectual and the emotional were one." (2000, p. 3)

As you design innovative, inquiry-based assignments think of ways to bridge subject areas and communication formats. Romano suggests that students write a preface, foreword, or introduction to orient their audience. This opening should be engaging, reader-friendly, and informative. The document might provide background information, review the inquiry process, discuss collaborations, or share perspective. Then, the information graphic, scrapbook, map, diagram, poster, illuminated term paper, or other graphic communication can stand alone without the need for additional explanation.

Issues in Graphic Inquiry

Can I use this diagram in my project? Is it okay to crop this photo? Should I believe this graph?

Young people face legal and ethical questions during the inquiry process. They need to apply copyright laws, evaluate content, and solve problems. While it's important to respect differing opinions, students need to ask deep questions and draw their own conclusions about evidence.

Standards from AASL, ISTE, and content areas across the curriculum stress the importance of safe, respectful, and responsible inquiry activities. These elements must be woven throughout the inquiry process.

Emily, Kellogg. "Author Interview." Skype. Badger Exchange, 24 Feb. 2011. Web.

Cites sources and gives credit for the ideas of others.
Demonstrates legal and ethical behavior regarding the location and use of information.
Shows responsible use of information and technology.
Advocates and demonstrates responsible behavior in the use of technology.
Demonstrates leadership in the use of information and technology as a digital citizen.

To keep an open mind, it's important to maintain doubt and skepticism. Rather than blindly following information, it's necessary to develop evidence to support specific viewpoints. This is particularly true in an era where it's easy to crop and modify images electronically.

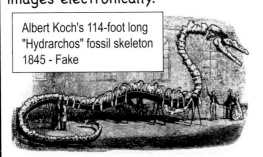

Albert Koch's 114-foot long "Hydrarchos" fossil skeleton 1845 - Fake

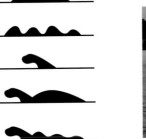

Loch Ness - Real or Fake?

Jamie McKenzie (2007) notes that constructive skepticism springs from a positive atmosphere of doubt. It encourages people to wonder about risks and pitfalls that could impact a project. Thinkers welcome constructive criticism and are constantly revisiting their goals, decisions, and directions. Uncertainty provides an opportunity to reflect on evidence and possibly come up with new arguments and approaches.

To make good decisions about evidence, young people need to be able to recognize prejudice, bias, and stereotyping. In **Visual Messages: Integrating Imagery into Instruction**, David Considine and Gail Haley stress that media literacy helps young people "raise important questions about how the media operate and how different audiences interact with the media." (p. 28, 1999) Standards associated with evaluating the validity of media claims are found throughout the curriculum.

We identified the advertising techniques that were applied to the visuals in television ads.

In my health and fitness class, we evaluated the claims of various fitness equipment.

We're also comparing the images used by various news media. Their choices reflect their different perspectives.

We found that the images and words worked together to form a persuasive argument.

I'm examining military recruitment posters to identify the techniques used to influence people. I'm looking at how African Americans have been recruited into military service since the Civil War.

After comparing news articles from today, I examined American Civil War era newspapers to contrast coverage in the North and South.

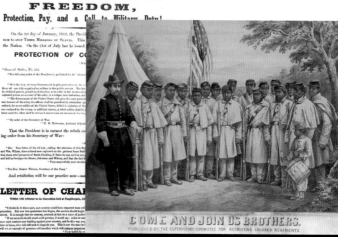

In **Visual Intelligence**, Ann Marie Seward Barry states "we must develop a critical understanding of how media can and does manipulate images that affect thought and emotion." (p. 333)

Google Books now provides access to many current and historical magazines. In my social studies class, we examined magazine covers looking for stereotypes and bias.

I want to be media literate. I always ask myself about the perspective of the people interviewed on the news.

How is the person portrayed?
Is the image an accurate reflection of the person?
Does the image show a stereotype or bias?
Why is he/she portrayed in this way?
How do associated words impact the experience?
How does this make you feel?

PBS has many programs dealing with ethics and media literacy. Go to http://www.pbs.org/teachers/media_lit/.

Harry Stein notes that "using stereotype is another way in which cartoonists convey their editorial opinions. A stereotype is an over-simplification of an idea, opinion, or judgment that does not allow for individualization. Stereotypes can take the form of a dangerous or misguided generalization about people and groups, but in cartoons, stereotypes are a quick, easy way to communicate ideas that many people recognize. Caricature is another cartoon technique used to promote a special message forcefully." (p. 39)

Go to **Daryl Cagle's Political Cartoons** at http://www.cagle.com/ to explore many recent examples.

Ethics involves addressing questions about morality. What is right/wrong, good/bad, just/unjust in human behavior? As students create their own images, they are faced with ethical dilemmas associated with the images they create.

Information. Is this information true/false? fact/opinion? accurate/distorted?

Choices. Will sharing be helpful/harmful? What are my reasons for sharing this image? Could this information be misinterpreted? Am I invading privacy or abusing a confidence?

Action. What's the issue and what's at stake? What value do I place on honesty and privacy? Who will be impacted by my actions? What is the moral reasoning for my decision?

I took photos of the war protest. I can make the crowd look large or small depending on how I crop the photos. What should I do?

Digital tampering is the practice of changing photos to meet specific needs. In the essay **When Your Eyes Tell Your Lies**, Timothy Maier discusses the issue of photo manipulation in our society noting that technology is raising new ethical questions about truth and deception.

I'm concerned about how the media connects beauty with self-worth. Many of the images in magazines are clearly modified in PhotoShop.

The Truth Behind The Photos: A Portfolio of Lies

By Sue Rae

I'm creating a portfolio of photographs to show young girls how images are manipulated for ads and magazine covers. I'm also showing photos of famous actors like Jamie Lee Curtis's "before" and "after" photo shoots.

Dove's Real Beauty project at http://www.dove.us/Social-Mission/ is designed to help young people explore different types of beauty.

Editing photos is a great way to involve young people in the photography process and help them better understand issues related to photo tampering. Explore how and why photos are modified.

Adjust the brightness and contrast

Crop a picture to focus attention

Remove a mark from an old photo.

Even these small changes can have a dramatic impact. Adjusting the brightness can bring out images you thought were lost. However adjustments can also result in removal of clues. Erasing a fold mark may also remove a feature from a photo.

Cropping the car out of the photo removes clues about when the photo was taken.

Cropped Photo

Uncropped Photo

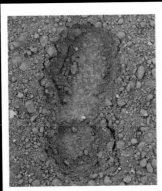

Small changes may not matter with personal photos, but what if the photos were going to be used as evidence in a trial or to justify a building development project?

Photo manipulation can be used to distort reality, deceive viewers, and lie to the public. Tampering began long before digital technology.

For lots of examples of **Photo Tampering through History**, read Hany Farid's Web page at http://www.cs.dartmouth.edu/farid/research/digitaltampering/.

Whether they're creating their own visuals or adapting the work of others, students need to be aware of the legal and ethical issues regarding property ownership. The Standards for 21st Century Learners (AASL, 2007) contain the following skill. **AASL 1.3.1** Respect copyright/intellectual property rights of creators and producers.

"The Congress shall have Power ... To promote the Progress of Science and useful Arts, by securing for limited Times to Authors and Inventors the exclusive Right to their respective Writings and Discoveries." *(United States Constitution, Article I, Section 8)*

Individual countries have varied laws related to intellectual property. Learn more about **United States Copyright** at http://copyright.gov/.

Creative Commons is a nonprofit organization working to increase the body of creative work that is available to the public for free and legal sharing, use, repurposing, and remixing. Learn more at http://creativecommons.org.

Students might wish to use CC licenses like this.

 by **Attribution**. You let others copy, distribute, display, and perform your copyrighted work — and derivative works based upon it — but only if they give credit the way you request.

 sa **Share Alike**. You allow others to distribute derivative works only under a license identical to the license that governs your work.

 nc **Non-Commerical**. You let others copy, distribute, display, and perform your work — and derivative works based upon it — but for non-commercial purposes only.

 nd **No Derivative Works**. You let others copy, distribute, display, and perform only verbatim copies of your work, not derivative works based upon it.

Plagiarizing images is an increasing problem in schools. Students need to understand the importance of citing the sources they use in projects and gaining permissions for images they plan to share outside the educational setting.

Software such as **HyperStudio** provides a way to incorporate copyright and Creative Commons information right into the document.

Direct students to look for copyright information related to the images they plan to use.

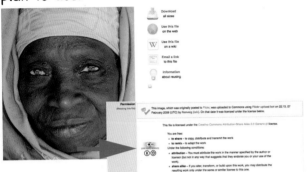

At the **Wikimedia Commons** website at http://commons.wikimedia.org/, each visual contains a copyright notice.

Online tools such as **Noodle Tools** at http://noodletools.com/ make citing resources easy. Styles include MLA, APA, and Chicago/Turabian.

As students manipulate photographs, remind them to think about their role as an ethical illustrator.
Who is the photographer?
Do I have the right to use and manipulate this photo?
What's the purpose of editing the photo?
How will readers interpret my changes?
How will I give credit to the original photographer?

Putting myself in the uniform of an astronaut made me wonder about this career. What would it be like to live on the space station?

The topic of intellectual freedom is important to both consumers and creators of graphics. Students need to understand both their rights and responsibilities. The AASL Standards for 21st Century Learners include a skill related to this topic.
AASL 3.3.7 Respect the principles of intellectual freedom.

I took an embarrassing photo of my friend, but I'm not going to post it on Facebook because I know how easy it is for others to see.

In a world of **Facebook** and **YouTube**, teens can easily have a global audience for their graphics. However, they need to consider both their own privacy and the privacy of others as they share.

The principles of intellectual freedom encourage the creation and sharing of visuals.

In **Kiss Clip Art Goodbye**, Bonnie Meltzer advocates the importance of children making their own original drawings and photographs rather than using clip art. She states that "the idea isn't to make all our students professional artists; the idea is to help them be better communicators and give them extra tools for life. The skills include making as well as reading visual language." (1999, p. 23)

Meltzer notes that some young people have difficulty getting started with drawing projects. She recommends providing specific assignments that help students focus their attention.

Some children may express concerns about their drawing skills. Provide photographs, artwork, and real objects young artists can use for inspiration. Provide an assortment of resources including books and websites to stimulate creativity.

Consider a wide range of visual assignments that provide opportunities for young people to express themselves using a variety of tools and techniques:
Symbols – create a symbol to represent a Greek god.
Portraits – create an illustration of your god that reflects his/her personality and attributes. What props might he/she be holding?
Posters – create a persuasive campaign poster to reflect the characteristics of your god.

Cathleen Soundy and Yun Qiu (2006) suggest coordinating drawing activities with thematically related sets of picture books. Suzanne McConnell's **Talking Drawings** (1992) is a research-based strategy for translating newly acquired knowledge into illustrations. Children draw, then discuss their pictures with peers.

Although it may seem like graphics are effective in all situations, it's important for educators to consider the individual child and the nature of the learning task. Andrew Stull and Richard Mayer (2007) found that involving students in reading graphic organizers can promote active learning and deep understandings of content. Students scored higher after reading a scientific article that contained graphic organizers than after reading a scientific passage in which they were asked to construct graphic organizers.

I'm a beginner, so graphic organizers help me see relevant information.

I have the basics, so I'm ready to apply my ideas to a graphic organizer.

Stull and Mayer explained that reading the text and remembering requires essential processing. Students spend their time reconciling the text with the graphic organizer, making direct comparisons and thinking about the content. When students create a graphic organizer, they are engaged in an extraneous process related to construction leaving less capacity for essential and generative processing.

Pamela Dunston (1992) studied a decade of research and found that graphic organizers provided before reading aided students in comprehension and recall of information. When students were asked to create graphic organizers after reading, their scores improved on recall, vocabulary, and comprehension. She found that when young people have in-depth instruction in constructing graphic organizers, the benefits of graphic organizers are highest.

Dunston stated that the graphic organizers are effective because of their ability to "organize information to be learned, connect it to what is known, and allow the reader to interact with the text" (1992, p. 59).

Patricia Mautone and Richard Mayer (2007) found that graphic organizers improve students' comprehension of scientific graphs, but students may need help in organizing the material found in graphics.

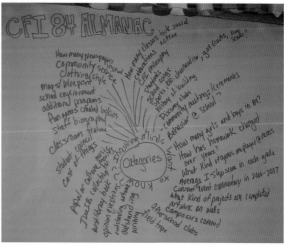

Because of their versatile use, graphics are helpful in differentiating instruction. Visuals can provide concrete examples for students who have difficulty with abstract concepts. They can also present information in a variety of ways to meet individual needs.

A learner who has difficulty communicating ideas through writing may excel at the development of graphic communications. The role of the educator is to connect the wealth of visual resources and tools with meaningful, inquiry-based experiences.

Graphic inquiry gives me the opportunity to question, explore, assimilate, infer, and reflect using effective, efficient, and appealing visual tools and resources.

With emerging technology tools like **Teen Second Life,** I can explore and even build amazing virtual worlds.

From engaging virtual worlds to complex visualizations, emerging technology tools and resources are providing new options for student information scientists conducting graphic inquiry.

Explore some interesting websites that will make you think graphically:

http://www.gapminder.org/
http://infosthetics.com/
http://www.visualcomplexity.com/vc/
http://www.fakeisthenewreal.org/
http://www.worldmapper.org/

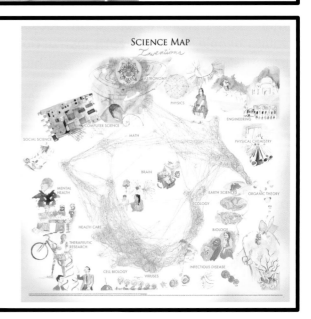

Afterword

The Original Idea

The original idea for "graphic inquiry" was to use the graphic novel format to illustrate a variety of information search situations. Cartoon characters would be involved in addressing both school and personal information challenges. Armed with information search strategies, these teen detectives would be aided by their pet blood-hounds, Valid and Invalid, to test the authority and credibility of various information clues and artifacts.

The reason for such illustrations of information literacy rested on the need to help students in all grades to visualize the information search and application processes. While many models have been created to help school librarians and their teaching colleagues understand the process, little exists to illustrate for students the processes of questioning, identification of information needs, selection and application of search strategies, and presenting the findings that lead to solving information problems.

The Expanded Application

While these ideas still have merit and may lead to future illustrated products, it became clear that the greater need was to establish examples of how illustrations in and of themselves pose an information inquiry maze that has not been fully explored. Visual literacy has certainly established the principles for critical analysis of images. Media literacy adds to this critical review by posing the need for analysis of visual communication in popular culture along with application of media production skills and techniques. Graphic inquiry builds on information literacy, visual literacy, and media literacy by applying the full information inquiry cycle to the use of visuals to address information problems.

The important difference in this application of elements of information inquiry to graphics and other illustrations is the demand placed on the student to complete the full information inquiry cycle. Not only is there the standard expectation to extract information from visuals and to present information findings in a visual manner, but through assimilation of new information (visuals), analysis of the value of the new information (visuals), and most of all, illustrating how the information selections made and how the information problem is solved, the student has the opportunity to go beyond just the print or oral products of information searching and presentation. They can graphically illustrate and explain the thoughts, considerations, and judgments made through the inquiry process. They can show their reflections on the visual information explored and illustrate how and why visual selections were made to extract and present ideas, arguments, proposals, stories, and conclusions.

Put simply, they can, as in math problem-solving, "show their work." They can graphically illustrate how they accepted or rejected information, how they assimilated it to their current knowledge, and how their findings are best illustrated for others who can gain new understanding with them. Reflections can include illustrations of the student's evaluation of his or her work and if they were successful or not in solving the original information need, and graphically show the raising of new questions for more extensive, in-depth information exploration.

The Product of Value

The collection of visual artifacts, application of learning standards to illustrations, and extensive examples of how graphics can be explored for information extraction and presentation gathered in this book provides a wealth of possibilities for students and teachers to fully employ the elements of inquiry. The most important aspect of assessment that can be applied to the inquiry process is that of illustrating new questions raised, new resources explored, and new graphics developed by the learner to convey his or her new understandings.   The learner is challenged to show his or her critical thinking, graphically.   Through graphic inquiry, learners can show their mind at work!

Great minds have used illustrations to convey their observations on the objects, events and meaning of their environment. Merriweather Lewis and his colleagues illustrated journals to document new plant and animal species. Charles Darwin relied heavily on illustrations as he analyzed relationships among animals. And the drawings of Leonardo Da Vinci conveyed ideas yet to become reality for hundreds of years. While few students will reach the genius levels of these great thinkers, the learning derived from application of methods to communicate with illustrations can be extensive, especially for some learners who are lost in print text.

Graphic inquiry includes the interaction among the learner and the multitude of visual messages pressed before him or her in our ever expanding electronic image world. Andrea Lunsford of Stanford University and John Ruszkiewicz of the University of Texas provide a vast assortment of examples for young adult exploration of the visual world in their exemplary text Everything's an Argument:

> Those who produce images shape the messages that those images convey, but those who "read" those images are by no means passive. Human vision is selective. To some extent, we actively shape what we see and have learned to see things according to their meanings within our culture. People don't always see things the same way, which explains why eyewitnesses to the same event often report it differently. Even instant replays don't always solve disputed calls on football fields. The visual images that surround us today and argue forcefully for our attention, time, and money are constructed to invite, perhaps even coerce, us into seeing them in just one way. But since we all have our own frames of reference, we resist such pressures. So, visual arguments might best be described as give-and-take, a dialogue, or even a tussle. (446)

It is that interaction with our visual environment that is captured in application of the elements of information inquiry applied to graphic inquiry. Graphic inquiry involves extracting information from and presenting information in visual formats such as political cartoons, diagrams, maps, photos, charts, tables, and multimedia. Through a recursive process of questioning, exploration, assimilation, inference, and reflection, students operating as information scientists along with instructional media specialists as their guides use graphic inquiry as a means to answer questions and to reflect on the process to reach conclusions.

Bibliography

Abilock, Debbie. "Visual Information Literacy: Reading a Documentary Photograph." *Knowledge Quest* 36 no. 3 (2008): 7-13.

Abilock, Debbie. "Applying Information Literacy Skills to Maps." *Knowledge Quest* 36 no. 4 (2008): 8-12.

Almanac Project. http://www.virtualinquiry.com/cases/almanac/.

Alvarado, Amy Edmonds and Patricia R. Herr. *Inquiry-based Learning Using Everyday Objects.* Corwin Press, 2003.

American Association of School Librarians (2007). Standards for the 21st-Century Learner. ALA.

Arnheim, Rudolf. *Art and Visual Perception: A Psychology of the Creative Eye.* University of California Press, 1974.

Arnheim, Rudolf. *Visual Thinking.* University of California Press, 1969.

Ausubel, David. *Educational Psychology: A Cognitive View.* Holt, Rinehart, and Winston, 1968.

Bang, Molly Garrett. *Picture This: How Pictures Work.* Chronicle Books, 2000.

Barry, Ann Marie Seward. *Visual Intelligence: Perception, Images, and Manipulation in Visual Communication.* State University of New York Press, 1997.

Baugh, L. Sue. *How to Write Term Papers and Reports.* Second Edition. Glencoe/McGraw Hill, 2001.

Bentley, Michael Lee, Christine Ebert, and, Edward Ebert. *The Natural Investigator: A Constructivist Approach to Teaching Elementary and Middle School Science.* Wadsworth/Thomson Learning, 2000.

Berger, John. *Ways of Seeing.* British Broadcasting Corporation, 1972.

Bromley, Karen D'Angelo. *Webbing with Literature: Creating Story Maps with Children's Books.* Second Edition. Allyn & Bacon, 1995.

Bromley, Karen, Linda Irwin-DeVitis, and Marcia Modlo. *Graphic Organizers: Visual Strategies for Active Learning.* Scholastic Professional Books, 1995.

Bromley, Karen, Linda Irwin-DeVitis, and Marcia Modlo. *50 Graphic Organizers for Reading, Writing & More.* Teaching Resources, 1999.

Buzan, Tony. *The Mind Map Book.* Plume Book, 1994.

Callison, Daniel. "Reflection." *School Library Media Activities Monthly* 16 no. 2 (1999a): 31-34.

Callison, Daniel. "Inquiry: Student-Centered Learning and the Media Center." *School Library Media Activities Monthly* 15 no. 6 (1999b): 38-42.

Callison, Daniel. "Information Inquiry." *School Library Media Activities Monthly* 18 no. 10 (2002): 35-39.

Callison, Daniel and Annette Lamb. "Graphic Inquiry: Standards and Resources." *School Library Media Activities Monthly* 24 no. 1 (2007): 39-42.

Callison, Daniel and Annette Lamb. "Graphic Inquiry: Skills and Strategies." *School Library Media Activities Monthly* 24 no. 2 (2007b): 38-42.

Callison, Daniel and Leslie Preddy. *The Blue Book on Information Age Inquiry, Instruction and Literacy.* Libraries Unlimited, 2006.

Cary, Stephen. *Going Graphic: Comics at Work in the Multilingual Classroom.* Heinemann, 2004.

Clauss, Patrick. *I-Claim: Visualizing Argument.* Bedford St. Martins, 2005.

Comenius, John Amos. *The Orbis Pictus.* C.W. Bardeen Publisher, 1887.

Caplow, Theodore, Louis Hicks, and Ben J. Wattenberg. *The First Measured Century: An Illustrated Guide to Trends in America, 1900 – 2000.* AEI Press, 2001. http://pbs.org/fmc/downloadbook.htm.

Carter, James Bucky. *Building Literacy Connections with Graphic Novels: Page by Page, Panel by Panel.* National Council of Teachers of English, 2007.

Considine, David M. and Gail E. Haley. *Visual Messages: Integrating Imagery into Instruction.* Second Edition. Libraries Unlimited, 1999.

Craver, Kathleen. *Using Internet Primary Sources to Teach Critical Thinking Skills in History.* Greenwood Press, 1999.

Creative Commons. http://creativecommons.org/.

CSI: Cemetery Scene Investigation. http://connections.smsd.org/csi/.

Dondis, Donis A. *A Primer of Visual Literacy.* The MIT Press, 1973.

Driscoll, Marcy. *Psychology of Learning for Instruction.* Fourth Edition. Allyn & Bacon, 2008.

Dunston, P. J. "A Critique of Graphic Organizer Research." *Reading Research & Instruction* 31 (1992): 57–65.

Eby, Lloyd. "In the Mind's Eye: Our Emerging Visual Culture." *The World and I* 14 no. 9 (1999), http://www.worldandi.com/public/1999/September/visual.cfm.

Egan, Timothy. *The Big Burn: Teddy Roosevelt and the Fire that Saved America.* Houghton Mifflin, 2009.

Eisner, Will. *Graphic Storytelling and Visual Narrative.* Poorhouse Press, 1996.

Elkins, James. *How To Use Your Eyes.* Routledge, 2000.

Endy, Drew, Isadora Deese, and the MIT Synthetic Working Group. "Comic 1. Adventures in Synthetic Biology." *Nature* (November 24, 2005), http://www.nature.com/nature/comics/syntheticbiologycomic/.

Fitzgerald, M. "Evaluating Information: An Information Literacy Challenge." *School Library Media Research* 2 (1999), http://www.ala.org/ala/mgrps/divs/aasl/aaslpubsandjournals/slmrb/slmrcontents/volume21999/vol2fitzgerald.cfm.

Frey, Nancy and Douglas Fisher. *Teaching Visual Literacy: Using Comic Books, Graphic Novels, Anime, Cartoons, and More to Develop Comprehension and Thinking Skills.* Corwin Press, 2008.

Friedman, Myles I., Diane H. Harwell, and Katherine C. Schnepel. *Effective Instruction: A Handbook of Evidence-Based Strategies.* The Institute for Evidence-Based Decision-Making in Education, Inc., 2006.

Gallavan, N. and E. Kottler. "Eight Types of Graphic Organizers for Empowering Social Studies Students and Teachers." *Social Studies* 98 no. 3 (May 2007): 117-128.

Gardner, Howard. *Frames of Mind.* Basic Books, 1983.

George-Palilonis, Jennifer. *A Practical Guide to Graphics Reporting: Information Graphics for Print, Web, & Broadcast.* Focal Press, 2006.

Gerlic, Ivan and Norbert Jausovec. "Multimedia: Differences in Cognitive Processes Observed with EEG." *Educational Technology Research and Development* 47 no. 3 (1999): 5-14.

Gorman, Michele. *Getting Graphic! Using Graphic Novels to Promote Literacy with Preteens and Teens.* Linworth Press, 2003.

Greek Mythology. http://mra-ancient-greece.wikispaces.com/.

Gunning, Thomas G. *Creating Literacy Instruction for All Students.* Sixth Edition. Allyn & Bacon, 2007.

Hanks, Kurt. *The Rapid Vis Tool-kit: An Intriguing Collection of Powerful Drawing Tools for Rapid Visualization of Ideas.* Crisp Productions, 2003.

Hanks, Kurt and Larry Belliston. *Rapid Viz: A New Method for Rapid Visualization of Ideas.* Thomson, 2006.

Harrell, L. *Teaching Touch: Helping Children Become Active Explorers of Tactile Materials.* American Printing House for the Blind, 2002.

Harris, Robert L. *Information Graphics: A Comprehensive Illustrated Reference on Visual Tools for Analyzing, Managing, and Communicating.* Oxford University Press, 1999.

Haven, Kendall. *Story Proof: The Science Behind the Startling Power of Story.* Libraries Unlimited, 2007.

Holmes, Nigel. "The State of the Chart." *IMPRESS* 3 (2000), http://www.nigelholmes.com/.

Hyerle, David. *Visual Tools for Constructing Knowledge.* Association for Supervision and Curriculum Development, 1996.

International Society for Technology in Education. *National Educational Technology Standards* (NETS), 2007.

Jacobson, Robert, ed. *Information Design.* MIT Press, 2000.

Koechlin, Carol and Sandi Zwann. *Info Tasks for Successful Learning.* Pembrook, 2001.

Koechlin, Carol and Sandi Zwann. *Q Tasks: How to Empower Students to Ask Questions and Care About Answers.* Pembroke Publishers, 2006.

Krashen, Stephen. *The "Decline" of Reading in America, Poverty and Access to Books, and the Use of Comics in Encouraging Reading.* Teacher's College Record, 2005.

Krygier, John and Denis Wood. *Making Maps: A Visual Guide to Map Design for GIS.* Gilford Press, 2005.

Kuhlthau, Carol. "A Principle of Uncertainty for Information Seeking." *Journal of Documentation* 49 (1993): 339-355.

Kuhlthau, Carol C., Leslie K. Maniotes, and Ann K. Caspari. *Guided Inquiry: Learning in the 21st Century.* Libraries Unlimited, 2007.

Kuhn, Deanna. *Education for Thinking.* Harvard University Press, 2005.

Lamb, Annette. Digital Photo Safari. http://eduscapes.com/sessions/safari/.

Lamb, Annette. "Wondering Wiggling, and Weaving: A New Model for Project and Community Based Learning on the Web." *Learning and Leading With Technology* 24 no. 7 (1997): 6-13.

Levstik, Linda and Keith Barton. *Doing History: Investigating with Children in Elementary and Middle Schools.* Third Edition. Lawrence Erlbaum Associates, 2005.

Lunsford, Andrea A. and John J. Ruszkiewicz. *Everything's an Argument*. Bedford St. Martin's, 2010.

Maier, Timothy W. "When Your Eyes Tell You Lies." *Insight on the News* (October 16, 2000), http://findarticles.com/p/articles/mi_m1571/is_38_16/ai_66241129/.

Martinello, Marian L. and Gillian E. Cook. *Interdisciplinary Inquiry in Teaching and Learning*. Second Edition. Merrill, 2000.

Marzano, Robert J. and Debra J. Pickering. *Dimensions of Learning Teacher's Manual*. Association for Supervision and Curriculum Development and the Mid-Continent Regional Educational Laboratory, 1997.

Marzano, Robert J., Debra J. Pickering, and Jane E. Pollock. *Classroom Instruction that Works: Research-Based Strategies for Increasing Student Achievement*. Association for Supervision and Curriculum Development, 2001.

Mautone, P. and R. Mayer. "Cognitive Aids for Guiding Graph Comprehension." *Journal of Educational Psychology* 99 no. 3 (2007): 640-652.

Mayer, Richard E. "Problem Solving Principles." In *Instructional Message Design: Principles from the Behavioral and Cognitive Sciences,* edited by M. Fleming and W. H. Levie, 253-282. Educational Technology Publications, 1993.

McCloud, Scott. *Understanding Comics*. HarperCollins, 1994.

McCloud, Scott. *Reinventing Comics: How Imagination and Technology Are Revolutionizing an Art Form*. HarperCollins, 2000.

McConnell, Suzanne. Talking Drawings: A Strategy for Assisting Learners. Journal of Reading 36(4). December 1992/January 1993, p. 260-269.

McKenzie, Jamie. "Grazing the Net: Raising a Generation of Free Range Students - Part Two." *From Now On* (1994), http://www.fno.org/grazing2.html.

McKenzie, Jamie. "A Questioning Toolkit." *From Now On* (1997), http://questioning.org/Q7/toolkit.html.

McKenzie, Jamie. "The Great Question Press: Squeezing Import from Content." *From Now On* (2004), http://questioning.org/questionpress.html.

McKenzie, Jamie. "Good Doubt and Bad Doubt." *The Question Mark* (2007), http://questioning.org/jan07/doubt.html.

Meltzer, Bonnie. "Kiss Clip Art Goodbye." *Learning & Leading with Technology* 27 no. 4 (1999): 22-27.

Meltzer, Bonnie. "Cheating the Kids." *Library Talk* 13 no. 2 (2000): 31-32.

Michalko, Michael. *Thinkertoys*. Ten Speed Press, 1999.

Micklethwait, Lucy. *I Spy Colors in Art*. Greenwillow Books, 2007.

Moline, Steve. *I See What You Mean: Children at Work with Visual Information*. Stenhouse Publishers, 1995.

Monmonier, Mark. *How to Lie with Maps*. Second Edition. University of Chicago Press, 1996.

Moscovici, Hedy, and Tamar Nelson Holmlund. "Shifting from Activity Mania to Inquiry." *Science and Children* 35 no. 4 (1998): 14-17, 40.

Mosenthal, Peter B. and Irwin S. Kirsch. "Understanding Documents, Graphs and Charts, Part I." *Journal of Reading* 33 no. 5 (1990): 371-373.

National Press Photographers Association. Code of Ethics. http://www.nppa.org/professional_development/business_practices/ethics.html.

National Research Council. Inquiry and the National Science Education Standards: A Guide for Teaching and Learning. National Academy Press. 2000.

National Research Council. *Learning to Think Spatially: GIS as a Support System in the K-12 Curriculum*. National Academy Press, 2006.

National Science Teacher's Association. National Science Education Standards. National Academy Press, 1996.

Nesbit, J. and O. Adesope. "Learning With Concept and Knowledge Maps: A Meta-Analysis." *Review of Educational Research* 76 no. 3 (2006): 413-448.

Noodle Tools. http://noodletools.com/.

Novak, Joseph D. and D. Bob Gowin. *Learning How to Learn*. Cambridge University Press, 1984.

Paul, Richard. Pseudo Critical Thinking in the Educational Establishment. http://www.criticalthinking.org/articles/pseudo-ct-educ-establishment.cfm.

Paul, Richard and Linda Elder. Critical Thinking: Tools for Taking Charge of Your Professional and Personal Life. Prentice Hall, 2002.

Pavio, Allan. *Mental Representations: A Dual Coding Approach*. Oxford University Press, 1986.

Pearce, Charles R. *Nurturing Inquiry: Real Science for the Elementary Classroom.* Heinemann, 1999.

Photo Tampering through History. http://www.cs.dartmouth.edu/farid/research/digitaltampering/.

Places & Spaces: Mapping Science. http://scimaps.org/.

Porter, Bernajean. *DigiTales: The Art of Telling Digital Stories.* Bjconsulting, 2005.

Read-Write-Think. http://readwritethink.org/.

Roam, Dan. The Back of the Napkin. http://www.thebackofthenapkin.com/.

Romano, Tom. *Blending Genre, Altering Style.* Heinemann, 2000.

Sarkar, Somnath and Richard Frazier. "Place-Based Investigations and Authentic Inquiry." *Science Teacher* 75 no. 2 (2008): 29-33.

Schnorr, J. A. and R.C. Atkinson. "Repetition versus Imagery Instructions in the Short- and Long-term Retention of Paired Associates." *Psychonomic Science* 15 (1969): 184.

Smith, M. W. and J. D. Wilhelm. *Reading Don't Fix no Chevys.* Heinemann, 2002.

Soundy, Cathleen S. and Yun Qiu. "Portraits of Picture Power." *Childhood Education* 83 no. 2 (2006): 68.

Stein, Harry. *How to Interpret Visual Resources, A Social Studies Skills Book.* Franklin Watts, 1983.

Stull, Andrew T. and Richard R. Mayer. "Doing Versus Learning by Viewing: Three Experimental Comparisons of Learner-Generated Versus Author-Provided Graphic Organizers." *Journal of Educational Psychology* 99 no. 4 (2007): 808-820.

Taskonomy of Tasks. http://webquest.sdsu.edu/taskonomy.html.

Titanic in the Classroom. http://connections.smsd.org/titanic/.

Tufte, Edward R. *Visual Explanations: Images and Quantities, Evidence and Narrative.* Graphics Press, 1997.

Tufte, Edward R. *Beautiful Evidence.* Graphics Press, 2006.

Tufte, Edward R. *The Visual Display of Quantitative Information.* Second Edition. Graphics Press, 2001.

United States Copyright. http://copyright.gov/.

Using Pictures in Lessons. http://www.ncrtec.org/tl/camp/lessons.htm.

Vaughan, Brian K. *Pride of Baghdad.* Vertigo, 2006.

Veccia, Susan H. *Uncovering Our History: Teaching with Primary Sources.* ALA, 2003.

Versaci, Rocco. "Literary Literacy and the Role of the Comic Book." In *Teaching Visual Literacy,* edited by Nancy Frey and Douglas Fisher, 96. Corwin Press, 2008.

Vygotsky, L. *Thought and Language.* Cambridge, MA: MIT Press. 1962

Wagner, Jon. "Constructing Credible Images: Documentary Studies, Social Research, and Visual Studies." *American Behavioral Scientist* 47 no. 12 (2004): 1477-1506.

Weaver, Marcia. *Visual Literacy: How to Read and Use Information in Graphic Form.* Learning Express, 1999.

WebQuest. http://webquest.org/.

Wolsey, Thomas DeVere. In *Teaching Visual Literacy* edited by Nancy Frey and Douglas Fisher. Corwin Press, 2008.

Wright, G. and R. Sherman. "Let's Create a Comic Strip." *Reading Improvement* 36 no. 2 (1999): 66-72.

Wyman, Richard. *America's History Through Young Voices: Using Primary Sources in the K-12 Social Studies Classroom.* Allyn & Bacon, 2004.

Zelazny, Gene. *Say It with Charts.* Fourth Edition. McGraw-Hill, 2001.

Zemelman, Steven, Harvey Daniels, and Arthur Hyde. *Best Practice: Today's Standards for Teaching & Learning in America's Schools.* Third Edition. Heinemann, 2005.

Image Credits

ARR - All Rights Reserved
Author - Indicates that the visual is part of a personal collection or donated for use in the book
BLM - Bureau of Land Management
CA - Courtesy of Clipart.com @2010 Jupiter Images
CDC - Center for Disease Control
DE - United States Department of Energy
DHS - Department of Homeland Security
EPA - Environmental Protection Agency
HHS - United States Department of Health and Human Services
IRA - International Reading Association
LOC - Courtesy of Library of Congress, ID provided with each image
NARA - National Archives and Records Administration
NASA - National Aeronautics and Space Administration
NCES - National Center for Educational Statistics
NCI - National Cancer Institute
NIH - National Institute for Health
NOAA - National Oceanic and Atmospheric Administration
NPS - National Park Service
OCA - Open Clip Art openclipart.org
PH - Courtesy of Photos.com
RWP - Reproduced with Permission
USC - United States Census Bureau
USDA - United States Department of Agriculture
USDC - United States Department of Commerce
USGS - United States Geological Survey
WEB - Web page screen image
WM - Wikimedia Commons
WMPD - Wikimedia Commons, Public Domain

Title Page:

i. Starved child by Dr. Lyle Conrad: CDC; Map: PH; Martial arts: CA; Carrot comic: Author.

Introduction:

vii. Classroom group; PH; Bridge: Author; Photographer, Pen: PH. viii. Girl, Teen with bandana, Boy, Bulb: PH; Light bulb diagram, Thomas Edison's patent, Edison image: WMPD; Energy Use: DE; Drawing: Author. ix. Photographer 1 & 2: PH; Jupiter, NASA; Mind Map by Tony Buzan, 1996: Plume. x. Gliffy.com; Boy picking berries, LOC nclc05419; Dragon: CA; Lizard, Venn, Cat: Author; Class: PH; Making biscuits: ppmsc-00260; Painting: PH; Diagram: Author; Acid rain: Author; Twitter.com; Mars Phoenix: NASA; Nubs: The True Story of a Mutt, A Marine & a Miracle by Major Brian Dennis, Mary Netherly, and Kirby Larson, Little Brown and Company publisher.

Section 1:

1. Woman holding book: PH; Boy in cannery: LOC nclc05356; Girls at weaving: LOC nclc01336; Boy picking berries: LOC nclc05419; 10 leading causes of death: CDC; Gliffy.com. 2. Snowman: CA; Graph, Map, Diagram: Author; Wheat, Teacher/Child 1, Teacher/Child 2, Teacher: PH. 3. Teacher, Nurse, Snail photo: PH; Snail diagram: Original by Al2, English captions & edits by Jeff Dahl; Child 1, Child 2, Child 3, Map: Author; Hand diagram: WMPD. 4. Orbis Pictus: WMPD; Teaching Visual Literacy: Using Comic Books, Graphic Novels, Anime, Cartoons, and More to Develop Comprehension and Thinking Skills by Nancy Frey and Douglas B. Fisher, Corwin Press, 2008; A Single Shard by Linda Sue Park: Cover @2001 Jean & Mousien Tseng, Clarion Books, imprint of Houghton Mifflin Harcourt Pub. Co. ARR; Map, Pottery, Landscape, Teacher/Child: PH. 5. Landform, Rock diagram, Red rock: Author; Cow, Balloon, Cow: PH; Cow 2: CA. 6. Frames of Mind: Theory of Multiple Intelligences by Howard Gardner, Basic

Books, 1993; Brain diagram by NEUTOtiker: WM; Irish Potato Famine, WMPD; Bank, PH; Poverty chart: USC. 7. Info Fluency, Act now: Author; Teacher, Student, Kiss, Joan of Arc, Sketchbook: PH; Tornado formation: NOAA. 8. Runway patterns: WMPD; Weather chart, Kitten, Bird, Fish: CA; I see What You Mean by Steve Moline, Stenhouse Publishers; 1995. 9. Land Monitor: NARA; Gettysburg: Author, Teacher, Student, Bridge: PH; Rio de Janerio by Ron Beck: USGS/NASA; Stars: USGS; 10. Black children playing: NARA 306-NT-171.611c; Graphs: Author; Teacher, Child, Watches: PH 11. Children, Librarian: PH; Guided Inquiry: Learning in the 21st Century by Carol C. Kuhlthau, Leslie Maniotes, and Ann K. Caspari, @2007. RWP ABC CLIO, LLC; Inquiry diagram by Annette Lamb and Daniel Callison. 12. Notes, Sketches, Mushrooms: Author; Girl, Boys: PH; The Catcher in the Rye by J.D. Salinger, Back Bay Books; Reissue ed. 2001. 13. Fire: PH; Man, Chart, Map: Author. 14. 3 Drawings, Computer screen: Author. 15. Teacher, Plate, Man, Compass man: PH; Floorplan, Bracket: Author. 16. Teacher, Map planning, Man, Woman, Land plan: PH; Hardiness map: USDA. 17. Roller coaster, Boy, Teacher,Grill: PH; Christmas card: Author; Weather map: NOAA; Label: WMPD. 18. Teens, Teacher, Dog: PH; WEB: USDA; Association, Dessert, Yoga, World: CA.

Section 2:

19. Girl, Teen, Cross section, Deer sign, Dragon, Skeleton 1, Skeleton 2: PH; Lizard: Author; Skeleton diagram: LadyofHats, Mariana Ruiz Villarreal, WM. 20. Teacher, Chalkboard: PH; Ugly logo, Video, Diagram: Author; The Visual Display of Quantitative Information by Edward R. Tufte, Graphics Press LLC, Chesire, CT, 2001, RWP; The Black Diamond Detective Agency, Art @ Eddie Campbell, RWP of First Second books. 21. Standards for the 21st Century Learner by the American Association of School Librarians, a division of the American Library Association. RWP; WEB: Chances Project, NCES; Information Design by Robert Jacobson & Richard Saul Wurman, The MIT Press, 2000; Teens: PH. 22. Scientist, Teen, Australia, Ruins: PH; Concept map, Chart: Author; Louisiana Purchase: NARA 594889; Arm, Computer, Recycle: CA. 23. Radio spectrum: USDC; Woman, PH; Chart, Graph: Author. 24. Charts: Author. 25. Moon, Man, Glasses: PH; Immigration statistics: DHS; Chart: Author. 26. Charts: Author; Sign: PH. 27. Blue prints, Teacher: PH; Skeleton: LadyofHats, Mariana Ruiz Villarreal, WM; House of fly: Aldo, WM; Pioneer 10 plaque: Designed by Carl Sagan & Frank Drake, Artwork by Linda Salzman Sagan, NASA. 28. Creatures, Plant: CA; Cell: LadyofHats, Mariana Ruiz Villarreal, WM; Exploded view: Rafael Augusto de Oliveira, WM; Eye in cross section: MesserWoland, Bedlay castle by Supergolden, WM; Drawings, Schematic, Diagrams: Author. 29. Giant plane comparison: Clem Tillier, WM; Glidden's patent: NARA; DNA replication: LadyofHats, Mariana Ruiz Villarreal, WM; Woman, Land cross section: PH. 30. Seasons: WMPD; Seasons 2: Cronholm144, WM; Stonehenge, WM; Drawing, Diagram: Author. 31. Woman 1-3, Man, Fish, Painting: PH; Progressive fallacies cartoon, NARA 306096. 32. Couple of bacteria: Gaspirtz, WM; Collage: Ines Zgonic, WM; Microscope, WMPD; Kunstformen de Natur (Plate 49) by Ernest Haeckel: WMPD; Graffiti: PH; Metro de Madrid: David Martin, transformation by Xauxa; Miss Annie Oakley, WMPD; Sunflower by VanGogh: National Gallery, London, WMPD; South Wind, Clear Sky by Katsushika Hokusai: WMPD; Deogratia: Art @ J.P. Stassen. RWP of First Second book; Rocky mountains: Author; FAE visualization: WMPD. 33. Teen: PH; Drawing: Author; All commissioned officers: NARA; Mona Lisa by da Vinci: Musee de Louvre, WMPD; Wikipedia visualization: Bruce Herr. 34. Ledger: PH; Pueblo Taos central portion (LOC cph3g0943); Painting: PH. 35. Woman 1-4, Boy 1-2, Treasure, Map: PH; Child drawing: Author; Melanoma research visualization: Kevin Boyack, Ketan Mane, Katy Borner. 36. Cartogram: Michael Gastner, Cosma Shalizi, Mark Newman of University of Michigan; Waterloo campaign: Ipankonin, WM; Scott's great snake: LOC g3701s cw0011000; General reference map: USGS 112733; Celestial map, World borders map: WMPD; Diagrams: Author. 37. Girl: PH; Oregon trail map: University of Texas Libraries, The University of Texas at Austin; Maps: The Way of Where: Knowledge Quest 36, no. 4; How to Lie with Maps (2nd Ed) by Mark Monmonier & H.J. de Blij, University of Chicago Press, 1996; Diagram: Author; Figurative map: Charles Minard; Utah shaded relief map: BLM, USGS 112461. 38. Journey North Project: WEB, Annenberg Media; The Tarantula Scientist by Sy Montgomery, Photos @2004 by Nic Bishop, Houghton Mifflin Harcourt Pub. Co. RWP; Distribution theraphosidae: Sarefo, WM; Maps: Author. 39. Plastids: LadyofHats, Mariana Ruiz Villarreal, WM; Sun, Rose, Plant, Cloud: CA, Teacher with child: PH; Others: Author. 40. Diagrams, Concept Maps: Author. 41. Girl: PH; Chicken sequence, Frog sequence: CA. 42. Needles, Leaves: PH; Others: Author. 43. Woman with x-ray, Woman with camera, Photographs album, Camera, Bomb, X-ray, Astronaut: PH; MRI: WMPD; Nixon and Elvis: NARA; Others: Author. 44. Washington, DC: USGS; Duck: Len Blumin, WM; Infrared: EPA; Radar: USGS; Hurricane Katrina: NOAA; Ultrasound: Sam Pullara, WM; Neck x-ray: Morbus Beckterew, WM; Motocross: Geraint Otis Warlow, WM; Stars, Microscope: PH; Others: Author. 45. Teacher, Plant, Cross-section: PH; San Francisco Earthquake of 1906: NARA 524395; Grinnell Glacier 1938: T.J. Hileman, Blase Reardon, USGS. 46. Klondike Gold Rush National Historic Park: NASA; The Call of the Wild, Macmillan Company; Jason's Gold @1999 by Will Hobbs, map illustrations by Virginia Norey, HarperCollins, New York, NY; Aerial view: PH; Shoreline: Author. 47. Symbols: CA;

Teen girl, Boy: PH. 48. Egyptian hieroglyphs: Jon Sullivan, Photos.org; A symbol: Mac Naylor, WM; Others: CA. 49. Man: PH; Symbols: CA; Map: Author. 50. Symbols: CA.

Section 3:

51. Class, Man with snake, Spider, Cricket, Mushroom: PH. 52. Child, Chick, Girl washing, Chick viewing: CA; Woman, Eggs: PH; Chicken sketches: VxD, WM; Others: Author. 53. Owl: PH; Owl: CA; Owl pellet: edwaado Flickr; Owl pellet dissection: North Island Wildlife Recovery Association RWP. 54. Buffalo Bill's wild west: LOC cph3h00057; The Scout Buffalo Bill by Forbes: LOC cph3g06424; Flags, Globe: CA; Others: Author. 55. Woman: PH: Child 1-2: CA; Aesop for Children 1919 by Milo Winter: Project Gutenberg; Others: Author. 56. Man: PH; DigiTales by Bernajean Porter RWP; The Storm in the Barn @ 2009 by Matt Phelan, Candlewick Press, Somerville, MA RWP; Old totem poles: LOC cph3c35989; World's largest totem pole: WM; Soccer ball, Joystick, Singer: CA; Others: Author. 57. Story Proof: The Science Behind the Startling Power of Story @ 2007 by Kendall F. Haven, ABC-CLIO, LLC RWP; Bronze, Braille, Toilet paper: PH; The Magical Life of Long Tack Sam: An Illustrated Memoir by Ann Marie Fleming, Riverhead Trade; Map, Laura Wilson comic: Author. 58. American Born Chinese: Art @Gene Yang RWP of First Second books, Teen, Adult: PH; Chinese history, Fortune cookies: PH; Library of Congress: WEB LOC. 59. Molecule, Girls, Bus ride: PH: KABAM Project: WEB CDC. 60. I Want You To Be SunWise: Arizona Department of Health Services; Others: Author, Cans, Paper, Bottles, Boy: PH; Mohandas K Gandhi: WMPD. 61. Girl: PH; Paws: CA; Weather map: NOAA; The Declaration of Independence: The Words that Made America, Scholastic Inc. @2002 by Sam Fink RWP; The Constitution of the United States @2010 inscribed and illustrated by Sam Fink. Welcomebooks.com; A Field Guide to Animal Tracks 3/E @1974 by Margaret E. Murie Houghton Mifflin Harcourt Pub. Co. RWP; Map: NationalAtlas. gov: Others: Author. 62. Square of Life: @2011 the Trustees of the Stevens Institute of Technology Hoboken, NJ; Boy, Girl, Australia: PH; Diagram: Author. 63. MyPyramid: WEB PD; Periodic table, Boy, Girl, Mitosis: PH; Others: Author. 64. Plant buds classification: LadyofHats, Mariana Ruiz Villarreal, WM; Girl, Woman: PH; Kidspiration project: Author. 65. Life cycle: LadyofHats, Mariana Ruiz Villarreal, WM; Egyptian boat: NOAA; Canoe manned by voyageurs: Archives Canada; Ship: PH. 66. Girl, Tomato sign, Compost: PH; Hardiness map: USDA; Chart, Diagram: Author. 67. Woman, Telephone 1-2: PH; Franklin D. Roosevelt with Eleanor Roosevelt 1910: NARA 195545; Others: Author. 68. Boy, Camera, Building, Pencil: PH; Abdomen-head-thorax: SuperManu WM; Drawing: Author. 69. Coins, Boy, Man: PH; Bicycle evolution numbers: Aldo WM. 70. Ancient Egypt map: Jeff Dahl WM; Egypt 1450 BC map: Andrei Nacu WM; Man, Teen, Costume, Painting 1-2, Boast: PH. 71. Bee collecting pollen: Joe Sullivan WM; Admongo.gov: WEB; Apples, Girl, Boy: PH; Sign: Author. 72. Beautiful Evidence 2006 by Edward R. Tuft, Graphics Press LLC, Chesire, CT RWP; Human-allosaurus size comparison: Marmelad WM; Pacific map: CIA World Facebook; Notes: Author. 73. iClaim: visualizing argument by Patrick Clauss, Bedford/St. Martins, 2005; Theodore Roosevelt and John Muir: LOC cph3g04698, Teen 1-2, PH. 74. Cancer chart: NIH; Lung cancer: NCI; Malignant mesolthelioma: Stevefruitsmaak WM; Respiratory system: LadyofHats, Mariana Ruiz Villarreal, WM; Not a cough: Stanford School of Medicine, Lane Library; Boy, Ashtray: PH. 75. Man: PH; Cattails, Diagram Cattails photos: Author. 76. Woman, Child: PH; Who Sank the Boat? by Pamela Allen, Putnam, 1996; Lego bathtub: Author; Duck, Pencil, Coin: CA. 77. Boy, Insect: PH; Drawing, Timeline: Author. 78. Letter carrier: NARA 165-WW-269B-15; Typist: NARA 165-WW-269B-16; Record book of patients, NARA 18; Pandemic map: David Chrest, RTI International, NIGMS Image Gallery; Boy, Bee: PH. 79. Potter 1-3, Artist, Elevator, Breads, Harvesting, Corn, Map: PH, Children: Author. 80. Teen girl, Teen boys, Child: PH; Comic: Author. 81. Teacher, Boy, Teen, Animal care: PH; Knapping, Graphic: Author. 82. Couple, Teen: PH; Fruit symbols: CA.

Section 4:

83. Woman with child, Painting: PH; Making biscuits: LOC fsa8c52415; Primer of Visual Literacy by Donis A. Dondis, MIT Press, 1973. 84. Teen, Ship 1-2, Viking: PH; Viking maps: Max Naylor WM; Yggdrasil: Erkadio WM. 85. Rip current diagram: NOAA; Boy, Girl, Car: PH; Wezel tkacki knots: Bastian WM: Cycle of ticks: CDC; UV: NOAA. 86. Teacher, Family, Painting: PH; General store: LOC fsa8c42415. 87. Woman, Drawing: PH; First vote: LOC ppmsc 00037; Daisy Dow: Holsinger Studio Special Collection University of Virginia Library; Woman with horses: Author. 88. Sector 7 @1999 by David Wiesner Clarion Books, Houghton Mifflin Harcourt Pub. Co RWP; Right Here on this Spot by Sharon Hart Addy @1999 by John Clapp Houghton Mifflin Harcourt Pub. Co. RWP; The Mitten 20th Anniversary Edition by Jan Brett, Putnam, 2009; The Visual Thesaurus @2011 Thinkmap ARR; Quintura for Kids: WEB. 89. Man, Teen, Fish: PH; We can do it: NARA NWDNS-179-WP-1563; Picturing America: WEB NEH; Symbols: CA; Graph: Author. 90. Columbus by L. Prang: LOC pga02388; Christopher Columbus: LOC cph3a05534; Christophorus Columbus:

LOC cph3a10965; Teen: PH; Graphic: Author. 91. Map: CDC; Man, Teen: PH; Graphs: Author. 92. Teen, Dining: PH; Diagrams: Author. 93. Teen girl, Boy: PH; Stem cells: Mike Jones WM; Hooverville: LOC fsa8b28022; Civil War project: Author. 94. Woman, Child, Panda: PH; Project Panda (Adventures of Riley by Amanda Lumry and Laura Hurwitz, Scholastic Press 2009; Conservation central: WEB Smithsonian; Map: Author. 95. Teen: PH; Mountain: CA; Drawing: Author. 96. Teen: PH; Cactus: CA. 97. Friends, Boy 1-2, Intern: PH; Astro camp: NASA; Venn, Inspiration, Basket: Author. 98. Chart: PH; Distance, Desert, 3 people: Author. 99. Child: PH; Concept map: Author; Bubbl.us: WEB. 100. Cactus 1-3: My life so far, Notes: Author; Marie Curie Nobel Portraits: WMPD.

Section 5:

101. Teacher: PH; NARA: WEB; Smoke: NARA 545469; Abandoned corvair: NARA; Air quality map: airnow.gov; Acid rain, Venn: Author. 102. Family, Crocodile, Landform: PH; Crocodile skull: Alexei Kouprianov WM; Airplane, Train: CA. 103. Devices Make Electronic Images Files Accessible to the Blind @Robert Rathe, NIST; Tactile board: NASA/JPL; Talking tactile tablet: Touch Graphics & National Geographic Society; Tactile Graphics @1992 by Polly K. Edman AFB Press RWP ARR. 104. Woman, Duck: PH; Uno's Garden @2006 Graeme Base Abrams Books for Young Readers. 105. Woman: PH; Mount St. Helen Images: USGS; Bronze shield: LOC cai 2a11797; Cernan jump salutes: NARA AS17-134-20380. 106. NARA Digital Vault: WEB; National parks preserve wildlife: LOC cph3f05639. 107. Woman: PH; Profits on child labor: NARA; NARA: WEB; Worksheets: NARA; Doing History: Investigating with Children in Elementary and Middle Schools 2005 3rd ed by Linda Levstik, Lawrence Erlbaum Associates. 108. Laika: art @Nick Abadzis RWP First Second books an imprint of Roaring Brook Press; Teacher and child: PH; Wright brothers: LOC cph3c01163; Balloon Manhattan: LOC. 109. West, Durer painting, Child: PH; Emigrants to the west 2: LOC cph3c01163; Masterpiece by Elise Broach and Kelly Murphy RWP Henry Holt and Co. LLC; Bread and Roses, Too by Katherine Paterson @2006 by Minna Murra, Inc. RWP Clarion Books Houghton Mifflin Harcourt Pub. Co. ARR; Strike in Lawrence, LOC cph3b44256; Collage: Author. 110. Woman: PH; The Administrator's promise: LOC; Walt Whitman diary: LOC; Kearney's men wounded: LOC cwpbh-03386. 111. Teen: PH; Discrimination images: LOC; Loose lips poster, NARA; 113. Man: PH; Charts: Author; The First Measured Century: An Illustrated Guide to Trends in America 1900-2000 by Theodore Caplow, Louis Hicks, Ben J. Wattenberg @2000 American Enterprise Institute for Public Policy Research, Washington, DC. 114. Boy: PH; Health: HHS; Matchstick graph: PH; Charts: Author. 115. Teen: PH; US Census: USU. 116. Teen, Slide: PH; Weather symbols: CA; Barometer: PH; Hyperstudio project: Author. 117. Man: PH; FedStats.gov: WEB; CreateAGraph: WEB. 118. Gears, Bike: PH; Chart: Author. 119. Man: PH; USASpending: WEB usaspending.gov; Statistics Canada: WEB statcan.gc.ca. 121. Man, Tiger, Middle east: PH; Astronaut: NASA; Teen experiment: NASA; Kennedy children: NARA 194343; Mars: NASA/JPL MRPS94103; Civil War: LOC cwpb04326; Depression mother: LOC fsa8b29516. 122. Teen: PH; ERA: LOC ppmsca01952. 123. Man: PH; Pearl Harbor: LOC fsa8e00810; Basket weaving by Laurie Minor-Penland: Smithsonian 92-8804; Tomatoes: NASA/Marshall MSFC-9805058; Depression era 4: LOC. 124. Speaker, Model: PH; Edward Curtis – 5: Smithsonian; Music: Author. 125. Cape D-Or Cliff IV by Metal Cowboy Flickr; Zoo: Author; Flooding, U.S. Air Force. 126. Teens, Roller coaster, Bird, Owl: PH; Others: Author. 127. Woman: PH; Drought images: NASA/JPL PIA04379; Piclits: WEB piclits.com. 129. Man, Maps: PH; Pays de Josselin: lavilleatlady flickr; Iditarod map: BLM. 130. Capitol Reef National Park map: NPS; Map: NOAA; Drawing: Author. 131. Manhattan maps: LOC; Geodata: WEB geodata.gov. 132. Woman, Indian empire: PH; Global vegetation map: NASA GPN-2003-00029; Learning to Think Spatially National Academies Press 2005; India: dawpa2000, flickr. 133. Student: PH; Chlorophyll concentration: NASA; North America tapestry time and terrain, USGS. 134. Vietnam: PH; Soldiers: LOC; Ho Chih Min Trail: Flickr; African American girl: PH. 135. Teachers, Boy, Aerial View: PH; Shackleton: Author. 137. Calcium: NASA MSFC-0300075; Kidspiration examples: Author; Calder photo: PD. 138. Animals: CA. 139. Prehistoric horse: CA; Artwork, Bird: PH; Mind mapping Africa: Appfrica, flickr; Inspiration: Author. 140. The web of agreement: Paul Downey, flickr. 141. NY Times 2009 Visualization: blprnt_van flickr; Concept maps: Author. 142. Man, Child: PH; Mercy Watson to the Rescue @2005 Kate DiCamillo @2005 Illustration by Chris Van Dusen Candlewick Press, Somerville, MA RWP. 143. Titanic in the Classroom project and website: Nancy Bosch and students; Group of survivors: LOC cph3b45387. 147. Clipart: CA; Hidden Treasure: @2011 Discovery Comics; Resistance: art@ Carla Jablonski and Leland Purvis RWP First Second books; Olympians Zeus: art@ George O'Connor RWP First Second books; Cartoon, WMPD; Page "Robert Tamandua": Miwer WM; Gunston Street Comics: Zaciski WM; On the Trail of the Missing Ozone: EPA. 148. Going Graphic: Comics at Work in the Multilingual Classroom by Stephen Cary Heinemann 2004; The Photographer: art@ Emmanuel Guibert RWP First Second books; Building Literacy Connections with Graphic Novels: Page by Page, Panel by Panel James Bucky Carter 2007 National Council of Teachers of English RWP; Bound by Law? Keith Aoki, James Boyle, Jennifer Jenkins, et al, Eds 2008 Duke University Press RWP. 149. Teen: PH; Graphic Storytelling and Visual Narrative by Will Eisner

Poorhouse Press 1996; Ready Kids comic: DHS; The Fishin' Season: NARA. 150. Stylized map: PH; Comic 1: Adventures in Synthetic Biology Nature nature.com/nature/comics/syntheticbiologycomic/; Making Smart Choices: SAMHSA. 151. The Vietnam War: A Graphic History by Dwight Zimmerman, Gen. Chuck Horner, and Wayne Vansant Hill and Wang 2009; Stiches, A Memoir @2009 David Small RWP W. W. Norton & Co, Inc.; Comic: CA. 152. Boy: PH; My Friend Toby: Bat Bites: MCACC; Pixton: WEB @2008-2011 Pixton Comics PIXTON.COM; Boy with worms: CA; Fire safety comic: Author; Worm comic: Author. 153. Teen: PH; Batman: NARA 595420; Journey into Mohawk Country art@ George O'Connor RWP First Second books; Student comic: Author. 155. Man: PH; Triangle Shirtwaist Factory @2006 Capstone Press ARR; Fish, Mad Hatter: WMPD; Mapping Penny's World by Loreen Leedy RWP Henry Holt and Co. LLC; Peter Pan: N. Kasp WM; Burl comic: Washington State Department of Transportation; Picture This: How Pictures Work @2000 by Molly Bang RWP Chronicle Books LLC San Francisco; Zoom by Istvan Banyai Puffin Books 1998; The Wall: Growing Up Behind the Iron Curtain by Peter Sis Farrar, Straus and Giroux 2007; The Stuff of Life: A Graphic Guide to Genetics and DNA by Mark Schultz, Sander Cannon and Kevin Cannon Hill and Wang 2009; The United States Constitution: A Graphic Adaptation by Jonathan Hennessey and Aaron McConnell Hill and Wang 2008. 156. Teen, Stamp, Ben Franklin: PH; Student project: Author. 157. Symbols: CA; The Great Graph Contest by Loreen Leedy Holiday House 2006; What Do You Do With A Tail Like That? Steve Jenkins and Robin Page art@ 2003 Steve Jenkins RWP Houghton Mifflin Harcourt Pub. Co. ARR; Graphic: Author. 158. Teen: PH; Henry's box 1-2; WMPD; Pride of Baghdad by Brian K. Vaughan and Niko Henrichon Vertigo 2008. 159. Forest: PH; Mouse Guard Volume 1 Fall 1152 (v. 1) by David Petersen Archaia Entertainment LLC 2009; Uglies RWP Carissa Pelleteri; Girl: OCA; Tuck Everlasting by Natalie Babbitt A Sunbirst Book /Farrar, Straus and Giroux 1988; 1984 by George Orwell, Signet Classic, 1961; 1984 map: WMPD. 160. Man: PH; Receipt, Coin, Security, Driver's license, Journal, Artwork: PH. 161. Civil War drawings: LOC; Courage and Responsibility: WEB civilwarlit.wikispaces.com; Houdini: The Handcuff King by Jason Lutes and Nick Bertozzi Hyperion Books 2008; Houdini: LOC cph3g03277; Biocube: ReadWriteThink.org Thinkfinity by IRA.

Section 6:

163. Woman: PH; Inquiry graphic: Callison 2002; Twitter.com: WEB; Mars images: NASA/JPL-Caltech/UofA/Texas A&M. 164. Hero's Journey: ReadWriteThink.org Thinkfinity by IRA; The Natural Investigator: A Constructivist Approach to the Teaching of Elementary and Middle School Science by Michael Bentley, Christine Ebert & Edward Ebert Wadsworth Publishing 1999; Model boat: Eileen McVey NOAA fish5013. 165. Boy: PH; The Frog Scientist by Pamela S. Turner @2009 Andy Comins RWP Houghton Mifflin Harcourt Pub. Co. ARR; Youthful Admirer: J. Alarcon or D. Benetti NOAA fish5301; Student projects: Author. 166. Girl holding berries, Science teen: PH; Anaphase 1-4: WMPD. 167. Heart diagram: CA; Heart: PH; Human heart, Kidspiration: Author. 168. Crispin: The Cross of Lead by Avi Hyperion Book 2002; Crispin: At the Edge of the World by Avi Hyperion Books 2008; Keying up by William Merritt Chase, Jester with a Lute by Frans Hals, Portrait of the Ferrara Court Jester Gonella ny Jean Fouquet, A Jester Holding a Flute by Peter Wtewael, Fool's Cap: WMPD; Fools Are Everywhere by Beatrice K. Otto University of Chicago 2007. 169. Child by water, Child with butterfly, Man with fish: PH. 170. Child thinking, Firefigher, Sea turtle, Boys & dog: PH; Turtle: OCA. 171. Hole in the ozone: NASA 049; Newseum: WEB newseum.org; Lion 1-2, Teen at board, Man thinking, Mummy photo: PH; Mummy drawing, Mummy historical, Mummy wrapping: WMPD. 172. Molly Pitcher: LOC cph3104439; Molly Pitcher: NARA, 532935; Girl: PH; Bats: Neville W. Cayley, WMPD; Q Tasks: How to Empower Students to Ask Questions and Care About Answers by Carol Koechlin and Sandi Zwaan Pembroke Publishers 2006. 173. ATV images: PH. 174. Jeep, ATV, Mountain bike. 175. Boy, Closeup teen, Dead fish, Fish sign, Two girls: PH. 176. Girl outside, Girl in library: PH; Darwin Australia: Australian War Memorial 044607. 177. Woman with child: LOC; Negro baseball player: LOC; Satchel Paige: Striking Out Jim Crow @2007 James Strum and Rich Tommaso RWP Disney@Hyperion ARR; Teens, Re-enactor: PH; Printer: Author. 178. PLFP 1-2: LOC Look-Job69-5080; Teen boy, Girl writing, Pads, Corkboard: PH. 179. Boy: PH; Sketch of John Ross Key: NOAA theb3923; Virus background, Crime screen, Boyle's law: Author. 180. Mummy 1: WMPD; Mummy 2-3, Teen: PH; Question-Explore: Author. 181. Boy reading, Fishmonger, Girl drawing: PH. 182. Boy building, Girl and teacher, Teen reading, Keyboarding: PH. 183. Girl monster, Girl writing, Dragon 5: PH. 184. Teen, Pomeiock: PH; Pomeiock warrior: LOC cph3b23278; Chief: The Trustees of British Museum. 185. Sew, Child and parent; Tree sap series: PH; Graphs: Author. 186. Earth's city lights by Craig Mayhew and Robert Simmon: NASA/GSFC. 187. Shoe, Child: PH; Fish gear: NOAA fish 2200. 188. Show, Testing, Scientist 1-2, Student: PH; National Invasive Species Council: WEB invasivespeciesinfo.gov; Notes: Author. 189. The Big Burn @2009 by Timothy Egan RWP Houghton Mifflin Harcourt Pub. Co. ARR; The Greatest Good: fs.fed.us/greatestgood/; Fire photos: PH; Concept map: Author. 190. Child: PH; Coin: US Mint; Forces of Flight: Smithsonian National Air and Space Museum airandspace.si.edu/howthingsfly. 191. Child: PH; Colonial Williamsburg Bricklayer game and slideshow: The Colo-

nial Williamsburg Foundation 2011. 192. Two people, Teen: PH; Assimilate-Infer: Author. 193. Man with fish, Boy: PH. 194. Teens, Mask: PH; Timeline: Author. 195. Teen, Man with butterfly: PH; Comic song: LOC cph3g03591; Garage band project: Author; Desert: Author. 196. Girl, Man: PH; Chandra X-ray Observatory: Flickr; Symbols: CA; Project: Author. 197. Woman, computer, dog: PH; computer: CA; AVMA: WEB avma.org; Florida Dept of Agriculture: WEB doacs.state.fl.us; AAAS: WEB aas.org; CDC: cdc.gov. 198. Man, Butterfly: PH; Inquiry project, map project: Author.

Section 7:

199. Teens, Woman: PH; Nubs: The True Story of a Mutt, A Marine & a Miracle by Major Brian Dennis, Mary Netherly, and Kirby Larson, Little Brown and Company publisher; Child drawings: Author. 200. Jellyfish, Child: PH; Jellyfish diagram: WMPD; Voices: Author. 201. Doctor and child: PH; Drawings, Map photo: Author. 202. Woman: PH; Inspection: LOC cph3a10026; Ellis Island comic: Author. 203. Woman: PH, Goat project: Author. 204: Shark tooth, Teachers: PH; Shark project photos: Vikki Tucher; Shark video: Author. 205. Boy leaf, Girl snake, Teen guitar, Instrument: PH; Fish: Smithsonian; Snake drawing: WMPD. 206. Child, Chinese drawing, Plant drawing, Dog: PH; Inquiry-based Learning Using Everyday Objects by Amy Edmonds Alvarado and Patricia R. Herr Corwin Press 2003; Leaf inquiry: Author. 207. Girl draw, Boy, Evidence: PH; Calliphora stygia, Calliphora augur, Space shuttle: WMPD; Sculpture, Candle, Washtub: Author. 208. Mandala: PH; Unfinished Lincoln: NARA; Smithsonian's History Explorer: WEB historyexplorer.americanhistory.si.edu; Within These Walls: WEB americanhistory.si.edu; Artificial heart: Smithsonian ABIOMED 2003.0166.01.1; Wood 1-2: Author. 209. Girl working: PH; Flow, Dinosaur, Exploding diagram, Nuclear fuel: WMPD. 210. Shells in sand, Teacher and student: PH; Rock cycle: WMPD; Diagram, Candy photo: Author. 211. Teen on rock, Teen boy, GPS: PH; Measuring Penny by Loreen Leedy RWP Henry Holt and Co. LLC; NRCS painting by Scott Patton: USDA/NRCS NRCSIA99545. 212. Montana girl: LOC cph3b19833; Wetlands project: USDA/NRCS NRCSSD01007; Water samples: USDA/NRCS NRCSIA99414; Graph: Author. 213. Science class, Teen: PH/ Titian Ramsay diary: LOC; CSI: Cemetery Scene Investigation: Nancy Bosch; Inventory: USDA/NRCS. 214. Boy, Boy holding flag, Emergency sirens, Girl holding camera, Freedom trail: PH; Mural: purioticorico flickr; Girl videorecording by Louise Kane: NOAA r0006602. 215. Girl at pond, Algae, Map, Woman: PH; Drawing, Chart: Author. 216. Teacher, Fish, Student: PH; Idaho Town 1-2: LOC; A River Ran Wild @1992 by Lynne Cherry RWP Houghton Mifflin Harcourt Pub. Co. ARR. 217. Man, Coal photo: PH; Google Earth Hero: WEB youtu.be/AzmrohA0aNc; Child drawing: Author, Quest for coal: Author. 218. Girl: PH; HEPA filter: LadyofHats, WM; Roman toga: LadyofHats, WM. 219. Inventors & Inventions Elisha Hardy, Fileve Palmer, Julie Davis, Katy Borner, Indiana University. 220. Boy 1-2: PH; Powow: National Museum of American Indian S22-21; Easter morning: Smithsonian PH 2003.7078.058; Bubbl.us: WEB. 221. Ancient Greece: WEB mra-ancient-greece.wikispaces.com; Google Earth: WEB earth.google.com; HyperStudio. 222. Photos 1-5: Author. 223. Children, Teen: PH; Sir Cumference and the First Round Table Text @ 1997 Cindy Neuschwander Illustrations @ 1997 Wayne Geehan RWP Charlesbridge Publishing, Inc.; Project: Author. 224. Clara Barton: LOC; Trail of Tears: LOC; Apple, Hot dog, Shell, Boy with shell: PH; Digestive System: WMPD; Nuclear fuel, WMPD. 225. MyPyramid: WEB mypyramid.gov; Grapes, Gambling, Banana, Milk, Cheese 1-2, Potato, Tomato, Fruit bowl, Carrots, Burger: PH; Concept map: Author. 226. Child drawing, Boy: PH; Pixton: WEB @2008-2011 Pixton Comics. PIXTON.Com; WebQuest.org: WEB webquest.org; Girl smiling, Comic, Georgia project: Author. 227. Student projects: Author. 228. Weather map, Map: WMPD; Soldier, Uniform, Teen, Snake: PH. 228. Japanese internment project: Author. 230. Symbol, Cottage, PH; Teen, Map: Author. 231. Student: PH; Fake dinosaur: WMPD; Diagram: WMPD; Loch Ness by Pierre Brial: WM. 232. Man, Woman, Teen: PH; Colored Free Men: NARA; Come and Join Us Brothers: NARA; Siege of Vicksburg: WMPD. 233. Family, Student: PH; Google Books; WEB books.google.com; Interviewing: PH; Flooey and Axel: LOC cph3c13875. 234. Teen boy, Teen girl, Model: PH; Protest photo: Author. 235. Historical photo: Author. 236. Creative Commons: WEB creativecommons.org; Hyperstudio project: Author. 237. Wikimedia Commons: WEB Ferdinand Reus; NoodleTools: WEB www.NoodleTools.com @2011 by Noodletools, Inc. ARR; Astronaut, Child, Teen, Homeless boy: PH. 238. Vase: PH; Alex drawing. 239. Girls with diagram, Concept map: Author. 240. Teen: PH; Second Life images: Author; Science map inventions: Elisha Hardy, Fileve Palmer, Julie Davis, Katy Borner Indiana University. We've done our best to ensure that proper credit has been given to images included in this book. We apologize for any errors or omissions.

Index

About the Authors

Annette Lamb has been a school library media specialist, computer teacher, and professor of education and library science. She is currently teaching online graduate courses for librarians and educators as a professor at Indiana University--Purdue University (IUPUI), Indianapolis, IN.

Daniel Callison has served as library media specialist for a high school program recognized nationally by the American Association of Secondary School Principals. He was director of the school library media masters program at Indiana University (IU), ranked among the top ten nationally since 1990; founding editor of *School Library Media Research*, the online reference research *Journal of the American Association of School Librarians*; and currently serves as professor and dean of the IU School of Continuing Studies.